OFFSHORING OPPORTUNITIES

OFFSHORING OPPORTUNITIES

STRATEGIES AND TACTICS FOR GLOBAL COMPETITIVENESS

JOHN BERRY

WILEY

JOHN WILEY & SONS, INC.

Library of Congress Cataloging-in-Publication Data:

Berry, John, 1960-
 Offshoring opportunities : strategies and tactics for global competitiveness / John Berry.
  p. cm.
 Includes index.
 ISBN-13: 978-0-471-71673-0 (cloth)
 ISBN-10: 0-471-71673-1 (cloth)
 1. International business enterprises. 2. Contracting out. I. Title.
 HD2755.5.B467 2006
 658.4'058—dc22

                                                        2005017416

For Gretchen and Kirsten Helitzer
Highlighting the market need
for an offshore service provider who specializes in diaper changing.

CONTENTS

See next page for instructions on using this card

Offshoring Value Delivery Framework Reference Card

Strategy Development	⇑	Selection Process	⇑	Relationship Building	⇑	Sustained Management
Phase 1 Think		Phase 2 Plan		Phase 3 Negotiate		Phase 4 Execute & Manage

❑ Strategy/Goals Alignment
❑ In-House or Out of House
❑ Organizational Readiness
  ❑ Strategic – workforce plan
  ❑ Operational – decisionmaking governance
❑ Business Case
		❑ Develop Selection Criteria
		❑ Selection Process
		❑ RFP
		❑ Site Selection
				❑ Pilot Project
				❑ Security Framework
				❑ Revise Business Case
				❑ Contracting
				❑ Relationship Model
				❑ Exit Strategy
						❑ Transition Strategy
						❑ Performance Tracking
						❑ Internal Governance
						  ❑ Strategic
						  ❑ Operational
						  ❑ Just-in-Time

READERS NOTE: OFFSHORING VALUE DELIVERY FRAMEWORK REFERENCE CARD

The Offshoring Value Delivery Framework is a concept discussed frequently throughout this book. Although its formal introduction can be found in Chapter 4, readers are provided another copy of this critical, visual management concept so they might remove it from the book and use it as a reference. Because the pattern of the book is to delve deeply into each phase of the framework, then back out to introduce subsequent phases, readers might find the process of being introduced into a new phase, diving deep into all its details, then coming back up to the surface for the introduction of the next phase a bit disorienting. This reference card acts as a kind of navigational and orientation tool so that readers can understand at what point in the evolution of an offshoring initiative they find themselves in as they read the text.

Feel free to cut out the back of this page along the dashed guideline. Keep the card on your desk, tack it to an office wall or use it as a bookmark. Turn to the reference card any time you feel the need to reestablish your bearings as you explore the principles of offshoring.

PREFACE

What is this book about? Strategies, tactics, and issues around offshoring. This book is designed for C-level and operational managers (all others are welcome too, however) in need of information and decision frameworks necessary to navigate the thicket of issues surrounding an offshoring strategy. Critics will say that this book is for offshoring and everything it impacts when, in fact, the book is for the illumination of an economic phenomenon and business trend that can improve a company's competitiveness or worsen it. An implicit advocacy of offshoring by dint of providing strategies and tactics to successfully execute it does not mean advocacy for massive layoffs of U.S. workers, no more than being for mild winter weather in a traditionally cold climate means advocating that ski lift operators go out of business because of the absence of snow. The fact is that for a variety of reasons explained shortly, offshoring is a real economic phenomenon and legitimate management discipline. It demands the editorial attention only a book can provide, so I decided to write one. Managers who ignore the subject do so at their own peril and that of their employers.

If managers have spent any time researching this subject, they might have found that the media offers conflicting signals about what is happening in the offshoring marketplace. For example, *CFO Magazine* runs a story that says the pharmaceutical industry is risk averse to offshoring because of, among other things, its standards of near perfection sought in all processes involved in the creation of a drug.[1] Perfection can be ensured only if the processes are under the company's direct control. Walk to the other end of the newsstand and the *Wall Street Journal* has published a story on the front page of the second section stating that the drug industry

---

1. Alison Rea, "Outsourcing Risks Worry the Wary," CFO Research Services, October 14, 2004.

is offshoring R&D to Asian service providers to meet operational and strategic needs.[2] Which is it? Both. Another example. The conventional wisdom says a company should never offshore its core competencies or those processes that deliver strategic value to the firm. But value hardly gets any more strategic than R&D, and these key processes are enjoying long but pleasant journeys to exotic locations with increasing frequency, as readers will discover. Joining research offshore is the D in R&D. More and more technology companies are sending product development work to offshore service providers. Never offshore the strategic says the little man in one ear; by all means offshore any set of business processes that deliver value to the organization, says his twin sister in the other. Which is it? Both.

Offshoring is highly contextual, influenced by many business circumstances: company cost structure, competitive environment, internal capability and resource availability to deliver value, new product introductions and the time-to-market issues surrounding them, a need for physical proximity to international customers, and the list goes on. Conventional wisdom is just that—conventional—and one person's peach is another's poison. In this kind of reality, the only hope from a book such as this is to provide the ideal, a framework for thought and discussion, and let managers apply it to the pressure-packed real world in which they toil. If they follow the framework, managers will discover if offshoring presents a compelling value proposition.

---

2. See Laura Santini, "Drug Companies Look to China for Cheap R&D," *Wall Street Journal*, November 22, 2004.

APPROACH OF THE BOOK

Another set of challenges in writing a book about offshoring emerges: one, the need to tackle the relevant issues with enough specificity that readers feel satisfied that they can apply the advice to their individual circumstances, whether the debate involves offshoring routine human resources (HR) processes in a chemical manufacturer or the offshoring of fulfillment and customer support in a financial services organization; two, the need to keep the information strategic enough that readers walk away with a solid decision framework applicable to any offshoring circumstance that presents itself. Positioning the book at the proper altitude somewhere between 50,000 feet and sea level is not easy, but hopefully readers will see that this text at least attempts to situate itself at an elevation suitable to providing both strategic and practical advice regardless of industry or circumstance by way of sharing plenty of examples of offshoring scenarios in many industries driven by various business needs. The job is made slightly easier by the fact that there are only so many business drivers motivating managers to offshore—cost cutting, time-to-market, and capturing capabilities not found in house are three common themes that emerged during the research for this book. Hopefully, the commonality of goals sought from offshoring will make the information in these pages relevant, even if specific scenarios involve industries far from a manager's own.

STRUCTURE OF THE BOOK

Another challenge is narrative and stylistic. Chapters 1 through 3 are introductory chapters, which provide an understanding of offshoring and its popularity in U.S. business today. The remaining chapters then turn sharply toward practical advice and guidance. These chapters are structured around the Offshoring Value Delivery Framework™, a strategic and tactical decision framework and model I created, which guides managers through critical issues at all points within the offshoring lifecycle. For example, readers will see in the Table of Contents that after Chapter 3, the book is separated into the 4 phases which makes up the whole of the Offshoring Value Delivery Framework. These phases constitute most of the book, Chapters 4-12. Each phase in the book is comprised of chapters which confronts and analyzes the specific offshoring management issues proscribed in the delivery framework. In a way, a visual of the Offshoring Value Delivery Framework, which appears more than once, is another kind of Table of Contents for the book. Because the book's contents map to the delivery framework, concepts might be introduced before a fuller explanation is provided. For example, an early chapter addresses the construction of a business case and economic model for any offshoring initiative. This chapter naturally illustrates all the costs, both obvious and hidden, that management must consider when deciding whether to offshore certain business processes. A complete explanation as to how certain costs arise and why they are important is covered in detail in later chapters. Some readers will read Chapter 6 on business case construction before having a complete grasp of all the costs that must appear in that business case. So, you might ask why not cover all the cost issues first and then address the business case? Because the book's structure is mapped to the Offshoring Value Delivery Framework, which has its own process-driven step 1, step 2 logic to it. Business case development happens to be one of the very early offshoring decision-making activities management undertakes. As you get into the text, it should become apparent why structuring the book this way is far superior for total comprehension than any other narrative approach.

The good news is this narrative structure should not at all hinder the reader for a number of reasons: One, the concepts are not exotic or difficult to understand and are at least familiar to many managers. Two, any time a concept is introduced and given just cursory attention at that point in the book, I point out that the topic will be covered in more detail later, so there is no need to panic. Three, once the whole book is read, all the pieces should fit together. Readers might undergo that "lights on" experience when suddenly it all makes sense. Managers will have a complete grasp of the breadth and complexity of the issues involved in deciding to offshore, executing an offshoring initiative, and managing that initiative for value, whether the offshoring is captive, that is, done in house, or through the auspices of an outside service provider. So, I won't stand in your way any longer. Discover and enjoy.

ACKNOWLEDGMENTS

This is my second book, and while experience is supposed to make the journey easier, it doesn't really. Writing a book is still much like swallowing a watermelon. The experience is made more digestible with the help of knowledgeable people who point me in the right direction around a specific topic, who provide interesting insights and information that adds value to the project, and who validate or challenge ideas I have been turning over in my head. For this, individual thanks are in order. They are presented in alphabetical order.

Barbara Beech, a group manager in IT vendor management at AT&T's Consumer Lab, was very helpful in sharing her hard won wisdom in crafting service level agreements with vendors. Bill Bierce of Bierce & Kenerson walked me through the legal minefield of contracting with offshore service providers. The crew at Cincom iOutsource—CEO, Ashish Paul, his colleague, Greg Rhodes, and communications executive, John Tepe, devoted the most time of any people interviewed, eight interviews in all, explaining call center offshoring. As a native of India, Ashish offered particularly useful insights about the culture and business climate of that country. Jay Doherty, a partner at Mercer Human Resource Consulting delivered once again (he helped me out with my first book). His site selection knowledge enhanced this part of the book. He also provided numerous offshoring insights with a human capital twist to them which also found their way into the book.

Further thanks must also be apportioned to the IT research house Gartner, which was very generous in sharing the CD from a 2004 Outsourcing Summit it hosted in Las Vegas when it turned out that I could not attend. Some of their insightful ideas are footnoted in these pages. Other ideas simply validated concepts I had already worked out which was helpful in keeping up the writing pace. Beth Hayes, IT practice leader at The Hackett Group, was generous with her time, allowing me to bounce ideas off her. (Also, thanks to Gary Baker, Hackett's communications guy, for feeding me information). Jim Maloney, the chief security executive at Corillian in Portland, Oregon, who validated and enhanced the security framework in these pages, is one of the most articulate technical guys I have ever had the pleasure of interviewing. Really fun to listen to. Daniel Werner of Hillsdale Corp., another Portland area company, helped me very early when I wasn't sure of the direction I was headed in. And last, but certainly not least, (and deliberately pulled out of alphabetical order in order to save for last) a heartfelt thanks to David Wagner, CIO of ON Semiconductor, who invested an enormous amount of time in sharing the offshoring experiences of his company. If I did my job—telling his story—readers will reap numerous riches from David's advice in how to transition business processes to an offshore service provider. His is the story of how to offshore the right way, and the book is better for telling it.

Thanks to everyone who participated.

John Berry
June 2005

1

OFFSHORING AND ITS DISCONTENTS

How do we start to understand the subject of offshoring? Let's begin by saying that up close the face of offshoring can be an unpleasant one. Inspect the pages of the April 2004 issue of Fast Company in which was documented the real pain experienced by real, talented people, as they got pulled by the undertow of an economic force sure to loom large in our lives in this century and one that experts are only beginning to understand completely. People mostly in their thirties, forties, and fifties, employed as call center managers, software engineers, and network administrators, one day learned that their positions were being eliminated simply because equally trained and capable people in foreign lands, hungry for the work, were trained and ready. These displaced workers often found other work. But often it wasn't as nearly intellectually satisfying or financially rewarding. More than one story featured the cruel irony of an American supervisor being bestowed the responsibility of training the replacement workers.

Fast Company is one in a collection of monthly manifestos dedicated to the celebration of jungle capitalism and the creativity of the warriors who survive and prosper in it. Yet to its credit, the magazine didn't confine the offshoring narrative to stories of how companies succeeded in executing strategy and tactics, which the IT trade press drowns us in regularly. The magazine put a human face on the dislocation that offshoring causes. It was that much more powerful because it is this kind of narrative that crystallizes fear people have over this subject.

The furor over offshoring has its roots in many places, and they are worth exploring:

- While causation is not precise, the outcry over offshoring seemed to have emerged just as the United States was recovering from a recession in 2001. As pundits, interest groups, and others sought answers as to why a recession occurred, offshoring activity by U.S. companies became a popular component of the explanation, however wrong-headed that particular explanation was.[1]

- The negative impact of offshoring is specific and immediate, but the benefits are diffuse and deferred. A software programmer loses his job. Bad. The money the organization saves over several years results in capital that can be plowed into new products or a new business requiring the hiring of people. Good—but speculative because this kind of trade in services is new behavior in the U.S. economy and also, because it may be causally difficult to link these job gains to the original move to offshore. Aggregate job growth data can allow one to deduce gains from offshoring, yet all people see is the pain, not the gain.

- Many of the tensions in U.S. society are about class and those tensions manifest themselves with offshoring. A steel worker with an 11th grade education loses his job? Well, that's our modern economy, people lament. The contents of your head, not the size of your fore-arms, will determine success in the New Economy, everyone asserts. But then the razor-sharp, highly skilled, four-years-of-college-and-some-grad school software programmer loses his position in company X as it decides to pay a comparably skilled India-based pro-grammer in Hydrabad 60% less for exactly the same work. This isn't the way I was told the world would operate, says the disillusioned, MIT-educated programmer. If rigorous programming work which requires more often than not a four-year college education is off-shored, what's next, surgery?

- The offshoring need is less urgent and so the act of doing exactly this is perceived as cruel and heartless. As much as unions scream about plant shutterings and domestic layoffs, the reality of global competi-tion stares manufacturers in the face. In some industries the domestic cost structure of some companies is unsustainable in the face of com-petition from China and elsewhere and that is why some industry sec-tors shrivel into shells of their former selves. These operations must take drastic measures or go out of business altogether. The proposition is simple: we move offshore or die. No such impending doom seems to loom over managers in organizations that decide to offshore routine back office functions. Rather, offshoring is just another arrow in the quiver of management tactics to reduce the company's cost structure. In fact, the company may be printing money because business conditions are so good. Microsoft, for example, offshores a number of technology projects to Infosys and Wipro, two Indian service firms.[2] Although its stock price has been moribund for a couple of years, it is not exactly a distressed company bleeding cash for which offshoring would do some real good. The pain felt by a seasoned IT professional is demonstrably more acute when seemingly the only reason why the employer made the offshoring move was to save some money, not save the business. The cloth out of the social pact between employee and employer has been unraveling for years. Moves to offshore corporate functions under these business conditions rips it.

- At the most visceral level, the United States is aware that no corner of the economy is immune from the forces of globalization. It is one thing for manufacturing jobs to disappear, since manufacturing does not represent the bulk of economic activity in the country. It is far different to witness the very same results in service sectors comprising skilled people that no one even 10 years ago could have conceived were vulnerable: health care, financial analysis, software design and creation, graphic design, legal support, and journalism. The breadth of job classes vulnerable to offshoring is far greater than was the case in manufacturing. Offshoring is symbolically powerful, for it conveys far greater economic uncertainty than we have known in the past because what it portends is a global marketplace for white-collar, skilled workers. Whether reality will fulfill these perceptions it is too early to tell.
- The pace and rapidity of job loss in services offshoring might dwarf the slower but inexorable decline of domestic manufacturing. The reason is that services offshoring is generally less complex to establish and manage than overseas manufacturing.[3] The alarm provoked by services' offshoring will rise in pitch and volume in proportion to the speed at which jobs leave for overseas.

The conflation of these factors has provoked a federal and state legislative response that has been, swift, predictable, and hysterical—in both the funny and alarmed sense. Attempts to either stop offshoring completely or blunt its effects have taken the form of proposals to stop the federal government from doing business with companies that offshore.[4] Ex-Senator Tom Daschle proposed the Jobs for America Act, which among other things give U.S. workers at least three months notice before a company laid off more than 15 workers and sent them overseas.[5] During the 2004 election, presidential candidate John Kerry argued for elimination of tax breaks to corporations on income earned abroad.[6] In one interesting twist to offshoring, a Connecticut Democratic congresswoman, Rosa DeLauro, pushed for legislation that would have required guest workers being "inshored" to receive the prevailing wage of the workers they would replace.[7] This particular example has a more historical pedigree in the HB-1 visa debate several years ago in which U.S. technical workers were complaining, with some justification, that simply to save on labor costs employers were replacing domestic technical workers with comparably skilled workers from other countries by granting foreigners work visas.

What is the subtext of these ideas? One, the federal government should not reward U.S. companies who export jobs. Two, workers should be given a transition time before their jobs are exported. Three, American corporations should not be given special tax treatment for business activity in a country that might be the target of offshoring. Four, if offshoring is wrong, so is inshoring. The politician's impulse to intervene when U.S. jobs are at stake is simply too irresistible for discretion to have its way; there isn't a politician in business who would not like to boast that he or she has saved thousands of Americans from unemployment, having stopped the exportation of American jobs.

While these examples happen to be the more reasonable of proposals, others illustrate how ill-considered are the attempts at stopping this economic force. In the "let's keep our head while all about us are losing theirs" department the Democrat Governor of Indiana, Joseph Kernan, canceled a contract with an Indian firm to process unemployment claims. Instead the contract was given to a U.S. company who will charge 50% more for the same work. Here are the results. The public workers kept their jobs at a subsidized cost of $8 million to Indiana taxpayers. Doesn't seem like much for protecting jobs, except that the state incurred an opportunity cost of $8 million that will not be spent on what Indiana arguably needs more of than state government workers processing unemployment claims— teachers, police officers, and assistance to the poor. What is the gain to Indiana in this scenario?[8]

Indiana's subsidy play is not unlike the myriad economic development efforts across the country. Distressed communities reach out to mostly low-paying industries (call centers being a popular example) and offer generous tax breaks in exchange for relocation to the area. A town gets 500 jobs and pays 100 times that in subsidies. This kind of folly, unfortunately, has insinuated itself into the offshoring scene with results that are both comical and scary. Consider the case of a New Jersey state senator, Democrat Shirley Turner who learned that a firm the state contracted with to provide job assistance to welfare recipients had shifted jobs from Wisconsin to Bombay, India. She introduced legislation requiring the state contractor to hire only U.S. employees. Never mind that a New Jersey politician is elected to concern herself with the interests of her district—in New Jersey. Her proposal caught the attention of the Phoenix-based vendor, who proceeded to agree to move the jobs from Wisconsin not to India but to—wait for it—New Jersey. In exchange, New Jersey paid the company $880,000 more than the original contract for those jobs. The state subsidized the creation of new jobs, a frequent occurrence. The obscenity of this story, however, is found in this one fact. The total number of jobs saved from offshoring? Nine. Nine jobs. New Jersey essentially paid almost $100,000 in taxpayer money to create each of the nine new jobs that arguably should have been Wisconsin's to keep or lose.[9]

From the xenophobia file comes proposals making the rounds in a number of state legislatures that would require call center workers in companies with offshore call center operations to identify where they are located. You call your favorite apparel vendor to check on the status of an online order and the rep greeting you would have to divulge that she is a Filipino working in a call center outside Manila. This should be highly effective legislation because it sure passes over the heads of those dullard Americans on the phone to a favorite vendor that the customer service rep with that thick accent might actually be sitting in a call center located in some exotic location very far away from Omaha.

Not only does the idea insult the intelligence of Americans, it assumes that the discovery that the rep is indeed a friendly Indian working in Delhi will inspire a kind of activism in which outraged customers take up arms against the offending company—a product boycott, perhaps—that will show the organization the error of its ways. The presumed result is a chastised company, which ends its offshoring service contract and rehires Americans. It is more likely that the caller will take up arms because the rep couldn't resolve whatever problem she called about (personally, I find Indian call center workers to be uniformly excellent, in spite of a sometimes very heavy accent that makes them hard to understand). It simply isn't a secret to anyone who under-goes a call center experience that many of those positions are already in India and elsewhere, and it is unclear if the consumer response politicians hope for would actually materialize to stop a company's rational economic decision to seek a lower cost answer to high operational expenses. Americans seem to like offshoring when they are not casualties of it. A vivid example of this is how E-Loan gives customers the choice of having their home equity loans processed domestically in 12 days or 10 days overseas. Nine out of 10 cus-tomers choose the quicker loan processing option, which means the work is done in Chennai, India. What can we conclude? Fear over offshoring is real. But would Americans prefer that companies not offshore if it meant a drop in convenience or increase in cost of a service? Apparently no.[10]

Furthermore, state-level legislative resistance to offshoring might very well be illegal, not that this would stop anyone in state legislatures. On behalf of the National Foundation for American Policy, two attorneys argued that these proposed laws would likely violate the U.S. constitution's Foreign Commerce Clause;; states are prohibited from making their own trade policies.[11]

All these examples offer a simple reminder: a broad, one-size-fits-all policy response to an economic trend that inflicts real pain on real people is problematic because offshoring encompasses so many contextual circum-stances. Responses to offshoring are akin to an antibiotic that not only kills the disease but the patient too. Hopefully, this will be made clear in the next section, which defines what offshoring actually is.

WHAT IS OFFSHORING?

There are two ways to understanding offshoring—that is, understanding what offshoring is, not its impact. One way is to consider it in the context of economics, which defines offshoring as international trade in *services, not products*, which is still international trade, it is just not offshoring. The second way bypasses the economic theory and is much more grounded in tactical business activity. The second approach is what most of this book is about. However, a brief look at the academic explanation can only help enhance our comprehension.

Economists Weigh In

The international trade explanation goes like this: a country imports services when its domestic companies hire foreigners to do service work otherwise performed by a domestic worker. Conversely, a country exports workers when its citizens perform service work for a company located in a foreign country. An example of the import of services: a U.S. company opens a technical support center in India and hires locals to do the work. An example of the export of services: a lawyer in New York is hired by a German car company to handle some legal work. In the context of the word "offshoring," a U.S. company offshores technical support center services in the first example. A German company offshores legal services in the second example. Economics looks at both the import and export side of the equation in explaining offshoring international trade in services, because, trade is a reciprocal arrangement.

The lawyer example is an interesting one because it reminds the reader, as they will be reminded throughout the book, that the cost imperative is not the only motivation to offshore. People assume that companies offshore to secure lower cost services abroad, because most of the media coverage about offshoring illustrates this very reason. In most cases this is true. However, other reasons exist to offshore. It might be that the New York attorney has unique legal abilities the German car company might find difficult to find domestically. Filling a skills gap happens to be another reason why a domestic company will engage in international trade in services rather than deploy domestic help, as we shall see later.

Arm's length international trade in services actually comprises more than one context[12] yet the examples above are representative of types of offshoring that fall within the trade in services definition. It seems like pretty basic stuff, understandable to all but the most uninitiated in the ways of economics and business. But this kind of services trade is fairly new to people. We are used to discussing trade in terms of importing cars or large containers in big ships making long voyages across vast and treacherous seas. Yet to the economist there is no difference between importing furniture or appliances in ships crossing the Pacific and importing architectural renderings crossing the Pacific in a beam of fiber-optic light. The economics are essentially the same. This fact should become clear to people as the scope and breadth of offshoring increases. There is little doubt that it won't.

Confusion Is Sewn

Plenty of definitional confusion has been created around offshoring. Point of confusion number one is the failure to distinguish between direct foreign investment and offshoring. Direct foreign investment occurs when a U.S.

company shuts down a plant in the midwest and opens one up in China or when a company chooses to open a plant in Singapore instead of Sacramento. The redeployment of capital in foreign lands describes direct foreign investment. In either case, local production workers would most likely be hired to replace the laid-off production U.S. workers. American jobs are offshored to the extent that foreign workers in a manufacturing setting do the work that Americans did, but in economics, technically, the hiring of foreign workers to run the factory floor is not outsourcing or offshoring. Neither is that labor procurement direct foreign investment. It is simply the add-on economic activity of the business who made a direct foreign investment in that country.[13] Had the company been a legal and medical transcription operation which closed its U.S. offices and opened a headquarters in India using local labor to service U.S. lawyers and doctors this would be true international trade in services. But this scenario would also be describing direct foreign investment if the company decided to invest in a building and local equipment to establish the operation too. To the economist, offshoring is concerned with international trade in *services*.

Another point of confusion is the increasing use of the word outsourcing to mean offshoring. Outsourcing has a much more specific meaning in business, especially in information technology. Companies have outsourced IT services and activities for many years. They contract with a domestic service provider such as IBM to handle various IT activities such as renting software (the Application Service Provider Model) or performing infrastructure and maintenance tasks. The company offloads these distracting obligations onto a third party who specializes in delivering these services. While the two words are often used interchangeably, the difference between outsourcing and offshoring is real but also very simple; in offshoring, a domestic company contracts with a provider to assume management of business functions off American soil, in some foreign country, presumably because the overseas location offers a compelling cost advantage (but not necessarily just cost savings as various parts of the book will show). Outsourcing is confined to the procurement of services within the domestic marketplace. Therefore, offshoring is a subset of outsourcing but they are not synonymous. Nitpicking though this may be, the book concerns itself explicitly with offshoring, even if many of the management principles applied to offshoring are rooted in outsourcing. The word outsourcing has its own meaning and will be used only to mean hiring a service provider domestically. Later, this chapter introduces a full list of definitions of offshoring and variants of it.

The conceptual confusion between pure offshoring—international trade in services—and direct foreign investment is found in many places. Critics use events in international trade as ammunition against the offshoring phenomenon when it really represents a small portion of total international trade economic activity. The rhetoric of CNN personality Lou Dobbs is a good case in point. He inventories the companies that "ship jobs abroad" without distinguishing between direct foreign investment, such as a domestic company building a manufacturing plant somewhere else in the world, and true offshoring. Consider this from a September 10, 2004 commentary on CNN's website:

> Instead of expanding our nation's manufacturing and textile base by opening new markets for products and services, all this administration and its predecessors have accomplished over the past decade is a series of outsourcing agreements. The principal beneficiaries of NAFTA and the World Trade Organization are U.S. multinationals that are exporting American jobs to cheaper labor markets overseas.[14]

Is outsourcing in this context synonymous with offshoring? Presumably yes, but again each term has a specific meaning. Does the expansion of foreign markets for domestic products and services mean that the United States should negotiate more favorable economic conditions for direct foreign investment so that our manufacturers can invest capital in foreign local markets—as well as invest in local labor—and in turn sell what those subsidiary manufacturing facilities produce? Or does Dobbs mean that if only the United States could open foreign markets currently closed we could expand our domestic manufacturing base? Or both, perhaps. If the latter, then Dobbs' argument assumes this: if foreign markets were opened, international demand for our domestically manufactured products would be so large as to presumably expand this type of manufacturing in the United States, and the number of domestic workers who are employed in this activity. This is an assumption large enough to drive a TV camera truck through.

While increased demand for our products in some imagined closed market can drive unit costs down, there is a limit to how low manufacturing costs in the United States can go (think the several thousand dollars in health care costs for auto workers embedded in the price of many automobiles) and that limit might prevent the domestic manufacturer from lowering its cost structure in line with global competitors whose cost structure is profoundly lower. Opening foreign markets to U.S. goods does not mean that the U.S. manufacturer is going to be cost competitive with all other competitors worldwide; U.S. jobs might still be lost even with the opening of new markets because the manufacturer's costs were still higher than the competitor based in China. Also, just because worldwide demand for domestic goods rises—maybe sharply—does not necessarily translate into large domestic employment increases. America's companies are the most productive in the world, and they would surely leverage a productivity advantage over competitors first before hiring incrementally more workers to satisfy this demand. The productivity payoff in U.S. manufacturing has been alive and well for some time. American companies make more with less, so the higher employment impact might very well be blunted.

There is a handful of economic concepts Dobbs juggles in this website statement. None directly deal with arm's length international trade of services—offshoring, except for perhaps an underlying displeasure that it is occurring at all.

His screed also overlooks fundamental realities of labor's mobility in our current world. The United States exports far more services than it imports in services today. That is, U.S. companies sell about $130 billion in services that include such activities as telecom, management consulting, software programming, and legal services. The U.S. imports about $77 billion. The United States is running a services trade *surplus* with the rest of the world to the tune of $50 billion.[15] Were Congress to erect barriers to offshoring and the purchase of services overseas, the likely response from trading partners would be swift retaliation. The possible result is that the United States saves jobs that otherwise would have been offshored but loses at least an equal amount of economic growth from the disappearance of foreigners' consumption of domestic services and perhaps the entire services trade surplus we now enjoy. That's worse than a zero sum game, but this possibility is seldom introduced into the offshoring discussion.

UNDERSTANDING OFFSHORING THE WAY
A MANAGER WOULD

Offshoring is best understood not in the conceptual jargon of economics but in the brass tacks of business application. Below are a number of scenarios that constitute offshoring. Technically, a scenario involving a manufacturer of products who sets up shop overseas and hires local workers does not constitute international trade in services. But for the purposes of this book, we will depart from the path of economists and take the license of including such cases because often a manufacturer will use local labor not only on the shop floor where it is directly tied to manufacturing activity but also in back-office operations. A manufacturer with a global presence might decide to consolidate finance operations in a foreign country and lay off U.S. workers performing these functions to capture significant operational cost savings. This is a common offshoring scenario. In this case, the manufacturer is offshoring because it is using foreign workers to perform finance *services* otherwise performed by domestic workers. In the context of business need, it matters little that one, the company is a manufacturer, and two, the offshoring is an internal reshuffling of staff rather than a procurement of such services from a third-party provider based in that foreign country. The art and science of economics makes no distinction between offshoring when the company procures labor from a service provider in that foreign operation and when it hires internally.[16] Both scenarios are international trade in services and offshoring, insofar as the fact that international trade in services and offshoring are synonymous to the economist.

Summarizing Economic Concepts of Offshoring

The following list provides some key economic concepts to consider related to international trade and offshoring:

- Direct foreign investment occurs when a company invests capital for some operation in a country other than its own. Direct foreign investment is not offshoring.

- International trade in services occurs when a company directly procures labor in a foreign country to handle internal services operations or engages a local service provider to run those services: HR, finance, IT, R&D, training, billing, logistics, call center customer support, and so forth. To the economist, international trade in services is the technical name for offshoring. Much offshoring in the United States today is typified by a company's shifting internal service work to an office in a distant land to capture cost savings or other efficiencies—no service provider is involved.

- Outsourcing is not offshoring because it describes procurement of a domestic third party to run some operation on its behalf. Offshoring is a subset of outsourcing because it represents an evolutionary step in the process of turning over the operation of services to an outsider.

Offshoring is evolutionary in that turning out the work to an outsider is not done with a domestic provider but one based in a foreign land.

• When a manufacturer closes a plant in the United States and opens one in Asia, any money spent on facilities and equipment is direct foreign investment. The hiring of local workers in that facility is a follow-on economic activity, not offshoring. However, if a manufacturer hires local labor directly or a service provider to run an internal service on its behalf, this is offshoring.

Offshoring Scenarios

Fast Company painted the face of the impact of offshoring. Here are short portraits of offshoring business activity. All examples are distilled from real-world scenarios.

Scenario One.   A New York–based investment bank hires an overseas service firm to produce equity analyst reports for its client base. Junior analysts at the home office are either reassigned to other responsibilities or laid off. Senior analysts in New York are freed up to spend more time on the phone with company CEOs and less time crunching numbers. The firm spends one–fourth the labor cost on offshored analysts.

Scenario Two.   A startup has an idea for a sophisticated niche software application to serve the biotech industry. Market research tells it that the domestic market would support such a product at a price point below its ability to make a profit and recoup the significant development costs if it hired U.S. software talent to develop the product. The company builds the product using offshore software development professionals and sells it domestically.

Scenario Three.   A domestic search engine company opens an R&D services facility in India. Although the cost differential in using foreign technical workers is significant, the primary motivation was the ability to tap into deep technical expertise in specific R&D disciplines without expending a lot of energy on recruiting.

Scenario Four.   A publisher of editorial material aimed at application developers sets up a trial with an Indian editorial firm to produce articles for the publisher's website. While the trial lasted, the vendor absorbed about half of what the publisher otherwise would have spent. While dollar savings was a big consideration, since the cost of freelance article procurement is the single biggest discretionary cost item, vendor management issues are figured into the decision. The publisher found it far more efficient to work with one source for editorial material rather than a stable of freelancers.

Scenario Five. A third-party U.S.-based radiology services company manages a stable of Australian-based radiologists who read x-rays, MRIs, and other images on behalf of the company's U.S. hospital clients. The U.S.-based health-care providers save no money in this arrangement because laws require that workers analyzing medical images for U.S. health-care facilities be trained and licensed in the United States. So, who did the third-party services company hire? American-trained and -licensed doctors living in Australia. On its face, this business model would not appear to offer the customer a cost advantage for radiological services, which drives much offshoring activity. In truth, it doesn't. American radiologists in Australia earn about as much as their colleagues in the United States. But then cost reductions were not a need the service provider sought to fulfill. It turns out that radiological services in Australia provide health-care providers "follow-the-sun" capability. That is, important radiological images are being analyzed when everyone in the States is asleep. Having around the clock service is an important value-added capability for U.S. health-care companies and is another motivation driving service providers to establish offshoring capabilities for U.S. companies.

Scenarios Tell Us . . .

The examples above deliberately avoided stories of companies who jettisoned half their information technology staff and hired a foreign service provider in their place, because those scenarios are so common. This might be what most people think of when they hear the word offshoring. Yet offshoring actually offers a richer set of case studies, involving more nuanced and less obvious motivations than simply the swing of the budget axe, and their very subtlety makes them worth exploring.

A few conclusions can be made from all the preceding examples. While it is small comfort to the U.S. worker out of a job from offshoring, cost savings are just one driver of the move to offshore services, albeit a large one. The labor cost differential in some industries is astonishing. A medical transcriptionist in the United States might fetch ten cents a line while a counterpart in India earns three. A junior investment research analyst in the United States might earn $90,000 versus $25,000 in India. Yet, often a company has a multiplicity of strategic or operational needs it seeks to fulfill. In fewer instances, cost is simply the push that sends an organization over the offshoring edge when other strategic considerations are in the center of the debate to offshore. It should also be clear that offshoring is not necessarily a zero sum game; a worker need not necessarily lose a job for a foreigner to take it. The startup did not lay off one worker; it simply hired overseas labor to fulfill a need no one else could, to reach its market objectives. Yet these examples are clearly offshoring—the procurement of arm's length international trade in services.

Mentioned earlier was the idea that one of the alarming aspects in the growth of offshoring is the fact a wide swath of the labor market is vulnerable to it. The breadth of offshoring, that is, the percentage of service job categories out of all occupations in existence that are candidates for migration overseas, is far greater today than its depth—the total number of jobs moving abroad as a percentage of total number of Americans employed in those categories. Out of approximately 500 occupational categories tracked by the Bureau of Labor Statistics, more than half are offshoreable, according to one research firm.[17] People are realizing that it's not just about call center reps and software programmers.

BUSINESS PROCESS OFFSHORING

One of the best definitions for offshoring is this: the delegation of ownership, administration, and operation of a process to a third party.[18]

If we shift our perspective from job categories to the business processes and services for which offshoring is a viable option, we capture yet another perspective and a deeper understanding of its scope. The offshoring of services is also called business process outsourcing or offshoring (BPO). Since this text is concerned explicitly with offshoring as a type of outsourcing, BPO will always refer to business process offshoring, unless otherwise specifically noted. Exhibit 1.1 illustrates the breadth of functions that BPO represents today, and Exhibit 1.2 provides definitions of BPO.

Business Process Offshoring Models

It is worth exploring the various offshore service delivery models briefly, if only to acquaint readers with the shades and gradations of this business trend:

- **Onshore Outsourcing.** This occurs when one company engages a service provider within the same country to provide business services.

Customer Facing Processes	
Sales Processes	**Customer Support Processes**
Sales activities—prospect, negotiate and close	Field support
Outbound telemarketing—sales on the phone	Call center customer and technical support

Internal Processes	
Supply Chain Processes	**Enterprise Processes**
Logistics and distribution	HR–payroll, benefits, staffing activities
Warehouse management	Finance–payables, receivables and other financial operational activities
Procurement	Information technology
Inventory management	Product development–R&D, design

EXHIBIT 1.1 SCOPE OF BUSINESS PROCESS OFFSHORING

	IS	IS NOT
BPO . . .	About business processes across the organization	About IT functions only, like application development, even thought IT represents a large percentage of offshoring today
	About information technology, to the extent that IT supports and influences business processes	Application hosting, software rental, staff augmentation
	Strategically important, involves many business needs	Concerned exclusively with cost savings and cheaper labor
	Emerging as a legitimate management discipline	A below C-level subcontracting function
	A set of competencies a service provider should have mastery of	A vendor repositioning ploy designed to exploit the interest and hype around the subject

EXHIBIT 1.2 BUSINESS PROCESS OFFSHORING DEFINED

SOURCE: Adapted from Gartner presentation "Evaluating and Selecting a BPO Provider: Be Careful What You Wish For," Gartner Outsourcing Summit 2004, May 17–19 2004, Las Vegas, NV.

Hire IBM Global Services to manage your mainframes, and you have onshore outsourcing. This used to be called simply outsourcing, but some felt compelled to add the onshore adjective to distinguish this scenario from offshoring. For the purposes of this book, outsourcing means the same thing as onshore outsourcing, a cumbersome word in the outsourcing taxonomy.

- **Near Shoring.** This describes a company of one country offshoring to a country proximate to itself. A U.S. company that near shores would contract with a service provider in Mexico, Central America, or Canada. This is still offshoring.

- **Cosourcing.** This scenario describes a situation in which data sits in a company's domestic data center but workers outside the company's country perform business process functions on that data. A bill-processing service provider might house its workers in Eastern Europe and have them log in to the data center of the U.S. client somewhere in the United States to perform the offshored work.

- **In-House or Captive Offshoring.** Companies with global operations engage in this scenario. They consolidate business process functions to a company office in a low-cost foreign country, for example when a semiconductor manufacturer offshores U.S. accounting work to its operation in the Czech Republic. Captive offshoring may or may not involve layoffs of domestic employees.

- **Service Provider Offshoring.** This is the most complex scenario. A company forklifts business processes and the supporting IT infrastructure out of its domestic operation and into the service provider's overseas operation. Much of this book deals with this very scenario. This, and the previous descriptive term captive offshoring, are often collectively referred to as "offshore outsourcing," but this seems redundant. Therefore, the entire book will refer to in-house or service provider offshoring outsourcing simply as offshoring.

CONCLUSION

As the pace of offshoring accelerates, you are likely to see more goofy ideas from politicians as well as loud reaction from pundits arrayed against the free flow of international trade in services. Readers will be equipped to sort through the erroneous and confusing rhetoric in possession of a deeper understanding of what offshoring as an economic phenomenon actually is. A thing cannot be understood fully unless it is defined accurately. For managers who want to offshore business processes, this has to be the first stop.

NOTES

1. Jagdish Bhagwati, Arvind Panagariya, and T. N. Srinivasan, "The Muddles Over Outsourcing," Economics Working Paper Archive, August 28, 2004, page 12. http://econwpa.wustl.edu/eps/it/papers/0408/0408004.pdf.

2. "Labor Group Presses Microsoft on Use of Offshore Contractors," Dow Jones News Service as published in the *Wall Street Journal*, July 28, 2004.

3. "The New Wave of Outsourcing," research report, Fisher Center for Real Estate and Urban Economics, University of California at Berkeley, Fall 2003, p. 10.

4. "Outsourcing Roundup: Proposed Legislation," *Wall Street Journal*, April 7, 2004.

5. Ibid.

6. Ibid.

7. "One Man's Crusade Against Outsourcing American Jobs," Christian Science Monitor, Marilyn Gardner, April 20, 2004.

8. George Will, "The Economics of Progress," *Washington Post*, February 20, 2004.

9. Michael Schroeder, "Unions, States Seek to Block Outsourcing of Jobs Overseas," *Wall Street Journal*, June 3, 2003.

10. "For Many in the US, Money Talks Even as Jobs Walk," *New York Times*, May 6, 2004.

11. "Outsourcing Attacks Not Over," *National Review* Online, Stuart Anderson, February 11, 2005.

12. The World Trade Organization (WTO) has delineated four modes of trade in services, but this book is mostly concerned with Mode 1, so discussion of the other three is deliberately skipped. For a fuller understanding of all international trade in services see "The Muddles Over Outsourcing," where the various definitions created by the WTO are explained in detail.

13. James Anderson, Neenan Professor of Economics, interview, Boston College, April 25, 2005.

14. www.cnn.com/2004/US/09/09/land.opportunity/index.htm.l.

15. Michael M. Phillips, "More Work Is Outsourced to the US Than Away From It, Data Show," *Wall Street Journal*, March 15, 2004.

16. Interview with Peter Morici, Economist and Professor of International Business, Robert H. Smith School of Business, University of Maryland, April 26, 2005.

17. "Shaking Up Trade Theory," *BusinessWeek Special Report* Aaron Bernstein, "The China Price," December 6, 2004.

18. From outsourcinginterests.org, www.sourcinginterests.org/research_reports.htm, a special interest group membership organization dedicated to outsourcing issues.

2

EVERYTHING YOU CAN SEND DOWN A WIRE IS UP FOR GRABS[1]

Let's start by saying that the U.S. economy comprises many professions that cannot be sent down the fiber-optic wires that traverse thousands of miles of ocean floors. Radiologists can read x-rays from distant locations, but it seems unlikely that surgeons will perform operations on patients in the United States from Eastern Europe anytime soon. The economy, in fact, is loaded with jobs that will never feel the gravitational pull of offshoring. Many of them are low paying: Wal-Mart greeters and clerks, convenience store cashiers and fast food cooks. However, some are not low paying but offer very good middle-class livings: upscale salon hair stylists, interior decorators, plumbers, car mechanics, and gardeners/landscape architects. In fact with the rising affluence of a broad swath of the U.S. population, some social and economic observers predict the resurgence of a craft economy, even if it represents a very small segment of the total labor pool. Here, people with very specific skills and capabilities but not necessarily considered part of "knowledge worker" population, since they are not necessarily college educated, earn very good wages providing unique products and services. There is a cultural bias toward obtaining as much postsecondary education as possible as a response to the perceived need for critical thinking skills and book learning in our new economic order. Indeed, most of the economy requires workers with the kind of conceptual thinking skills that a college education sharpens. But it is the trades, crafts, and other professions which don't require as much formal schooling but rather apprenticeship training that will perform well in a world which offshores.[2]

18

This irony is certainly a slap in the face to college grads who assumed that a college and postcollege education was the silver bullet of success and vaccine against any kind of long-term unemployment. Especially, those trained in rigorous professions such as software engineering, where the difficulties in mastering the skills necessary for credentials turn many people away and created nice labor shortages for those persevering and smart enough to stick with it. When layoffs hit IT professionals, they might have used the downtime for an extended vacation as they were little concerned about finding a new position elsewhere. The problem is there are a couple of inherent attributes of the profession, which mesh nicely with some of the conditions which make offshoring so compelling. The job characteristics of software programming joined to external forces which propel offshoring activity created a kind of perfect storm, which makes software careers so vulnerable. The conditions which support offshoring across many job categories are worth exploring in more detail for they provide insights about the suitability of an offshoring strategy in a manager's specific organization.

SETTING THE STAGE FOR OFFSHORING

A number of circumstances and conditions have arisen that should only accelerate offshoring. Each factor is not enough in itself to encourage offshoring, but each contributes to make arm's length procurement of services attractive.

Stark Wage Differential

For all the strategic reasons some companies might find offshoring compelling, the vast majority of companies send work overseas because it is profoundly cheaper to do so. Exhibit 2.1 illustrates just how stark are the differences in labor costs for specific service positions in the United States versus India. It is not just that workers in some foreign countries fetch much lower wages but rather that American companies can pay these wages and obtain comparably skilled people. If it were simply a matter of wage differentials alone, Sudan and Borneo would be offshoring candidates, but they are not—at least today.

Tax Policy

Companies can defer taxes (or never pay them) on foreign-earned profits. The tax code is structured in such a way so that U.S. companies do not have

Occupation	U.S. Hourly Wage	India Hourly Wage
Telephone Operator	$12.57	$1.00
Medical Transcriptionist	13.17	2.00
Payroll Clerk	15.17	2.00
Legal Assistant	17.86	7.00
Accountant	23.35	10.00
Financial Analyst	34.00	10.00

EXHIBIT 2.1   DIFFERENTIAL IN HOURLY WAGES FOR SELECTED
OCCUPATIONS BETWEEN THE UNITED STATES AND INDIA

SOURCE: Adapted from "New Wave of Outsourcing," research report from Fisher
Center for Real Estate and Urban Economics, University of California, Berkeley,
Fall 2003, p. 3. For simplicity's sake, some of the wages in this table are averages
taken from the Berkeley data.

to pay the full 35% rate when that money stays invested overseas. Say that an overseas subsidiary of a U.S. company earns $10 million with a tax rate of 20%, which it is obligated to pay the country in which the subsidiary does business. At a 35% domestic tax rate, the parent company's liability to the IRS for that foreign income is $3.5 million minus the $2 million already paid to the foreign government, or $1.5 million. The loophole is simple; the subsidiary is supposed to turn over all money made in a foreign country to the parent company, which kicks in, in this tax scenario. But if the subsidiary claims that the money it earned is going to be invested overseas, it never remits its earnings to the parent company and no tax liability of $1.5 million occurs, and the company's effective tax rate is lower because of the tax law. For instance, General Electric had $21 billion in unrepatriated earnings last year, which gives it an effective tax rate of about 22%.[3]

These are called unrepatriated earnings and are common. Astonishingly this policy was not crafted by President George W. Bush, or his father, or President Clinton or even President Reagan, one of whom most people might believe was the author of such a provision. This policy actually goes back to the establishment of the corporate tax in the early 1900s.[4] While tax policy is in itself not enough incentive for a company to offshore, it cannot be ignored.

Prevalence of the English Language

Someone once said that the language of money is English. Foreign workers' understandable desire to earn it results in a mastery of English that runs from good for some functions that don't require customer interaction, such as software programming, to excellent where workers are in direct daily contact with customers such as call centers in India. Often, it is enough for a supervisor or team manager working with foreign programmers to know English for communicating their project management interactions with the U.S. headquarters selling these services.

In the early days of offshoring, say 2001, English language proficiency wasn't as big an issue because the target for offshoring was Ireland. Now it is. The Philippines has emerged as a viable offshoring target because of its close cultural ties to the West as well as the fact that it has a vast English-speaking population. India is a country whose native tongue is not English but is a country comprising, rather, a stew of more than 20 native languages. Nevertheless, the legacy of British colonial rule left India with a pool of people with English-speaking skills, which is serving it well as a target for offshoring. One Indian businessman joked that he was glad the country was colonized by the British and not the French.[5] Actually, the French are probably glad that they colonized North Africa because the availability of French-speaking locals now makes it an attractive region for companies seeking to set up French-language technical and customer support operations for France-based companies.[6] North Africa is emerging as a go-to market for English and non-English call center operations. *Datamonitor* projects call center positions to grow nearly fourfold over the next four years in such locations as Egypt, Tunisia, and Morocco.[7] The world is fast discovering the need for non-English-speaking reps. One outsourcing service provider established a 70-seat call center in Tijuana, Mexico to accommodate clients who seek customer support for 40 million Americans whose first language is Spanish.[8]

While the reality that English is a second language to native workers has not materially compromised the service levels a company seeks from offshoring these activities, the language barrier does pose risks. Problems can be as innocuous as a U.S. customer needing a foreign call center rep with a thick accent to repeat him or herself. In fact, the language challenge is dictating what types of call center activity is assigned to various parts of India. Northern call centers are relied on more than southern centers for outbound activities such as marketing and sales, where the quality of English speaking skills can influence revenue targets a company has set. It is more likely that you will find that the majority of call centers in the southern part of the country will be responsible for inbound activity only, where English accents are more pronounced.[9] Apparently, companies are willing to assume greater risk in potential language barriers for incoming activities like tech support or billing questions.

The language challenge is also potentially lethal. A group of British hospitals contracted with an Indian outfit for medical transcription, but it bungled the service. Medical documents were dictated digitally, then sent to the service provider for transcription. Medical conditions were misinterpreted by the workers. "Below knee" amputation became "baloney amputation," and "phlebitis, (an inflammation of the vein), left leg" was transcribed as "flea bite his left leg."[10] The work was so bad that a spokesman for a U.K. medical professional association made the rounds in the local press to alert the public to the dangers of offshoring this kind of work.[11] This mangling of the English language is quite funny, until someone dies as a result of it.

Perhaps the likeliest risk found in the language issue is what might be growing American's hostility to foreign-speaking customer service personnel simply because an accent is an indication that the worker is located offshore. Will simple exasperation turn into outright hostility as U.S. workers perceive a growing vulnerability of domestic job loss to these countries and use their call center experience with foreigners as a pretext or reason to vent their fears and frustrations? It's simply too early in the life of offshoring to tell. Today, companies are willing to take that risk, low or high as it might be.

IT's High Comfort Level with Outsourcing

The outsourcing of some or all of IT functions has a storied history. In the early days of computing, few companies could afford expensive mainframes, so corporations eager to automate functions such as billing and payroll rented computation time from service providers. Workers manipulated information on "green screens." The age of client-server computing democratized these capabilities by making them affordable and available to the entire company workforce. Companies big and small invested in servers to run applications that automated workflow and desktop PCs to improve worker productivity. The introduction of IT into every corner of the organization profoundly improved the work environment in terms of efficiency and effectiveness but also introduced a level of complexity the people responsible for oversight of these assets were often times ill-equipped to manage. Bloated budgets, cost overruns, and the profligacy of capital left many senior managers with a crisis of confidence in the ability of IT to deliver value to the rest of the organization. Outsourcing became a popular IT strategy for a host of operational activities, including bug fixes, user interface changes, application development, and integration work. It still is. Some organizations see the migration of these activities overseas as an evolutionary step in outsourcing. Good outsourcing practices are a necessary prerequisite to good offshoring practices, and many companies are motivated to move activities already performed by a service provider domestically to those areas of the world where costs may be demonstrably lower than in the United States but where service is not sacrificed but comparable, or even better. Service providers have responded by adding offshore capability to their IT outsourcing management service offers. Organizations equipped with hard-won wisdom in how to do outsourcing right possess a strong foundation to leverage the cost and strategic advantages of offshoring, and this is an important reason why so many IT functions have already been sent overseas.

Big Drop in Telecom and Data Connectivity Prices

The labor rate differential in services between the United States and developing nations such as India has been wide for many years. It is not a new phenomenon. But a labor arbitrage to capture cost savings in services wasn't remotely possible until the precipitous drop in the cost of international telecommunications and data, which makes remote management possible. Oncept, a Bay area consulting firm (www.oncept.net), provided Exhibit 2.2, which shows how dramatically connectivity costs have dropped between Los Angeles and Prague, the Czech Republic, making Prague an attractive offshoring location today. Suddenly, arm's length service arrangements that transcend domestic geographic borders became possible. Fiber-optic capacity increased sevenfold in India between 2001 and 2002, for instance.[12] A trans-Pacific leased circuit with a 128-voice-line capacity cost more than $40,000 per month in 2002 and $11,000 per month in 2004.[13] Telecom was never a company's biggest operational expense, but it is even less so today, representing on average about 10% of operating costs in India. Price reductions are sure to fall further as new capacity is added in Asia. The drop in telecom prices in 2004 alone were dramatic in India.

While prices have dropped, capacity has grown exponentially. The drop in telecommunications costs cannot be overstated when explaining the growth of offshoring. In fact, some experts believe that cheap connectivity as a key ingredient of offshoring will fundamentally change the nature of work. This idea is explored more below.

Diminished Importance of Physical Proximity

It's just not the case anymore that managers need be in physical proximity to the managed every minute of the day for many kinds of work functions to

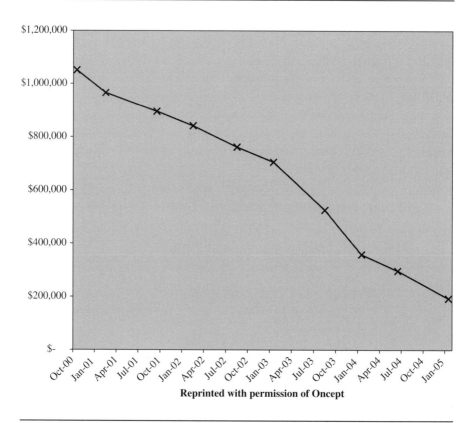

Reprinted with permission of Oncept

Exhibit 2.2   Annual Costs in U.S. Dollars for a 45-Mbps Data Connection
between Los Angeles and Prague

Source: www.oncept.net

get done because much work involves the manipulation of information
rather than the handling of physical goods. It would be difficult for the load-
ing dock foreperson located in Asia to direct stevedores offloading a cargo
ship at a dock in Los Angeles. Manufacturing still requires direct and regular interaction between manager and worker. A lot of work, however, either
in manufacturing back offices or in service industries simply does not
require the intensity of direct supervision. It probably never did, but managers hovered over people because the absence of cheap telecom or the lack of
outsourcing/offshoring service providers for many functions offered no
other arrangement. Besides, many managers are control freaks who believe
constant line-of-sight contact is the only way to manage people. Deep cultural biases built up over years of work practices lead many managers to

find it preposterous that their direct reports are not within a short walk. How else to explain why many information intensive businesses still require workers to show up at the office every day when distant relationships can be just as productive and manageable?

Deeper thinking about the concept of management and physical proximity emerged with the telecommuting craze in the mid-to-late 1990s. Cheap telecom, web-based applications such as intranets, as well as whiteboards and videoconferencing proposed tethering employees to the mother ship, while employees worked from home. The greatest resistance came from managers who did not like the idea of their direct charges working out of sight. Some managers were sure that workers would spend all their work time playing video games or taking care of their little children.

Yet, upon further reflection some managers discovered their fears were misplaced for this reason; a sizeable portion of the work conducted in a company is routinized and measurable, which means that people can be held accountable for results even from a distance. The most effective way to ensure an acceptable level of productivity and keep workers away from video games was to determine the measurability of work output and then set the appropriate performance metrics to track it. Medical transcriptionists, for instance, are paid by the number of lines of physicians' dictation that are typed up every day. A magazine writer is given a word count and is paid for the total number of words published. A software programmer might be responsible for a certain number of lines of code per week. A radiologist might be responsible for analyzing and reporting a certain number of medical images per week. The measurement is crude—raw volume, which doesn't account for quality—but the quality is assumed, which is why we have service level agreements (which will be discussed in more detail in Chapter 10). What is important is the idea of output measurability. This concept is closely tied to deliverables, one of the most common words in project management. In each example, the work product can be broken down into deliverables, which allows for measurability and remote management as the work is being completed. The deliverable could take the form of completion of a certain component of a larger software application, a first draft of a long feature article, a one-page written interpretation of an x-ray, five pages of medical or legal transcripts, and so on. Telecommuting or "offsiting" these functions is feasible because once the quality level is agreed upon, managers can leave these workers alone to do their stuff. Offshoring is an evolutionary phase in the growth of distributed work environments. In every example above, the final work product can be sent down the wire, and it matters little given the quality of telecommunications technology today that what is being sent down that wire travels 10 or 10,000 miles.

The fact that software programmers are getting caught in the same vortex as medical transcriptionists is one of the paradoxes of the offshoring phenomenon, but it is only a paradox when you assume that education levels and the content of intellectual effort involved in the work correlates with job security. As the examples show, there is no correlation between high credentialization requirements for a particular career and whether that professional is subject to international competition. The rigors of software training no longer offer an inherent barrier to entry to the pursuit of that profession, as the size of the foreign software worker population can attest to. The important job feature that transcriptionists and programmers share is its routinization and output measurability. What jobs are candidates for offshoring is explored in more depth in the "How Big Can This Thing Get?" section.

DRIVERS OF OFFSHORING ARE INTERDEPENDENT

None of the conditions explicated above by itself is enough of a business reason to offshore. Low wage rates in a distant land are great, as long as there exists affordable telecommunications whose cost would otherwise cancel out the benefits of a labor arbitrage. A vast supply of English-speaking workers offers less value if many of those workers have little formal education. Attractive tax policies will contribute to the bottom line from offshoring but only if the labor rate differential is substantial enough to offer a medium to long-term return on investment (ROI). If no labor arbitrage exists, the tax advantages alone may or may not be worth it. It is the confluence and interdependence of these forces, some which started 50 years ago and some far more recent, that collectively make offshoring a compelling strategy today.

Cummins is an example of a company who leveraged a number of interdependent and interrelated drivers of offshoring, which taken together drove strategic outcomes. It began with offshoring of application development of software that manages an engine's performance, including such functions as firing the ignition system in the most fuel-efficient way. The design is conducted in the United States, but the coding is done in Pune, India, where Indiana-based Cummins has a development facility. The money it saves on engine software is money that is spent on additional manpower to get the software made more quickly and, therefore, engines to market faster.[14]

The second strategic outcome grew out of a decision to reengineer its development efforts to rely less on physical prototypes and more on sophisticated modeling software, which simulates a prototype for engine development. The company squeezed $3 million out of development and reduced turnaround times from nine to six months—in the United States.[15] It offshored this work to highly trained engineers despite the business process performance improvements already here because Cummins could hire incrementally more engineers at lower cost. However, a chief driver of the decision to offshore this development work was a judgment that Indian engineers were hungrier and more enthusiastic in the face of these challenges.[16] Several intertwined conditions helped Cummins achieve its goals: lower software development costs, lower product development costs, the relative ease with which Cummins could replicate high-value business processes offshore, and the attitude and energy of the technical talent all fused to measurably improve the manufacturer's competitive position.

HOW BIG CAN THIS THING GET?

Quite big, depending on whom you talk to. The growth of the offshoring market should be looked at it in two ways. One, what is its growth potential in terms of revenue and/or job creation? Two, how high up what we can call the "cognitive food chain" can offshoring reach? Already mentioned in Chapter 1 was the idea that the breadth of offshoring is greater than its depth today. But if everything that can move down a wire is up for grabs, this exposure will impact not only a significant share of domestic job classifications but also a significant total number of American workers; that is, the impact from offshoring should deepen in relation to the total worker population as it also spreads across many job classifications. We have already seen hints of the idea that offshoring is not confined only to low-wage, low-skilled work, as any U.S. programmer who has been replaced by a comparably skilled worker in India can attest. Could it actually show up at the boardroom door?

In terms of revenue and job growth, estimates vary, but McKinsey estimates that the offshoring marketplace was already worth $32 to $35 billion in 2002 out of the estimated $3 trillion of total business functions that could be offshored[17] (about 25 to 30% of the U.S. economy). It expects growth at a rate of 30 to 40% a year, representing a $100 billion industry by 2008.[18] The Bureau of Labor Statistics, however, is having difficultly quantifying the aggregate numbers of jobs lost from offshoring so far. It began to track this phenomenon only in January 2004.[19] While uncertainty exists about the precise volume of job losses that will stem from future off-shoring, McKinsey tells us offshoring will be a big industry indeed.

COGNITIVE FOOD CHAIN

Another way to get a handle on the extent to which offshoring will affect the U.S. job market is first to visualize a cognitive food chain in which job functions are placed within a hierarchy of skill and intellectual demands. Then, in a second rendering, visualize the offshoreability of job functions against several critical criteria: the measurability of work output (the more measurable the more suitable for offshoring), the ability to manage and oversee the work from a great distance (the more manageable from a distance the more suitable for offshoring), and a related issue, the need for that job function to remain inside the organization's base of operation in order for that job to offer relevance and value (the less need for a job function's physical proximity the more suitable for offshoring). The purpose of this exercise is to compare and contrast the two conceptualizations, so that readers can see that there is no easy correlation between the cognitive demands of a particular job category and that category's suitability for off-shoring; many low skill jobs are ideal for offshoring, but so are some very cognitively demanding positions. Through this exercise, readers will understand better what drives the candidacy and suitability for offshoring by job class. There is another motivation for conducting this exercise: to disabuse anyone of the notion that a worker's ability to move up the cognitive food chain inoculates him or her from the forces of offshoring. This is not necessarily true.

It is essential to remind the readers of two important points here. One, the bulk of this book concerns itself not with offshoring job functions but rather business processes. The job functions follow naturally. And two, this specific analysis is best applied to those situations where the organization offshores to a third-party service provider. This exercise is less germane to a captive situation because the job functions are still under the direct control of the organization even if they are geographically disbursed, and we are interested in what job classes can be readily forklifted out of the direct control of the organization and overseen by a third party. A global company's move to consolidate business process operations in a foreign office to save money or capture other efficiencies—captive offshoring—is a popular and important flavor of offshoring, but this exercise is attempting greater comprehension of how large the impact across job functions offshoring presents to the U.S. economy.

Exhibit 2.3 represents a cognitive food chain, a hierarchy from low to high of the skills, education, and intellectual demands of particular jobs. The hierarchy is admittedly arbitrary—a software programmer might belong at the top of the pyramid, and some people might argue that CEOs who continually destroy shareholder value might belong in the same category as mail room workers, since they don't seem to exhibit any cognitive ability to manage the company. Someone is bound to get upset at where they are depicted in this hierarchy, so a couple of more points are in order. One, this construct generally holds true and does not require extactitude for the larger point to win merit. Yes, a call center rep fielding highly technical questions from semiconductor engineers requires high cognitive ability and would certainly warrant a bump up a couple of rungs in the hierarchy, but generally the placement of this job class is accurate. Two, this image is not a value judgment about the intelligence of anyone doing these jobs but rather speaks to the intellectual demands of the job itself.

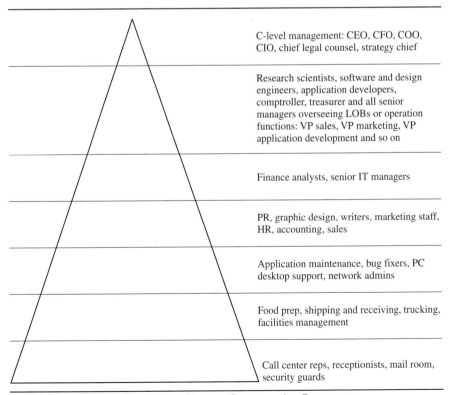

EXHIBIT 2.3   COGNITIVE DEMANDS OF VARIOUS CORPORATE JOB FUNCTIONS

Plenty of smart college-age kids work in a company mail room. You just don't have to be a genius to work in one.

Compare and contrast that figure with the following, Exhibit 2.4, which depicts the offshoreability of these job functions against the three important offshoring criteria described earlier: measurability of work output, ability for distance management, and little need for job proximity to any physical location.

In the offshoring sweepstakes, company truck drivers and security guards are the fellow travelers with the CFO and chief legal counsel. None of these positions are likely candidates for offshoring because they do not meet all the criteria. A receptionist's job is arguably offshoreable, but part of his or her value is assisting more senior managers in their work, which

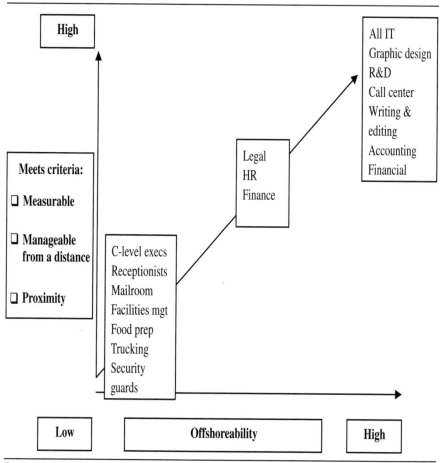

EXHIBIT 2.4   JOB OFFSHORABILITY FACTOR

might require heavy face-to-face contact in the course of a business day. Facilities managers are not likely to manage the company's boilers and air conditioning systems from a distance even though sensor and controls technology makes it possible to diagnose performance and problems from a distance. Someone needs to be around to fix problems as they arise (although this function could be outsourced). At the other extreme, all those job functions possess work output that is highly measurable, do not require physical proximity to a company's base of operations, and can be managed from a distance. In the middle are jobs that fall in between; the VP of HR is likely not an offshoreable function because of his or her consultative role with other senior managers. This requires a high degree of peer interaction. However, lower-level HR functions in payroll or employee benefits administration meet the three criteria. The chief in-house legal counsel is not likely going anywhere for the same reason. However, a lot of legal work is rote and boilerplate. Other regulatory obstacles might exist to stop the offshoring of legal work, but it is a work area that, in some respects, in theory meets all three criteria. Accounting is ripe for offshoring because of its criteria fit. As readers get deeper into the book, they should discover that the degree of offshoreability of different job functions within a particular domain such as HR, finance, IT, and so forth maps to the degree of offshoreability of the business processes these functions are tied to. In other words, some HR jobs such as help desk or payroll staff are highly offshoreable, and so are the business processes the jobs are responsible for. Some finance jobs in accounting or accounts payable or receivable are offshoreable, and so are the business processes these jobs are tied to. Again, the book's focus is directed toward business processes not job functions, but it is helpful to see the link between the two.

Some of these examples are so obvious that they bring into question why the exercise was done in the first place. One, the offshoring candidacy of job classifications is not so obvious in the context of the hysteria the subject seems to stir, as if every worker in the United States were vulnerable to its effects. Two, exploring jobs that are offshoring targets brings into question the conventional wisdom that education is the silver bullet against job loss from offshoring. Clearly, this construct demonstrates the partial fallacy of that argument, and this issue is definitely worth exploring.

INVINCIBILITY OF THE SYMBOLIC ANALYST?

Clinton administration labor secretary Robert Reich coined the phrase "symbolic analyst" to describe the type of job that requires a high degree of cognitive ability and education. It's a great phrase not only to describe the essence of the abstract and critical thinking that goes into the work of a significant swath of the U.S. labor force but also to capture the nature of our current economy, one that is built more on intellectual firepower and less on physical strength. It is not universally true but is true enough for a large part of our economy. One wonders if he trademarked it.

The danger is assuming that high cognitive demands equate to job security, that symbolic analysts will thrive in the future economy. We now know this is not necessarily true. The point here is not that high cognitive job functions are definitely going to be offshored but rather that they lend themselves to offshoring should the organization decide to try. In Reich's estimation, symbolic analysts are poised to dodge the offshoring bullet as long as they do not get trapped into job functions that are routinized.[20] Routinization, that which is an habitual or repeatable, equates with measurability, an important criterion in determining offshoreability. Take journalists, a job classification you would not think is ripe for offshoring. (We already saw that one technical journal is trying). The *New York Times* is unlikely to offshore its national political reporting desk. The idea is absurd. Those reporters do not produce routinized work even if the work output is measurable, and there is a high need for worker proximity to a base of operation in the Washington, DC, bureau. Less absurd is the idea of the *New York Times* offshoring copyediting, a lower-level but important editing function in newspapers. Intelligent, foreign workers fluent in English as a written and spoken language could perform this routinized and measurable work in Bangalore or Singapore and email the stories back to the United States. If managed properly they also do not need to work in physical proximity to the newspaper's headquarters. That the *New York Times* is unlikely to offshore copyediting does not detract from the feasibility of offshoring it. This function meets the criteria.

OFFSHORING INNOVATION

Another related offshoring shibboleth is that organizations should not offshore that which is strategic to the organization. Those activities that help win customers and make money are best done in-house where the organization exerts complete control over these activities that directly influence these outcomes. How can we reconcile this belief with the growing amount of product design work American companies are offshoring to third-party specialists?

Companies like Dell, Motorola, and Philips are offshoring the design of key products to third-party outfits, several are in Taiwan, adopting these designs in their products and slapping their brands on them.[21] Intense price competition in digital gadgets—MP3 players, cell phones—is driving companies to seek cost reductions in the most strategic activities of the company.[22] It isn't that these organizations don't view R&D as strategic, but rather R&D's productivity, the ROI in the form of high-impact products for the amount of money invested in the research and development activities that produces them, is lower than senior management would like. Organizations have the means, through offshoring and other techniques, to control internal costs with a fair amount of precision and have at least attempted so in every corner of the company. R&D is just about the last controllable expense companies have, and they are inclined to cut it unless internal R&D produces more. And this trend is not confined to electronics. The China Pharmaceutical Economy Research Center estimates that through 2005 drug companies will either outsource or offshore up to 65% of R&D.[23]

A deeper analysis of offshored R&D shows us that, just as in the case with other business processes like HR and finance, some job functions are more offshoreable than others. Companies today are deconstructing the entire R&D workflow to determine who stays in-house and who is offshored to a service provider. A design collaboration software company commissioned a study looking at this very question for a hypothetical company whose R&D operation is composed of 1,000 engineers and the results were summarized in a March 2005 issue of *BusinessWeek*. The results were as follows: approximately 150 were deemed most critical to the organization.[24] These jobs included the managers who direct and oversee product development strategies and manage R&D project milestones and budgets. System engineers are also critical because they establish the performance standards for products. Less critical job functions included mechanical engineers who stress test products and engineers who turn designs into prototypes. The most suitable R&D jobs for offshoring, the study, found were engineers who figure out reductions in manufacturing costs and documentation specialists who draw product renderings for the factory and write operating manuals. The least critical job functions in R&D share certain attributes that readers should be quite familiar with now: the work is measurable, it can be managed from a distance, and the job responsibilities do not require high face-to-face interaction with others in the base of operation. In the end, the study calculated that nearly 30% of that hypothetical company's R&D staff could be offshored.[25] .

CONCLUSION

The perfect storm for offshoring bears down on the U.S. economy. Cheap telecom, availability of English-speaking and educated foreign workers, the cost proposition of sending in house work to an outsider, and the fact that many job functions share the characteristics of measurability, distance manageability, and low need for proximity come together perfectly like pieces of a giant jigsaw puzzle. The only element left to determine whether offshoring will remain in our sights for years to come is whether companies can pull it off successfully. Offshoring is still an emerging management discipline even though its roots are found in outsourcing, a practice with which many organizations have experience. So, it's time to leave the theoretical and enter the practical. What are the strategies and tactics an organization can employ to gain maximum value out of offshoring? The rest of this book explores this very question.

NOTES

1. Nandan Nilekani, CEO of Infosys Technologies speaking at the 2004 World Economic Forum, as reported in Steve Lohr, "Many New Causes for Old Problem of Jobs Lost Abroad," *New York Times* February 15, 2004.
2. *See* C-SPAN's "In-Depth" with social scientist Charles Murray, which aired February 6, 2005. During a three-hour conversation, Murray discussed the value of a college education and the possibility that far too many people unsuited for college attend anyway because of the belief that it is the vehicle for upward mobility. These comments were made in the context of a caller to the program suggesting the need for apprenticeship training in high schools, which Murray supported. Webcast archive at www.booktv.org/indepth/archive_2005.asp; click on the Charles Murray link.
3. Steve Liesman, "US Tax Code Provisions Encourage Offshore Jobs," *Wall Street Journal*, March 4, 2004.
4. Ibid.
5. Andy Meisler, "Where in the World is Offshoring Going?" *Workforce Management*, January 2004, p. 45.
6. "Offshoring from France to Africa," Commweb, October 22, 2004, www.commweb.com/news/51000367.
7. "Profiting from the North African Option," *Datamonitor* report, March 2005.
8. www.mphasis.com/news_rooms/Outsourcingcenter.htm.
9. Interview Ashish Paul, CEO and managing director, Cincom, February 9, 2005.
10. Fran Foo, "Offshoring: Don't Shoot the Messenger," *ZDNET Australia*, August 24, 2004.

11. Ibid.
12. Jesse Drucker, "Global Talk Gets Cheaper," *Wall Street Journal*, March 11, 2004.
13. Ibid.
14. Michael Oneal, "From Indiana to India: Why 1(One) Firm Leapt," *Chicago Tribune*, April 5, 2004.
15. Ibid.
16. Ibid.
17. Vivek Agrawal, Diana Farrell, and Jaana K. Remes, "Offshoring and Beyond," *McKinsey Quarterly* special edition, 2003.
18. Ibid
19. Joseph Rebello, "Job Losses from Outsourcing Prove Hard for US to Quantify," *Wall Street Journal*, November 22, 2004, p. A2.
20. Robert Reich, "Nice Work If You Can Get It," *Wall Street Journal* OP-ED, December 26, 2003.
21. Pete Engardio and Bruce Einhorn, "Outsourcing Innovation," *BusinessWeek*, March 21, 2005.
22. Ibid.
23. Laura Santini, "Drug Companies Look to China For Cheap R&D," *Wall Street Journal*, November 22, 2004.
24. Pete Engardio, "R&D Jobs: Who Stays, Who Goes?" Online Extra "Outsourcing Innovation" issue of *BusinessWeek*.
25. Ibid.

3

COASE AND THE CHANGING NATURE OF WORK

Nobel Prize economist Ronald Coase posed a very simple question in a 1937 article—written when he was in his late twenties—entitled "The Nature of the Firm"[1] that resonates still. Why do we have corporations? What is their purpose? What economic logic brought them into being? Capitalism itself does not explain why economic activity inheres to an operational, social, and legal arrangement called a company. Why couldn't the manufacture of cars and ovens have taken a different form? For instance, why couldn't the creation of a product be the sum result of the economic interactions of a number of independent workers who could rely purely upon market mechanisms to negotiate the price of their services in the assembly line?

Although simple, the question was incredibly insightful and his answer deepens our understanding of offshoring today. The answer is transaction costs. Throughout history, companies controlled most if not all the processes of production because the cost to them was far lower than having an outsider perform them—if even an outsider existed to offer the service. Coase reminded us that the cost to make something is not confined to production costs or labor costs but also encompasses information and search costs and the time it takes to negotiate contracts and the terms of engagement between business entities. Policing and enforcing contracts is another set of transaction costs. Theoretically, a worker on the assembly line responsible for pistons in engines could negotiate pricing and other terms with another worker responsible for piston rods or piston rings in a market arrangement that would move toward the goal of building a car engine but this scenario wasn't practical. It would have taken far too much time to resolve this kind of arrangement to mutual satisfaction—one result of any market transaction—and time-to market considerations in automobile manufacture are quite important. A series of market transactions such as this might have led to it taking months instead of hours to build a complete car.

It was far easier for companies to internalize many production activities in a kind of central planning model.[2] Much economic activity was best completed where organized groups of people performed different production or back-office functions in a hierarchy of decision making. All the important decisions were made at the top and those below carry them out. This kind of capitalism resembles the Army far more than it does a collection of independent market actors pursuing efficiency in a complex world. This is no accident. Early management structures in the modern corporation resembled a military hierarchy because managers were comfortable with this arrangement.

Coase learned from talking to managers that they understood well the tradeoffs between doing things in-house and contracting with an outsider.[3] Although these insights were formulated in the context of "production," they are powerfully applicable to companies who "make" services rather than products. Many functions conducted internally are now candidates for outsourcing, and by extension, offshoring precisely because the transaction costs are low enough to make these arrangements feasible and cost-effective.

One conclusion that observers might draw is that as companies externalize functions through service provider relationships they will inexorably become smaller. Clearly, the evidence is the opposite in many cases. Companies are more gargantuan than ever. Perhaps the scale of some companies today speaks more to the need to leverage market size and scope to compete effectively and the impulse to grow through acquisition rather than organically. Despite volumes of empirical evidence that suggest mergers of large organizations destroy value as often as they create it (HP, Compaq, and its firing of Carly Fiorina is a recent example) companies continue to walk down the marriage aisle and put on organizational pounds in the process. Coase himself observed in his paper that "changes like the telephone and the telegraph which tend to reduce the cost of organizing spatially will tend to increase the size of the firm".[4] Telecommunications and Internet technologies, which make outsourcing more feasible, don't necessarily decrease the size of organizations. These forces might actually help make them bigger. But the causal relationship between the ability to outsource/offshore and the size of companies is not the point. The salient point is that some transaction costs are low enough that traditionally internalized functions—software development, finance, HR, order fulfillment, call centers, and the list goes on—are routinely exposed to market arrangements today in which companies negotiate with service providers to fulfill these activities and minimize transaction costs in doing so, i.e. offshoring. Search costs are lower because of the Internet and proliferation of firms offering outsourced/offshored services that make themselves known in the marketplace. Negotiation and bargaining costs are lower because of the proliferation of service level agreements and contracts between company and service provider. Policing and enforcement costs are lower because of information technologies that provide operational data access for companies to keep service providers honest.

It is doubtful that we will ever live in a world where discrete and very granular business activities such as the assembly line example above will all become subject to a daily market function in order to complete them. But we might very well end up in a world where work is far more distributed and borne by myriad service delivery relationships than we ever thought imaginable. The movie industry is often cited as a vivid example of this distributed, market-driven work paradigm, outsourcing of a kind. While the motion picture companies might be centralized and hierarchical, the aggregation of talent required to bring a production to the screen is subject to price signals and market negotiation because almost no one associated with a movie works for a movie company per se but is either a freelancer or an employee of a production house contracted with a studio to produce the film. The studios really act as banks to finance movies and as distribution arms to distribute the product to the theater chains across the United States. Professionals in this industry have been acclimated for some time in assuming the transaction costs required to set the terms for a movie to get made. Cheap telecom didn't drive this. Other forces were at work. But the result is still the same; market-force arrangements achieve the same results as command-and-control organizational hierarchies. The economic literature is unclear whether the reduction in transaction costs will tend to make companies bigger or smaller. The data is inconclusive.[5] What is clear is that important but distracting and costly business processes are candidates for offshoring, regardless of what size companies will become from it. And this will only accelerate.

WILL THE NATURE OF WORK CHANGE?

While this book does not expressly address this question, it is worth exploring briefly because many believe that the nature of work will change if outsourcing and offshoring continue to prove their mettle. Despite the introduction of automation and productivity-enhancing technologies into the enterprise, management guru Peter Drucker believes that knowledge workers are not nearly as productive as they could be and that this circumstance is the direct result of an historical bias on the part of companies toward doing everything in-house.[6] Outsourcing/offshoring is a good start in closing the productivity gap, but Drucker also believes that the focus on cost savings from labor arbitrage is misplaced. The real value of outsourcing/offshoring is that it raises the quality of the people who still work for you because those individuals will dedicate themselves to the critical work that determines the performance of the company such as R&D, innovation and market strategy.[7] Ideally, they will be more focused and effective in their jobs. Nonessential work, on the other hand, will be performed by outsiders who do nothing else but figure out the means of delivering support functions the most efficient and effective way possible. And service providers will deliver all nonstrategic functions better because they specialize in these functions for a wide array of customers and have developed a far deeper expertise in their execution than could ever be realized in a corporation.

This is the theory anyway. Outsourcing/offshoring and the cheap connectivity that makes it possible on a scale unknown in the past are a manifestation of a world in which, in some expert's estimation, companies can enjoy both the scale efficiencies of large companies and the benefits of small ones, including flexibility and freedom.[8] Distributed work arrangements mean that decision making and power should be decentralized as well. In this new world the best way to gain power might actually be to give it away because control freaks who micromanage—and they are legion in U.S. companies—will always receive active resistance or capitulation manifested in a lack of motivation from workers. In either case, the manager's goals are not realized.

Coupled with decentralized decision making is the use of market arrangements externally and internally to get things done, such as procuring more freelancers for project work, or in an internal scenario, using market mechanisms for employees to buy and sell products and services among themselves. In one example of this internal market scenario, an oil company declared that it would decrease greenhouse gas emissions 10% by a certain date. Managers handed out pollution permits to business units with each permit allowing for a certain amount of emissions per year. Using an electronic trading system, business units could buy or sell permits that would help them reach the stated target. A business unit that was having trouble reaching the company target could buy from another business unit the number of permits it needed to fall within compliance. In one year, the company business units traded 4.5 million tons of emission rights at an average internal price of $40 a ton.[9] This market arrangement not only helped the company reach and enterprise-wide target nine years before the deadline, but it also democratized decision making because it allowed each business unit leader to decide how much emission reduction was the optimal amount for that particular unit.[10]

SOFTWARE INDUSTRY OFFERS HINTS

How custom applications will be created in the future is another concrete example of how work will change in these new, decentralized work arrangements. Historically, an enterprise custom software program has moved through a series of stages as it evolved from tadpole to frog. A company starts with a needs analysis and a statement of business requirements, then proceeds in successive stages through design, coding, testing, documentation, training, and implementation. This methodology has been sacrosanct because it works. It is also very expensive for a couple reasons. One, although legacy code and other design elements quite applicable to the construction of a new software application are sitting around on someone's hard drive, they are seldom reused in a systematic fashion. Second, users are not called upon to weigh in with interface and functionality preferences until the software is almost completed. Changes tend to be very expensive when most of the application has already been built.

What is emerging is a new, more cost-effective approach to application creation, and offshoring is driving its adoption. Developers leverage object-oriented programming techniques to create canned, reusable software components that have unlimited reuse in future applications. Adoption of this approach fundamentally changes how application development work is done. Since large applications are created in discrete parts, not unlike cars assembled by companies from interchangeable parts, bugs and defects are discovered and fixed earlier in the process than the traditional testing stage, where the cost involved is factors greater. Junior engineers spend their time assembling software components, while the design is left to more senior programmers.[11] End user feedback can be solicited and acted upon much earlier in the development process, which cuts costs as well.

Indian application development houses are applying a manufacturing metaphor to what has been viewed as an art. The automobile metaphor is so strong that some experts argue that the software market might evolve into a collection of vendors each selling their component specialties that, when assembled, constitute a complete application. The way that software is made today is not unlike the approach of vertically integrated car companies in the early days of the industry; they owned operations for every facet of automobile making. Today, car companies rely upon a vast web of suppliers for everything from windshields to bumpers. Could the application development business, influenced by the work processes of offshore service providers, reconstitute itself in this new form?

It is not as if U.S. programmers were unaware of the power of reuse. But strong disincentives blocked broad acceptance of this development approach, not the least of which are fears of deep budget cuts in IT budgets arising out of the cost efficiencies derived from this new way of building programs.[12] IT professionals also face the obsolescence of ingrained and proven project management techniques used with traditional development methods—checklists, milestones, and a whole body of knowledge around software development using the old methodology. Apportioning project costs is another challenge; how much does the IT organization charge back to a business unit for a new application if half of it was built with software components from applications going back several years? None of these issues are insurmountable, but they involve change. Change is time-consuming and sometimes unpleasant, and there was no earthly reason in the minds of programmers why they should have to. People seemed satisfied with standard operating procedure around application development. Until offshoring.

The need for offshore service providers to inject process discipline to ensure quality is driving the adoption of these orphaned work techniques. They are simply too powerful to keep hidden in the attic any longer. Service providers realize that if quality is not at least comparable to that from domestic service providers or internal IT organizations, the cost advantage simply isn't compelling and the offshore value proposition disappears. Distributed work arrangements such as offshoring are changing the nature of work; the change in the nature of software development work will be complete when domestic service providers and IT organizations are forced to adopt the work methods of their Indian counterparts or . . . see the work offshored.

OFFSHORING ALSO OFFERS HINTS

The act of offshoring itself suggests how extensively the nature of work will change if it continues its growth path. Instead of a focus on the management of internal resources, mostly people and technology, the focus will shift to the search for a realization of value from another organization. Management shifts from decisions on labor and capital allocation directly to the management of a service provider who makes those labor and capital allocation decisions on its behalf. The offshoring organization is less interested in explicitly those decisions and more in cost cutting or more strategic impacts from the relationship itself. It's up to the service provider to worry about specific labor and capital deployment and how those decisions will capture the value that will please the customer. It is not the responsibility of the offshoring organization to dictate these decisions, since the service provider is presumably more expert than it in managing specific offshored business processes because it does so for many organizations and has developed particular expertise.

Because of this shift in management focus, the critical question for the offshoring organization is not, how do we allocate labor and capital to drive performance and meet operational and strategic goals? But rather, how do we manage effectively the outside organization with who has been entrusted with the management of our critical business processes? Answering this question reveals the shifting nature of work as different management and work skills are required of the offshoring company. Think of the change as managing the managers and decision makers or "metamanagement." If offshoring proliferates into many company operations, the managers of the offshoring organization might do well to manage those offshoring relationships as a portfolio of cost center activities and capital investments with expected net present values (NPVs) attached.

As readers will see when they dive into the chapters directly addressing offshoring strategies and tactics the new required skills and operational processes brought about by this shift in management focus are extensive. At the highest level, companies with more offshoring in their future will need to figure out the optimal decision-making governance that determines a yes or no to any offshoring initiatives. Who is involved? What is their say in the decision? Companies will need to be as adept at hiring the right service provider, as they have been skilled at hiring the right employees. That is, companies will develop new recruiting skills, since they are recruiting vendors, not people. What kind of vendor selection framework does the organization use in recruiting new offshoring talent to mitigate the risk that the relationship will fail and that value will not be realized? This is an acquired skill and not just the application of common sense. Companies will have to figure out the right combination of carrots and sticks with which to motivate the service provider to provide excellent service. What is the optimal contracting relationship that ends up as a win-win for both parties? Too often organizations are intent on grabbing the last nickel on the table during contract negotiations, and they are finding out that this attitude in many offshoring experiences proves the cliché that you get what you pay for. Developing sophistication in service provider contracting is an acquired skill, and because this is work that some organizations have had little experience in conducting they haven't acquired this newly needed expertise.

Then we get into the squishy concept of company culture. It certainly will change in a world of offshoring. Today, offshoring in many organizations is ad hoc. Decisions are not arrived at under any consistent strategic framework that considers an offshoring initiative's alignment and support for a company's overarching goals. This should change as companies recognize that offshoring is no longer about hiring third parties to do application development and graphic design but far more strategic activities like research and development. The company will need to figure out how to balance the strategic vision of offshoring as a long-term viable management practice against the desire to empower and motivate employees to perform in the face of prospective layoffs down the road. Figure *that* out. A company culture will also change if by virtue of offshoring the organizational hierarchy flattens because fewer people work in the company. As was already alluded to, decision rights are likely to be distributed instead of centralized. What is the correct decision rights and authority blueprint where offshoring is concerned if, as readers will see, so many centers of power and organizational control are involved in the decision?

In every example just provided—strategic, tactical, and cultural—fundamentally new skills and new capabilities are asked for when companies, desiring to succeed, offshore. Companies find that new skills and capabilities are required all the time as market conditions and its goals change over time. Why so different with offshoring? For the simple reason that management in the U.S. corporation over the past 100 years has been built around the motivation and direction of people and exploitation of assets. In offshoring, management is built around the motivation and direction of service providers (unless, of course, the offshoring remains inhouse—captive offshoring). The company is no longer managing people and assets of certain business processes; it is managing relationships. Very different. And the fact that this management shift requires new skills and new capabilities means that the nature of work is evolving because new skills and capabilities are a response to what work the organization performs and how the work is performed.

CONCLUSION

Over time offshoring might prove to be both cause and effect of how the nature of work will change. Offshoring is a cause of changes in work because as a management discipline the oversight of outsiders represents the need to conduct different in house activities to make these relationships successful and this imperative requires different skills and organizational arrangements. Extensive offshoring of business processes and work activities that historically might have appeared inconceivable might be the catalyst for many more market-driven, less hierarchical work arrangements as well—perhaps the virtual corporation concept we have heard of so many times in the past but that has yet to be realized. If we offshore, the nature of work will change. Offshoring is also an effect of changes in work because it represents the impact and outcome of decisions to exploit interdependent business conditions facing organizations today: low-cost, high-quality international labor, cheap telecom, measurability of some work processes, and the need to focus on core competencies are a few.

Peter Drucker declares that every function that does not offer a career track into senior management should be outsourced[13] (and by association, presumably, offshored). Surely, the nature of work will change for companies who follow his advice.

NOTES

1. Ronald Coase, "The Nature of the Firm,"1937. This paper is widely available on the Internet. This text sourced people.bu.edu/vaguirre/courses/bu332/nature_firm.pdf for its copy.
2. Hal Varian, "A New Economy With No New Economics," *New York Times*, January 17, 2002.
3. Thomas W. Hazlett, "Looking for Results," *Reason Magazine* interview with Ronald Coase, no date provided.
4. Coase, "The Nature of the Firm," p. 8 (PDF form).
5. Varian, "A New Economy With No New Economics."
6. Brent Schlender, "Peter Drucker Sets Us Straight," *Fortune*, December 29, 2003.
7. Ibid.
8. Thomas W. Malone, "The Future of Work: How the New Order of Business Will Shape Your Organization, Your Management Style and Your Life," Harvard Business School Press, 2005. From Malone's website at ccs.mit.edu/futureofwork.

9. Ibid, page 92.
10. Ibid.
11. See the "Quality Relies on Process, Planning" section of Michael Oneal, "From Indiana to India: Why 1 (One) Firm Leapt," *Chicago Tribune*, April 5, 2004.
12. Chris F. Kemerer, "Reusable Asset," *InformationWeek*, September 22, 1997.
13. Schlender, "Peter Drucker Sets Us Straight."

Phase I

STRATEGY DEVELOPMENT: THINK

An offshoring strategy asks: How can business process offshoring complement and add value to the overriding business goals? Where is the alignment between business goals and an offshoring idea? This alignment question is now routinely asked of the IT organization when expensive capital investments are proposed. It stands to reason the inquiry should extend not only to the offshoring of IT services but also to any business process domain that might prove to be an offshoring candidate.

A well-defined offshoring strategy is designed to identify new capabilities that offshoring could provide directly, either through a service provider or in-house. A clear strategy should also point the way to indrect benefits such as the deployment of offshore capability freeing up internal resources for higher value-added work. As Chapter 1 demonstrated, companies offshore for a variety of reasons beyond simple cost reduction. An offshoring strategy maps out the deployment and management of external resources that support internal efforts to reach the strategic goals of the organization. That strategy might include such things as long-term cultivation of overseas technical talent to support a company's product innovation path or an alliance with a service provider who can provide fulfillment and logistical services near a new market a company is just entering.

An example of offshoring alignment to innovation strategy occurs when the company cultivates human capital where local labor demonstrates considerable strengths. Like most tech companies, Intel has a voracious need for technical talent. It continuously builds relationships with quality centers of technical training as seed beds for future innovation in the company. A relationship Intel has forged at one state university in Russia, for example, has a team helping Intel scientists develop software for wireless applications.[1] Intel often starts with an equipment donation, then the partnership evolves into its development of curricula and the joint projects. While Intel is well schooled in building global manufacturing capabilities around the world, its offshoring of research activities (which does not necessarily mean any layoffs of U.S. scientists) is part of its long range goal to cultivate the best scientific talent it can find. Historically, Russia has produced some of the best technical talent around, this despite its history of stifling totalitarianism, and more recently, a crippled economy marred by corruption. It can't get much more strategic in any organization, however, than building a pipeline of talent eager to go to work for it. Whether Intel calls it offshoring or personnel development, there is clearly alignment between this use of foreign workers and the goals of the company, which, as anyone who follows technology trends knows, demands constant innovation.

In another example, it was shown that by offshoring logistics and fulfillment business processes locally, a company improves its on-time delivery now that delivery is closer to customers. Freed from the distractions of building a fulfillment capabilty internally, it can devote more internal resources and energy to market entry activities such as channel development and sales. Offshoring supports a strategic goal of opening a new market overseas.

The offshoring strategy, ideally, is baked before a specific need ever arises. In this way, strategy sets the direction for future decisions about all the tactical stuff companies can get bogged down in such as country site selection, skills assessment of the offshore talent, cost/benefit models, and so on. If decision activity around offshoring is standalone and done in the context of an immediate business need, by definition, these actions are tactical and ultimately myopic because they do not see the forest for the trees. An offshoring strategy is a set of principles and guidelines aligned with critical business goals that indicate which business processes make sense to offshore, suggest the kind of relationship that should be developed to offshore and set the direction for the ongoing management of that offshoring relationship.

---

1. Jason Bush, "A Renaissance for Russian Science," *BusinessWeek*, August 9, 2004.

4

POURING THE FOUNDATION: THE OFFSHORING VALUE DELIVERY FRAMEWORK

Examples in Chapters 1 and 2 convey the idea that although in intent and impact much of offshoring is about cost cuts, clearly there is more going on. Business need is varied and so are the types of processes and resources companies seek to offshore. Because of the breadth of both the business problems and the processes and activities designed to solve those problems out of which a company decides to make an offshoring move, it would seem difficult to establish a planning and decision framework that could satisfy every context-specific scenario. Nevertheless, any company interested in building a methodological approach to offshoring is invited to explore the framework presented in Exhibit 4.1.

Exhibit 4.1 represents a phased-based look into the major areas of management decision making and activities to build an effective offshoring capability, with a beginning that requires offshoring strategy and ending with the proper maintenance of an established offshore relationship. Within each phase are the important activities that require tactical execution in order that the phase fulfill its mission and that all phases collectively fulfill the organization's overarching goals. Taken together, all four phases ensure that value is delivered from the offshoring effort, whether it be cost savings, operational improvements, strategic impacts, or a combination of these. The framework is applicable to any set of business processes: IT, call centers,

49

Strategy Development		Selection Process		Relationship Building		Sustained Management
Phase 1 Think	⇑	Phase 2 Plan	⇑	Phase 3 Negotiate	⇑	Phase 4 Execute & Manage
□ Strategy/Goals Alignment		□ Develop Selection Criteria		□ Pilot Project		□ Transition Strategy
□ In-House or Out of House		□ Selection Process		□ Security Framework		□ Performance Tracking
□ Organizational Readiness		□ RFP		□ Revise Business Case		□ Internal Governance
□ Strategic – Workforce Plan		□ Site Selection		□ Contracting		□ Strategic
□ Operational – Decision-Making Governance				□ Relationship Model		□ Operational
□ Business Case				□ Exit Strategy		□ Just-in-Time

EXHIBIT 4.1 OFFSHORING VALUE DELIVERY FRAMEWORK™

finance, logistics, and so forth within any business context or circumstance out of which the need to offshore first arose.

As you should see, the process-driven framework is iterative and causal; its guidance is designed to be repeated each time a new offshoring effort is considered. Repeatability provides structure to the process of managing offshoring activity, while raising the competency level of managers as mastery is gained through doing something again and again. The framework consists of an inherent circularity, although it is not rendered visually that way. Once an offshoring effort has been executed and is subject to ongoing management, managers can return to the beginning when a new offshore proposal has emerged and begin the process anew. The overall offshoring strategy is reviewed, and the planning, execution, and management process is launched all over again. The framework is also causal in that each phase's completion is dependent on the one preceding it. It's hardly likely a company would establish service level agreements (SLAs) in the third, or relationship-building phase, without first discussing in the previous phases either the nature of the project or the strategic value sought from offshoring, since SLAs are highly influenced by those issues. Offshoring value is only ensured when the right decisions are made in the right order.

The remainder of this chapter will explore developing an offshoring strategy and the issues of control that swirl around the offshoring debate.

STRATEGY/GOALS ALIGNMENT: A BALANCED SCORECARD APPROACH

The Balanced Scorecard (BSC) is not the only way to conceptualize the strategic alignment between business goals and offshoring moves, but it is a useful thinking tool because of the simple logic behind it. It provokes clarity in thinking in how offshoring might offer value to the organization by illustrating how alignment is actually achieved. Neither is it essential that the BSC be implemented in a company for some of the concepts in the methodology to offer value in constructing an offshoring decision process. For anyone unfamiliar with the BSC we will start with a brief review.

Exhibit 4.2 depicts one of the most important conceptualizations in the BSC. It is composed of four related operational perspectives applicable to any organization—Learning and People, Internal, Customer, and Financial. The logic of the BSC is simple. Any company from the largest multinational to the neighborhood mom-and-pop store shares the same goal—to make money. Companies are interested in a number of financial goals

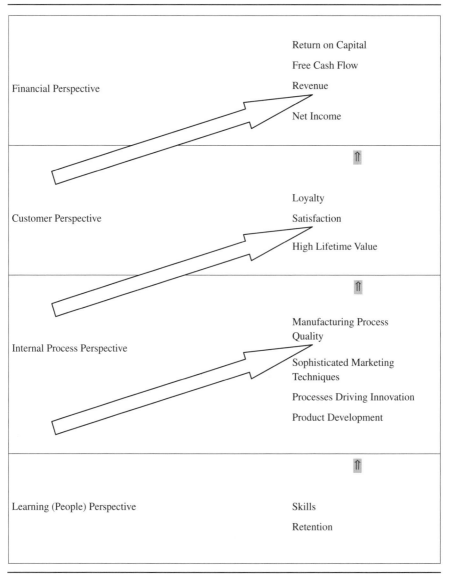

Return on Capital

Free Cash Flow

Financial Perspective   Revenue

Net Income

Loyalty

Customer Perspective   Satisfaction

High Lifetime Value

Manufacturing Process
Quality

Internal Process Perspective

Sophisticated Marketing
Techniques

Processes Driving Innovation

Product Development

Learning (People) Perspective   Skills

Retention

EXHIBIT 4.2   BALANCED SCORECARD

SOURCE: Adapted from Robert S. Kaplan and David P. Norton, "The Balanced Scorecard, Translating Strategy Into Action", Harvard Business School Press, 1996, page 31.

listed to the right within the Financial Perspective, depending on the type of company, size, and circumstances at any given time. Now the logic of the BSC kicks in; in order to achieve any financial goal what must a company do, in its most basic form? Provide products and services popular with customers, of course. In order to achieve this customer goal of creating great customer products and services, what must a company do? Establish effective internal processes across the organization that enables the creation of popular products and services. In order to build these internal processes what must a company do? It must hire, train, and retain the best people it can find, because ultimately it is people who create the workflows and processes that are a necessary condition for the organization to compete. Pretty simple stuff.

Exhibit 4.3 depicts how the simple logic of the BSC can be applied to the discussion of offshoring. We see the four perspectives once again as well as the success factors that lead to the outcomes a company seeks for each perspective. The need for customers to buy the things that makes the company money suggests that such indicators as loyalty and high lifetime value tell us that the company is indeed making popular stuff or delivering valuable services and that there is a likelihood of profitability because of this. But in order to win over customers the company must make products and services they will buy. In order for this to occur the necessary conditions for innovation or service excellence must be in place; the success indicators in the Internal Perspective acknowledge the organization's ability to make the stuff that draws customers because effective internal processes have been developed—perhaps over years of effort and trial and error on the part of managers. Because it is people and not machines who figure out what internal conditions must exist for the creation of products and services that will draw customers, companies take seriously the need to offer training and professional development, while providing not only paths for the advancement of key people but also policies to retain them in the organization.

Notice, the success indicators in any perspective are no guarantees of success—costs could far exceed revenue despite the popularity of a product or service. So, even though success indicators are achieved in the Customer Perspective, loyal customers at any given time might not necessarily translate into profitability. The same truth holds in the Internal Perspective. World-class manufacturing capability and the creation of high-quality products does not necessarily translate into market success if managers have misjudged consumer preferences. WebTV was a clever idea and it worked, but it hasn't been a smashing financial success for Microsoft. This reality speaks to the interdependence of success indicators across perspectives and the demands for excellence in all of them; for example, it is crucial that both an internal perspective process called manufacturing and the

BALANCED SCORECARD OBJECTIVES	WHAT BUSINESS PROCESSES SUPPORT ACHIEVEMENT OF OBJECTIVES IN EACH PERSPECTIVE?	IF OFFSHORED, RELEVANT KPIs
SUCCESS INDICATORS IN FINANCIAL PERSPECTIVE ⇨ **Return on Capital** **Free Cash Flow** **Revenue** **Net Income**	Not applicable—the ultimate results sought are financial returns. The business processes that support this are found within the three preceding perspectives	Increases in any financial measures
How does an organization achieve these financial goals? *By providing products and services popular with customers*	Business Processes	
SUCCESS INDICATORS IN THE CUSTOMER PERSPECTIVE ⇨ **Loyalty** **Satisfaction** **High Lifetime Value** **Marketshare Increases** **Decreased Churn and Defections**	**Call Centers** **Customer Service** **Marketing and Sales** **Logistics and Fulfillment**	Increases or decreases in any influencing metric, then same in any success indicator
How does an organization achieve customer goals?		

EXHIBIT 4.3 ALIGNING OFFSHORING WITH BUSINESS GOALS: A BSC APPROACH

By building effective internal processes that drive creation of those products and services

Business Processes

SUCCESS INDICATORS IN THE INTERNAL PERSPECTIVE ⇧

Manufacturing Process Quality—Six Sigma
ISO Certification
Exceed Industry Benchmarks
Design Awards

Working Capital Improvements
Cash Flow Improvements
Improvements in Receivables

Manufacturing
R&D
Product Development
Design

Finance

Increases or decreases in any influencing metric, then same in any success indicator

How does an organization achieve process excellence?

By developing skills and talents of employees who build these process capabilities

Business Processes

SUCCESS INDICATORS IN THE PEOPLE PERSPECTIVE ⇧

Retention of Best Employees
Recognition from Professional Associations
New Skills Capture Effectiveness
Reductions in Employee Departures
Productivity Lift

Training
Professional Development
HR

Increases or decreases in any influencing metric, then same in any success indicator

EXHIBIT 4.3 ALIGNING OFFSHORING WITH BUSINESS GOALS: A BSC APPROACH (CONTINUED)

customer perspective process called marketing work in conjunction to achieve the desired outcome of customer growth.

Balanced Scorecard Impacts Reveal Offshoring Value

Once an organization considers the success indicators that influence performance improvements across the perspectives, it is prepared to ask what are the actual business processes subject to offshoring that result in success indicator improvements? Exhibit 4.3 illustrates some of the business processes that influence success factors in each of the BSC perspectives. If the organization offshores specific business processes, is it confident a success factor improvement will ensue that leads to improvement in the perspective?

For example, will offshoring call center operations improve customer satisfaction? Could the offshoring move harm it? Do we care? Many don't, until complaints reach a critical mass, causing the organization to fold these processes back in-house or, at a minimum, choose a domestic service provider over an Indian one. What about HR, which represents a small portion of offshoring today but is expected to grow? How will offshoring HR processes improve our company's capacity to train and retain talented workers in the organization if we believe in the idea that high-quality personnel set the stage for success in successive perspectives? Will we be able to leverage any policy or operational innovations that allows us to manage our human capital more effectively? If so, what success indicator might improve from these business process innovations? And if the company is considering the offshoring of just training and education activities, what additional value will it capture in terms of retention and worker productivity and effectiveness?

When managers dig a little deeper into the answers around these questions, they will realize that a metrics-driven approach to offshoring analysis will require in some circumstances the identification of additional key performance indicators (KPIs) in order to make the proper link between the value in offshoring specific business processes and the desired outcome of improvements in specific success indicators. For example, by offshoring call center operations a company seeks improvement in the success indicator category called Customer Satisfaction. In order that offshoring call centers have any chance of actually improving customer satisfaction, managers will want to track intermediate performance indicators, or influencing KPIs that impact ultimate success indicators. In the case of call centers, those influencing KPIs would include efficiency and effectiveness metrics such as Average Speed of Answer, First Call Resolution, Hold Times, and others. (These are discussed in more detail in Chapter 13, "Calling All Low-Cost Reps.") So, the relevant question becomes: Can offshoring call center operations improve a number of efficiency and effectiveness metrics above what domestic operations already achieve? Exhibit 4.4 illustrates how influencing metrics can be mapped.

In the People Perspective, success indicators such as productivity improvement can be broken down into an influencing measurement of how much more of whatever work deliverable is produced per time period—hour, week, quarter, and so forth. If the workout is discretely measurable—products off the line, insurance applications processed, past due collections captured—productivity can be measured. Would offshoring the training, education, and professional development function equip employees to fulfill strategic goals? A company with a large international presence might want to hire a large training firm with a similar footprint for consolidation and one-stop shopping of all its training needs. An offshore training provider would be in a position to offer in-class training for a company's local workforce where face-to-face pedagogy is preferred to CD or over-the-wire content delivery. While such an arrangement cuts down on travel costs to bring international employees to a U.S. company's onsite training facility, cost is not necessarily the only reason to offshore this function. Organizations with rapid product introductions, such as Avaya, need efficient education delivery. The telecom equipment supplier hired Accenture

BSC Perspective	Success Indicators	Influencing Metrics
People	Productivity lift	Production of more units of work per time period
	Retention	Increase in promotions from within versus outside hires
	Skills capture effectiveness	Higher test scores in job categories, speed to proficiency
Internal	Manufacturing Process Quality	Six Sigma results, lower defects, higher yields
	Finance	Increases in Days Payable Outstanding
Customer	Satisfaction	On-time delivery
	Loyalty	Increases in contribution margin

EXHIBIT 4.4 LINKING METRICS TO SUCCESS INDICATORS

to manage workforce training and saw a 60% improvement in time to subject matter proficiency—a key influencing metric—for some courses
through better coordination of content development and delivery to its
product development processes.[1]

Moving to the Internal Perspective, a company considering offshoring
inventory management functions might want to ascertain whether the company will manage working capital more effectively. A relevant influencing
metric is in Days Payable Outstanding (DPO). This metric describes how
quickly organizations are paid by customers for products or service performed. Will an organization see improvements here were it to offshore
finance business processes? Many finance decisions are tied up in a web of
cross-functional business responsibilities. DPO improvements might actually derive from discounts offered customers for paying bills quickly, a
payment policy established by marketing and sales. Yet could a lift in DPO
come at the expense of lower revenue if this influencing metric is tied to
overly aggressive payment discounts? In the customer perspective, an organization determines that improved on-time delivery is a key influencing
metric in the customer relationship. It is not uncommon for manufacturers,
a semiconductor maker for instance, with a presence in multiple global
regions to establish a fulfillment capability nearby in order to boost ontime
delivery to regionally close customers. Over time, companies like the chip
maker can establish a direct causation between improved ontime delivery
and customer lifetime value. Clearly, a semiconductor company's customer, maybe a cell phone maker, values better delivery times, especially in
fast-paced industry sectors where time-to-market considerations for cell
phone handsets is key. The cell phone maker rewards its supplier that has
proven its ability to deliver with more business.

An organization interested in exploring strategic value will follow a
path from the business processes under offshoring consideration, to the
success factors they influence, to the next perspective in the logic chain of
the Balanced Scorecard on a journey toward total comprehension of the
implications from offshoring; if the organization offshores logistics, what
improvements or deterioration might emerge in the time-to-delivery success factor? Since in the logic of the Balanced Scorecard the financial perspective is directly impacted from improvements or deteriorations in
customer perspective success factors, the pertinent question is what
impacts to profitability might emerge through this chain reaction? These
questions are worth asking only if a company believes in the importance
of exploring offshoring for its potential delivery of value above and

beyond just cost savings. Yet, in all but the smallest offshoring projects, a Balanced Scorecard analysis is potentially useful because as a kind of view finder which looks at enterprise performance holistically it may cause managers to ask questions that might otherwise never get asked.

Value of Metrics

The BSC is obviously enamored with metrics and performance measures. In fact, its success depends on using them correctly. A reliance on metrics also assumes that companies have baseline results against which to assess the likely outcomes of offshoring. This is not always the case. Some companies deliberating an outsourcing or offshoring option on the table will bring in a consultant to benchmark performance and will in turn use the results as a starting point to think more deeply about offshoring's value. In spite of the BSC's metrics-driven approach, the idea is not to measure everything in sight. Overzealousness here will simply immobilize the company in analysis paralysis. The metrics Easter egg hunt could compromise building momentum for the overall effort. A company wants to focus on just those measures that are relevant to the question of offshoring's contribution to high-level strategic objectives.

The value of metrics is twofold. One, it gets managers thinking holistically about the impacts of offshoring, both obvious and not. Here's the obvious: a manufacturer might decide to consolidate all its fulfillment in one offshore location to better manage inventories. On-time delivery is certain to rise the further from fulfillment the customer is located. Is the offshoring move worth the risk? Here's the not-so-obvious: A company decides to disburse fulfillment into key locations close to manufacturing in order to please customers. On-time delivery drops drastically—good—but so does the time to payment because of a deep recession that begins several months later in the offshoring country—bad. Near term, the offshore investment in a new fulfillment capability is rewarded with neither more work nor quick payments from customers because of emerging economic conditions over which the company had no control. Metrics will not do anything to solve problems outside a company's control, but considering the economic conditions of the offshoring target country and the timing of the initiative at a minimum ensures that the issue becomes a risk factor in the total decision framework. Site selection is explored later, in Phase 2 of the Offshoring Value Delivery Framework. This might seem obvious, but it is often the obvious which is either overlooked or not given the level of scrutiny required. Reliance on metrics should provoke managers to attack the assumptions on which the proposed value of offshoring rests; if a customer states emphatically that big improvements in on-time delivery will win the company more orders, what does this expectation assume? That the customer will have a need for more orders because business is gangbusters. True or false?

Two, the metrics emphasis is useful for offshoring because it forces managers to support contentions of its strategic value with empirically derived data when a Balanced Scorecard analysis is included in a business case and cost/benefit analysis. Anyone evangelizing the strategic value of an offshoring initiative might offer the relevant key performance indicator (KPI) to prove the expected value of the initiative. Data-driven decision making can also act as a circuit breaker when an offshoring proposal throws every conceivable benefit at decision makers, even if those benefits have little chance of materializing. Managers feeling the heat to cut costs and believing offshoring is the answer will hype every point of value thinkable, anything to get approval. Prove it, senior managers will retort, and one of the most effective ways of doing that is to show how offshoring is expected to increase or decrease some metric. Managers are less likely to argue the value of offshoring if a KPI supporting some operational boost cannot be rationalized or an argument for a measure's numerical value lacks credibility. Because of the inherent reliance on metrics, using the BSC as a strategic decision making tool should raise the quality of business cases and inject accountability into decision making. This is no small feat when you consider that in at least a few well-known companies capital investment is, quite scarily, made on the basis of the quality of PowerPoint slides and how articulate the business sponsor is.

We see that any kind of strategic roadmap to offshoring provokes useful, probing questions. But obviously, these questions, like the ones asked earlier in this section, are valid only if the organization accepts, if not the potential strategic value of offshoring, at least the notion that offshoring might have operational implications—good or bad—beyond cost savings and that attempting to understand these implications is an exercise worthy of the time and effort it takes to explore them. Companies that want to save significant amounts of money from offshoring are often short-sighted, so the BSC is irrelevant. They simply need to determine whether they can get the same level of service quality for less cost and embark on the effort. (Sometimes organizations do not even deliberate the quality issue very deeply.) Much of today's offshoring is bounded by this limited scope. But not all offshoring.

The More Strategic the Offshoring, the More Sophisticated the Analysis

Because business process offshoring is such a new option for many companies, it would take a bold analyst to declare the widespread future adoption of strategic frameworks around this activity. Nevertheless, as offshoring moves up the cognitive food chain from processes requiring low skills to processes requiring great skill and sophistication involving the organization's most prized employees, by default the subject takes on a more strategic cast. For this reason, it just might turn out that offshoring's strategic importance in the organization—and the need for a strategic decision framework—will rise in direct proportion to how strategic is viewed the very business processes under offshoring consideration. For example, a large percentage of offshoring today involves information technology business processes—application maintenance, software upgrades, software business logic changes, and bug fixes and patches. For many organizations, IT is a utility services group; its operation is important, after all every business operation depends on it, but its work is not strategic to the organization. Information technology won't drive a new business model, revenue growth, or entry into a new market—today. Perhaps tomorrow, as the organization deepens its relationship with the service provider, it discovers the possibility of offshoring more strategic kinds of IT work such as application architecture and design. So, as companies discover the greater business value offshoring offers, the need for more formal strategy might emerge.

Offshoring Strategy Can Drive Process Reengineering

Another valuable result of analyzing offshoring in a strategic framework is the discovery that work can be done more effectively than had been so in the domestic operation before the offshoring effort began. Companies might not just forklift processes out and mirror them at a foreign location but rather see the potential in reengineering processes as an offshoring effort is forged. For example, if a company has the need to penetrate a new market segment or geographic region it might then ask how additional cost reductions can be achieved, even beyond the initial savings in the offshoring arrangement. One original equipment manufacturer (OEM) to the automobile industry realized that it could employee workers in the task of body welding instead of deploying capital-intensive and expensive robots.[2] This labor for capital substitution process reengineering made possible by the labor arbitrage in the offshoring move provided a dramatic cost savings that furthered a strategic goal. True, the company might have reached the same conclusion had it dove into an analysis from a more limited cost reduction perspective only, but that process change discovery would have occurred only if managers bothered to ask what business process changes could drop costs even further than the dramatic savings it was already capturing. It is arguably more intuitive to look at a strategic goal—market share capture—understand that entering as the low-cost leader is the way there, and then ask how that offshored cost structure could be lowered even further to achieve the goal. Reflexively, managers would direct their focus to production processes.

A more paradoxical result of a business process analysis is the *lessening of automation to support key processes.* The idea seems daffy and against every shibboleth of business process reengineering which argues that processes can be improved through IT automation. This is, of course, true when the relative cost of capital relative to labor is cheap, as is the case in the United States. Why have hundreds if not thousands of clerks filing claim forms in file cabinets when databases and software can handle the job far more cost-efficiently? This economic logic, however, is turned on its head in offshore target countries where the reality is just the opposite: labor is far cheaper than capital. Why shouldn't companies take advantage of this fact by employing less capital versus labor to achieve some business process? Less capital deployed in the labor-capital mix to achieve the same outcome makes capital more productive and capital productivity is a desired goal of many CFOs.

For example, a payment process service provider might have workers input cleared checks into an IT system rather than use capital-expensive imaging software because this labor-capital mix is cheaper, a complete reversal of the trend in the United States, where today people receive bank statements featuring pictures of checks rather than the checks themselves because of the cost-effectiveness.[3] Indian car companies use more labor and less capital in many automobile manufacturing processes—body welding, materials handling, and so forth, and save millions in assembly costs.[4] It is assumed that one of the tasks of a CIO is to help managers figure out any improvements in automation, that is IT, to be had in a business process offshoring situation because today IT is inextricably involved in every process the organization engages in. As counterinstinctual as it is, the CIO's value in some situations is also to figure out scenarios where the elimination of automation adds value to the offshoring arrangement.

Need for Process Mapping

A detailed explication of process mapping is beyond both this author's domain of expertise and the scope of this book. But it cannot be stated too often or emphatically enough: *successful business process offshoring is fundamentally dependent on management's complete and comprehensive understanding of how current business processes that are offshoring candidates are organized and executed inside the organization. It is only from a comprehensive understanding of business processes workflow that any basis for an understanding of the value of business process offshoring can be understood.* If readers take away nothing else from this book, let it be this. It seems so intuitive as to not merit mention. But it is amazing that any organizations initiate an offshoring analysis without understanding how work is currently accomplished today. Consider the story of the investment house Lehman.

The company offshored its internal IT help desk operation for its 7,500 employees to Wipro in Bangalore, India. Despite the seemingly deep managerial and technical experience of one of the world's largest offshoring service providers and the operational sophistication of one of the best-known U.S. investment banks, Lehman cut the cord after just eight months when performance levels proved dreadful. What sabotaged the effort? Among other things, Lehman failed to fully comprehend the complexity of calls to the internal help desk. The CIO simply did not understand in exquisite detail how business processes slated for offshoring are conducted in the organization—today.[5] A comprehensive understanding would have revealed business process complexity and might have changed completely the direction of offshoring decision making.

How can an organization make any meaningful judgments about the value of offshoring if it cannot grasp the expected ease or difficulty in replicating these processes in an organization that has never managed the processes before? Process mapping and flowcharting is an old discipline rooted in engineering, manufacturing, Six Sigma, and Edwards Deming, one of the giants in the art and science of quality management through measurement. If managers with offshoring oversight cannot find domain expertise within the organization, then they get it outside the organization. They eat the cost of consulting help in mapping and fully understanding complex processes targeted for offshoring. This cost becomes another drag in a fully burdened cost-benefit or financial model, but it is nothing compared to the costs Lehman ate.

Conclusion

Whether the company adopts a Balanced Scorecard approach or some other construct, it should realize that a framework should be adaptable to the changing goals and needs of the organization. Entering a new market is the goal today, but perhaps tomorrow it will be improving the pace of innovation and product introductions. Maybe the next day the goal is both simultaneously. Management might tinker with the framework itself to improve its relevance and effectiveness, but in the end its ultimate value is found in its ability to inject flexibility, consistency, transparency, and common understanding into the process of decision making. Proper offshoring is proving to require nothing less.

IN-HOUSE OR OUT OF HOUSE: ISSUE OF CONTROL

There are a couple of high-level ways a company can consider offshoring versus doing the job in-house, the old buy or build question that IT organizations have faced for many years. Many large companies have a global footprint, so when the decision is made to offshore, the proposition involves moving business process administration from its base of operations to a lower-cost foreign office. The organization retains complete control over the business processes. Many companies do not enjoy a global presence but see offshoring as a viable option nevertheless. The question for them is a binary one: offshore to a service provider or do not offshore. The merits of offshoring can be deliberated in two ways. One approach is to cast the "in-house or out of house" debate around control. The second approach is to place the issue in the context of existing strategic value of the business processes versus the competencies and capabilities of internal organizations to manage these processes and deliver that pursued value into the future.

So, does a company go it alone and construct an inhouse offshore capability or hire a service provider? Answers are so context-driven by business conditions and what processes are candidates for offshoring that a detailed explanation for each and every possible scenario comprises its own book. Consider offshoring in the context of control; does it cause the organization any concern that it would lose control of daily oversight of business processes where they offshored to a service provider? The concept of control is value- and culture-driven, not unlike the "not invented here" (NIH) syndrome in which some organizations are loathe to procure something as strategic as intellectual property (IP). The not-invented-here mindset tells the organization that if it cannot create the capability itself, then the IP is certainly not worth licensing from elsewhere. There is no valid defense for this stance. The pace of innovation and the limited budgets of R&D have diminished the pervasiveness of this bias but it hangs on in engineering-driven companies. The issue of control is likely less important or not an issue at all in organizations that seek large cost reductions by offshoring business processes. In fact, they are delighted to get these distractions off the books. From a simple control/cost savings perspective Exhibit 4.5 illustrates the tradeoff.

In the buy or build debate, there are only four choices: do not offshore and perform the processes in-house, "onshore" outsource the processes to a

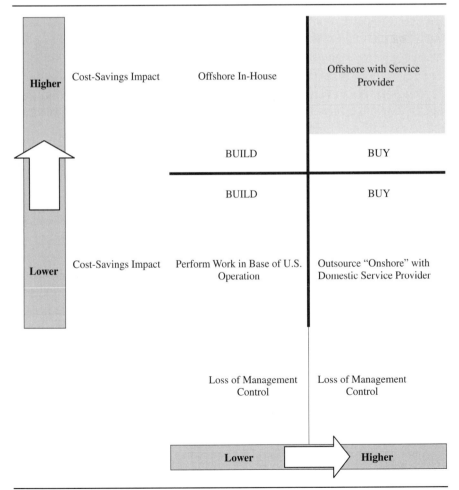

EXHIBIT 4.5 COST SAVINGS/MANAGEMENT CONTROL TRADEOFF

reputable domestic service provider, offshore in-house, or offshore with a reputable service provider in the target country (which might be a domestic service provider who has extended its presence to the foreign location). Most offshoring is company controlled today.[6] Large organizations with an international presence consolidate business process functions in a foreign office. In this way they enjoy significant cost savings while retaining operational control. Yet, the more control a company is willing to relinquish often means the larger the cost savings. The shaded box in the upper right of Exhibit 4.5 represents the sweet spot of cost savings but is also where the greatest amount of control is surrendered. This fact was revealed in Chapter 2, "Everything You Can Send down a Wire Is up for Grabs"; specialization in specific processes on behalf of myriad customers gives the service provider economies of scope and deeper insight into efficiencies that a company might take far longer to figure out given the competition for internal resources and the breadth of responsibilities it faces every day. The service provider is bound to do it better over time, so the decision is fairly clean; a service provider offers the greatest chance for the most cost savings in exchange for surrendering day-to-day control (but not responsibility) of the business processes. The pace of offshoring today suggests that many companies find this an equitable tradeoff.

We, of course, know by now that cost is not the only offshoring consideration on the company agenda. How might the buy versus build debate unfold if the issue of control were placed in the context of strategic value and not costs alone? Consider Exhibit 4.6. A company that seeks to determine the fit between offloading business processes and overarching corporate goals—perhaps using a Balanced Scorecard approach—might find that the greatest value can be captured in the same upper-right quadrant as in Exhibit 4.5; that is, the greatest strategic impact might reside in an offshoring scenario in which the organization hires a service provider somewhere in the world because as a global company it realizes the distinct advantages in building an alliance rather than relocating these processes in-house at that offshore location. This is not the most common scenario today; as stated earlier, most companies do offshore or relocate processes in-house. But as offshoring matures, service providers in specific business process domains will offer a compelling value proposition under certain circumstances. What if a company cannot offshore in-house because it simply does not have that global footprint? The control issues that loom large have not stopped some companies from plowing ahead with offshoring anyway. For example, venture capitalists highly encourage startups to offshore

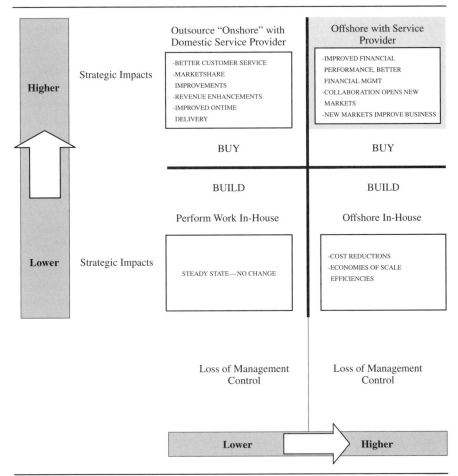

EXHIBIT 4.6 STRATEGIC IMPACT/MANAGEMENT CONTROL TRADEOFF

product development work—one of the most strategic activities a company engages in. Lower cost is a key driver here but with strategic implications; cash conscious startups can conserve cash and hire more technical talent for less, thus improving productivity, and in turn deliver products to market faster.[7]

The salient point here is that the locus of greatest strategic value in business process offshoring means ceding everyday management of them. This is a tradeoff the highest levels of management will have to resolve. Some companies simply will not relinquish control and ownership of activities they deem strategic. Others, such as startup companies, might prefer to conduct the work internally but because of their place in the business food chain and the maturing capabilities of foreign service providers, determine that the control tradeoff is more than worth it. In the context of control, the issue boils down to this: if the organization is confident that it can support strategic objectives by offshoring with a service provider, what is it really giving up control of if it could never capture these improvements without an alliance in the first place? The loss of everyday control does not mean ceding responsibility. In fact, as the stakes in offshoring rise, so does the need for a collaborative working arrangement between organization and service provider to achieve desired results. The importance of service provider management and the operationalization of an effective governance structure to ensure high-quality service delivery will become apparent in Chapter 12, "Start of a Beautiful Friendship."

But to clarify the point, let's assume that the higher the degree of offshoring correlates positively with the degree of strategic impact. Then the tradeoff is clearly one of impact versus control. Exhibit 4.6 depicts this tradeoff. We see that turning out business process management to a third-party offers points of value the organization would not be likely to capture were it to offshore in a captive arrangement or not offshore at all.

Other Buy or Build Considerations

The in-house or out of house debate will turn on more than the issue of day-to-day operational control. Other control issues loom large:

- **Ownership.** Business processes have emerged as bona fide intangible assets for some companies, even if they cannot be quantified financially.[8] If a set of processes confers some competitive advantage—and the company should know if it does—ceding control essentially means that a company is transferring an asset whose value cannot be leveraged in pricing negotiations with the service provider. There is no formal intellectual property protection for know–how as there is for patents and copyrights; therefore, the service provider in receipt of this expertise can apply it to other clients unless expressly prohibited in the offshoring contract. Then the challenge becomes one of monitoring and enforcement, which is itself difficult. It is not likely that a company would offshore business processes that already confer a competitive advantage, but the real risk lies in a company's inability to assess whether a set of business processes provides the potential for intangible asset value creation. On a cost basis, offshoring looks really compelling. But is it leaving future value on the table in the form of an intangible asset, presumably a source of value the company would want to control? Only senior management can answer this.

- **Knowledge Retention.** Companies who take intellectual capital seriously understand the difficult to quantify but nevertheless important idea that experienced employees are a source of knowledge and professional development of less experienced workers. Avon Products made a conscious decision to keep offshored programming hires in-house for this very reason.[9] It had the choice of whether or not to do this because of its global presence. It folded offshore programming work into already established operations. As Avon's CIO saw it, a seasoned executive in one part of the world could mentor within the domain of application development a less experienced worker in another part of the world.[10] The less experienced worker improves her productivity over time through this mentoring, while the know-how and knowledge remains within the tribe, unless one of the workers leaves, but then every company faces this risk whether it offshores or not.

In a service provider relationship, the value of knowledge transfer and mentoring is far more at risk. Risks are twofold; the knowledge provider receives no compensation for the provision of useful knowledge to a service provider's employee who then applies this hard-won know-how to other customers. This is perhaps less of a concern than the second issue: experiential knowledge transfer is useful only if the service provider can leverage the improved skills and productivity of the worker in receipt of that expertise from the customer. This is one reason why retention is such an important workforce goal for many companies. The service provider worker could be assigned to other customers or leave the organization, and the offshoring customer has no control over service provider turnover. Knowledge cannot be stored in a lock box. How important is it to retain control of knowledge assets, considering the inevitable leakage that occurs when offshoring business processes?

One way around knowledge leakage we saw emerge a couple of years ago was through the formation of offshore development centers (ODCs). The idea was for the service provider and offshoring client to form a deeper offshoring relationship in which the service provider dedicated assets and resources specifically to the one client in exchange for guarantees of steady work. Otis Elevator forged an ODC with Wipro Technologies for IT business process offshoring services after the project-by-project relationship grew to a portfolio of 30 applications. Among those dedicated assets are the workers involved in the business process work.[11] In this arrangement, knowledge is retained by a captive service provider team. An ODC is no guarantee the worker will not leave the service provider's organization, but it does provide assurances that the worker is dedicated to a specific customer as long as he or she works for the service provider.

Although one of the benefits of an ODC is the ability to retain domain expertise within the customer's operational fold, knowledge retention is not the sole criteria for establishing one. The benefit is residual, a follow-on to the more important benefit of providing an organization with the ability to more effectively manage a distance relationship.

- **Time-to-Market.** Can an organization reasonably expect to ramp up an in house offshore business process capability faster than can a service provider, who has at least some of the resource elements already in place? Moving to an offshore service provider is hardly a turnkey proposition. It takes months to a year or longer, depending on the complexities involved. Yet can the organization reasonably believe that it can get the needed business processes up and running any faster? So, the relevant question becomes: is it worth ceding some management control in exchange for a measurably faster time-to-market when a considered decision tells the organization it is simply not prepared to make the leap as quickly as it needs to? When a company needs to establish a logistics and fulfillment capability to support new market entry in some distant location, the time to ramp up that capability emerges as the key decision driver. Even in possession of in-house resources in that foreign location that would serve as a foundation for building the capability inside the organization, it might be better off offshoring to the service provider.

- **Resource Constraints.** This is simply another dimension that reveals the time-to-market issue. We saw that a startup has far fewer resources in time, people, or expertise to manage the establishment of an offshore design and development center. Clearly venture capitalists with big investments in these companies see no problem in farming out key product work to a reputable service provider overseas. Here is the relevant question; is the expected value from offshoring greater than the existing cost to operate these processes in-house plus the additional investment in new resources needed to elevate the performance of these business processes to a level sought from the service provider?

In-house or Out of House: Value versus Key Organizational Capability

An interrelated way to cast the "in or out" offshoring question is through the prism of organizational capabilities, popularly referred to as core competencies. Exhibit 4.7 illustrates how these two dimensions mix.

Scenario C.   In the C quadrant exist those business processes ripe for offshoring. The processes are not linked to any strategic goals of the organization nor are the processes themselves a key organizational capability. Payroll and routine support for nonstrategic software applications come to mind.

Scenario B.   Contrast this with B quadrant in which both the business processes support strategic outcomes and the employees responsible for

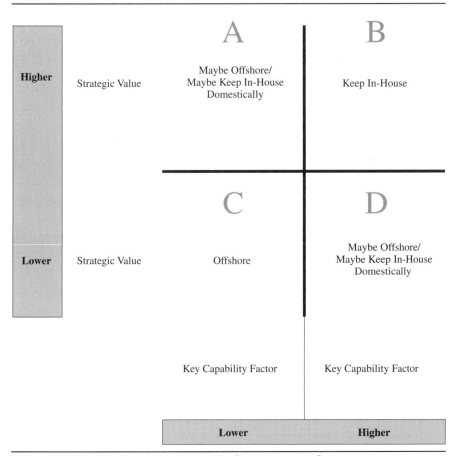

EXHIBIT 4.7   BUSINESS PROCESS VALUE AND KEY ORGANIZATIONAL CAPABILITIES

them have developed key organizational capabilities in delivering them. For example, consider a manufacturer that has built a homegrown application to manage all the processes around manufacturing. The application has been refined and perfected through years of use and the work of software architects and application development teams in the IT organization. The application is strategic to the organization insofar as it supports manufacturing capabilities integral to the company's success. Since the work of the IT organization in supporting and developing enhancements to the application is inextricably tied to the application's value, the company makes a conscious decision to maintain complete control over these activities. The IT organization has shown not only an ability to effectively support and maintain the application but also has served as a value-added business partner to manufacturing executives in figuring out feature and functionality innovations that over time have improved the effectiveness of the application and, therefore, the company's manufacturing operation. The hard-won experiental knowledge accumulated over years of operation would be very difficult to replace. Therefore, IT business processes are considered a key organizational capability and are not offshored even though on a pure dollar basis the company could save significant money in staff compensation.

While B and C quandrants represent fairly clean offshoring decisions, the situation in A and D quadrants is more subtle and complex.

Scenario A.   Does a company offshore business processes that are linked to strategic goals but are not a key organizational capability in and of themselves? Many companies are offshoring research and/or design and product development work, which is highly strategic but not necessarily a core competency or key organizational capability (which is precisely why companies are willing to offshore this work).

Scenario D.   Do there exist any processes that are not strategic if the goals they support are? Again, answers are highly contextual to the specific traits and attitudes of the organization.

Some companies have demonstrated that specific workforce recruitment, retention, and skills development strategies represent top and bottom line results through higher customer satisfaction and reduced costs. Given this circumstance, an organization which has created a new workforce strategy around these desired goals would need to create new business processes in order to bring the objectives off. The company decides to hire a new program manager reporting directly to the CFO. The company also decides that it seeks additional data-tracking capability to monitor progress, which requires tweaks to an HR system and databases. If this strategy proves a competitive differentiator, and it has for some organizations, it would think hard about offshoring this work. It may decide that this retention program's policy setting and oversight remain in the U.S. headquarters because of the CFO's ownership and keen interest in the program as well as the fact that the strategy represents a valuable trade secret. However, the organization determines that the administrative business processes necessary to support the program can join other routine HR processes that are already being managed by a service provider because of the high trust that has developed over time between the customer and vendor. The workforce strategy is a key organizational capability. Paperwork and administrative workflow supporting the strategy are not. Some business process jewels linked to this strategic goal are guarded closely within the palace walls. Others might be offshored.

Of course, the offshoring decision is made demonstrably easier in a captive scenario; does the organization keep control of processes in its base of operation or move them to an in house location in a low cost country where a lot of other HR activities are already being performed? Control in all its dimensions is not an issue. In this case, the company saves significant money on program execution and management because it taps this overseas HR resource instead of using its far more costly U.S. operation.

Turning to the lower-right quadrant, what circumstances have arisen in which some business processes have proven themselves key organizational capabilities but are not strategic to the company? Consider an IT scenario again. Supposing that an IT organization has a track record of delivering on time, on budget, and with the precise functionality line that the business or operation needs—excellent software design, application development, and project management processes. This well-honed machine is supporting outcomes—technological capabilities—that, although important to the success of the business, are not necessarily strategic. A company knows its IT organization service processes are key organizational capabilities because it has bothered to benchmark its performance against other IT organizations of similar size, budget, and sector type.

In this case, the organization will weigh the cost benefits and other potential efficiencies of offshoring against the hard work that went to the creation of a truly valuable internal services organization, no small feat when many IT organizations are not. Assuming that the offshore service provider can deliver at the same performance level as the internal IT organization, as a 30 to 50% potential cost reduction from offshoring stares the manager in the face, his head says, yes, offshore, but his heart says, no way, developing this IT organization was too much work. Managers might decide that the devil they know is better than the one it does not and, therefore, not offshore. More likely the cost savings at a comparable level of quality will be too much to ignore. The organization will offshore but slowly because of the higher risk that the service provider will not perform at the same level as the internal organization.

Control and Risk

When managers describe a loss of control from business process offshoring, they are expressing concern about the risks to the arrangement. And they are real. Companies risk weaknesses in a service provider's internal controls, especially where finance functions are concerned; the risk is magnified because of the Sarbanes-Oxley Act. Companies must certify not only the financial results but also the internal controls that influence the numbers being reported.[12] Loss of intellectual property (IP) is another real risk. Loss of IP could take the form of natural intellectual capital leakage and dispersion in the process of knowledge transfer described earlier or outright theft in which patents or trade secrets fall into the hands of outsiders. In one survey, IP theft is near the top of CFOs' concerns.[13] Similarly, companies are concerned with the loss of other kinds of sensitive information such as employee medical or financial information. Political instability looms to varying degrees; who was not concerned when India and Pakistan, two habitual combatants on the world stage, a few years ago stood eyeball to eyeball with nuclear weapons trained on each other? After years of financial commitment to building offshore capabilities, including a medical equipment joint venture and a research center to leverage local engineering talent, General Electric put the brakes on investment in India as a result of this very incident.[14] Other less dramatic but more palpable political risks, palpable because they have a higher probability of occuring, include a change in government that changes tax or employment laws, which makes offshoring conditions less favorable.

The issue of risk, although entangled in the concept of control, often emerges when management prepares a cost-benefit or Return on Investment Model to gain visibility into the costs and value-creating possibilities of an offshoring move. Here, these risks are weighted for the probability of actually happening, and some dollar value is assigned to these risks should they occur. The dollar value of these risk events is then subtracted from the total dollar value of the model. The possible offshoring returns are made more conservative. There is nothing stopping management from considering any risk issue during the in-house or out of house debate. In fact, given how exotic and new offshoring is to companies, they might decide that an infusion of risk analysis must occur at the strategy formulation stage of the Offshoring Value Delivery Framework rather than apply risk analysis only at the project-level phase when the organization is ready to construct a formal business case around specific business processes under offshoring consideration. It might make a valid determination that the sum total of identified risks is greater than the combined cost reduction and value-creation potential in a relationship with a service provider. Management is therefore directed toward a captive offshoring effort when possible, or, when the company has no global footprint, a decision not to offshore at all, at least in the near term.

CHAPTER TAKEAWAY

Here are some key concepts to leave this chapter with:

- Is offshoring an ad hoc decision based entirely on cost or does it require a systematic decision framework which considers possible strategic implications? Even organizations who view offshoring strictly as a labor arbitrage and cost-cutting option can benefit from considering these decisions within a more strategic framework. If nothing else, companies should view cost-cutting offshoring holistically, which provides an awareness of potential impacts on other parts of the organization.

- The Balanced Scorecard is a kind of Swiss army knife management tool. Its logic can be applied to many business situations, even if the organization has not fully operationalized the methodology to direct business activities and decisions. It provides a holistic performance perspective, which allows managers to place individual offshoring initiatives within a larger impact context.

- A strategic analysis should compel a detailed analysis of what specific steps compose the business processes under offshoring consideration. Failure to understand business process complexity leads to failure when the processes are finally offshored to a service provider. A debate might ensue as to whether or not processes can or should be reengineered before offshoring. If aggressive cost cutting is the primary motivation, the organization should explore the possibilities of deautomating processes as a way to rebalance the capital/labor intensity mix.

- Offshoring to a service provider is fundamentally about relinquishing control. What is it that organizations fear losing when control is given away? Control must be balanced against business needs that offshoring is attempting to fulfill. Since business needs are context-driven no magic template exists for every offshoring situation. Organizations will balance potential offshoring value against risks from surrending business process control.

- Conventional offshoring wisdom holds that you offshore routine business process activities and maintain those processes that represent core competencies or key organizational capabilities. Start with this argument as a baseline for discussion and run scenarios in which this advice is ignored.

NOTES

1. Staff, "Accenture Learning Offers Global Approach to Outsourced Training," Trainingoutsourcing.com, Supplier Spotlight, August 2004. http://www.trainingoutsourcing.com/to_spotlight.asp?ID=288.
2. Vivek Agrawal, Diana Farrell and Jaana K. Remes, "Offshoring and Beyond," MicKinsey Quarterly special edition, 2003.
3. Ibid.
4. Ibid.
5. Stephanie Overby, "Lost In Translation," *CIO Magazine*, July 15, 2004.
6. Ralf Dreischmeier, Tatjana Colsman, Ranier Minz, Harold L. Sirkin, "Achieving Success in Business Process Outsourcing and Offshoring," Boston Consulting Group, February 2005, p. 4.
7. Patrick Thibodeau and Sumner Lemon, "R&D Starts To Move Offshore," *Computerworld*, March 1, 2004.
8. I write about this fairly extensively throughout my book, *Tangible Strategies for Intangible Assets*, McGraw-Hill 2004.
9. Larry Dignan, "Avon: Offshore Twist," *Baseline Magazine*, October 30, 2003.
10. Ibid.
11. Stephanie Overby, "The Hottest Trend in Outsourcing Management," *CIO Magazine*, June 1, 2003.
12. Lori Calabro, "Looking Under the Bonnet," CFOEurope.com, December 2004, www.cfoeurope.com/displaystory.cfm/3444088.

13. Kate O'Sullivan and Don Durfee, "Offshoring by the Numbers," *CFO Magazine*, June 2004.

14. Jay Solomon and Kathryn Kranhold, "In India's Outsourcing Boom, GE Played a Starring Role," *Wall Street Journal*, March 23, 2005.

5

IS THE ORGANIZATION READY?

Readiness has a few connotations. At a very tactical level, the organization is ready to offshore when it actually begins transitioning the work to the service provider or in house foreign office. New job functions that meet the need for managing the offshoring relationship have been established, and the organization has constructed a timetable around the specific activities, which, collectively, take the company from the first step into the transition to the last step in which the service provider has assumed all process responsibility. More on these elements of offshoring value delivery later.

At a higher level, organizational readiness describes a company's preparedness to consider offshoring from a strategic and operational perspective. What elements of organizational preparedness are required to execute an offshoring strategy successfully?

STRATEGIC LEVEL READINESS

The most strategic definition of readiness is this: has the organization awakened its workforce to the idea that offshoring is a necessary operational and strategic objective in every facet of the business from this day forward into eternity? Job one should be (and often it is not, but you are reading this author's opinion) the creation of a message from the CEO outlining the broad strokes of the company's pursuit of offshoring. The content of the message should include the clear rationale as to why offshoring is suddenly on senior management's radar: offshoring is an economic force, and were any company to ignore it, this might constitute a most serious breach of management's fiduciary responsibility. As competitors adopt off-shoring in various parts of their business, it would be folly for this organization not to choose the same course; if our cost structure is seriously out of line versus the competition, this organization will cease being competitive. This is the plain truth. The message should be consistent—not one message for investors, suppliers, and customers, and another for employees. The message should also include the commitment to further regular communication with senior executives as plans are solidified to offshore operational or line of business functions.

It is in this point of offshoring execution that the wheels fall off. A communications plan cannot end with a yearly pronouncement from the CEO or annual report boilerplate and then the next thing employees know a business unit or operational area has decided to offshore business processes and their jobs are gone. Not only is it callous but it also creates the risk of driving other employees to distraction as everyone concentrates their minds on which plot of corporate land the offshoring bulldozer will overrun next instead of the job responsibilities in front of them. In the name of the humane treatment of employees and avoiding a corrosive drop in worker productivity, distant smoke signals around offshoring are not enough. High-level talk must be matched on the ground with ongoing tactical communications.

When ON Semiconductor was spun off from Motorola about six years ago, offshoring was just emerging as a real business trend in corporate America. Motorola actually had been offshoring for years, as far back as the early 1980s when it hired Filipino technical workers to manage its enterprise software system that supported manufacturing there.[1] This Phoenix-based manufacturer of chips with 15,000 distinct products across eight product categories demonstrated its commitment to offshoring when in the name of dramatically cutting costs, it decided to transition legacy application maintenance from a U.S.-based service provider to an India-based provider. The arrangement consisted of the creation of a partnership between ON Semiconductor's domestic outsourcer ACS and an Indian offshore company called Larsen and Toubro Infotech Limited. CIO David Wagner committed himself to regular communications with the internal IT organization when it was announced that this work was moving from ACS offices near ON Semiconductor's corporate headquarters in Phoenix to Mumbai. The legacy application maintenance was the first set of business processes ON Semiconductor as a standalone company had ever offshored to a service provider, so it was understandable when heads turned among his staff. Am I next? was the natural reaction.

The communications plan was not complicated. Wagner scheduled face-to-face meetings with the IT staff every eight weeks to answer questions, dispel rumors, and update them about the progress of this specific offshoring event and the company's future plans. "Honesty and openness is the best policy," says Wagner. "Rather than worry about ghosts and shadows it's better to tell it like it is."[2] The basic message, which remains in place to this day as these bull sessions continue, is that offshoring is a potential option at any time as ON Semiconductor attempts to keep its cost structure in step with the competition; the option is built into a set of IT organization operating principles signed off on by the board of directors. While the message is not completely sunny, it is honest and Wagner brings to this communications effort a credibility some other C-level executives might not; he reports directly to the CEO of the company. None of the information emerging from the highest reaches of the organization is either filtered or otherwise shaped and spun when he talks to his staff.

An example of a broad outline of a communications plan appears in Exhibit 5.1. Some of these activities are actually executed far down the offshore value delivery pipe, but the planning around that execution happens now. Communication is not an afterthought, coming on the heels of an offshoring move underway.

BUILDING THE SAFETY NET

Organizational readiness also means that the entire set of policies, procedures, and resource commitments with which the company will support its workers laid off from offshoring is in place before any offshoring begins. The extent of a company's financial commitment to this aspect of offshoring will depend on the genuine level of concern that senior management has for the fate of its laid off workforce and the quality and sincerity of the organization's values, which dictate the implementation of specific tactics and resources to support these folks when layoff notices are finally issued. Specific policies and procedures look like this:

- **Severance.** Standard severance package tied to the time of service at the company.
- **Transition Payment.** An additional financial inducement representing some percentage of severance to keep workers through the transition to the offshore operation. This tactic might prove critical, as readers will

PRINCIPLE	ACTION ITEM
Tell it straight	Prepare a truthful business rationale for why offshoring is an organizational reality
Tell the whole story	Communicating the broad principles of an offshoring stance loses its credibility when, on the heels of this the company suddenly announces a new round of offshoring layoffs, therefore . . . (*see next principle*)
Tell the story frequently	Frequently enough that employees feel satisfied that they have an accurate assessment where the company is and what the near future holds. Even in the face of an uncertain future, people feel they have some control to plan a course of action if they are provided candid updates of the status of specific offshoring initiatives and have ample time to prepare
Tell the story face-to-face	Impractical as it may be the larger the organization, face-to-face communication brings a credibility and empathy "all hands" conference calls, emails and broadcast voice mails do not; some f-to-f might be necessary if the pace and depth of offshoring increases and morale tanks
Tell the contingency story, make sure it is understood	Have a formal and generous safety net plan in place for all employees facing offshoring layoffs—outplacement and job search resources—communicate the availability of a safety net

EXHIBIT 5.1 How to Communicate Offshoring Plans

see when transition planning is explored later; knowledge transfer is a key component of successful offshoring. Forcing staff already aware of their layoffs to work as active participants in the mentoring of the new offshore workforce is audacious, but runs the risk of inviting sabotage during one of the most important phases of the whole project. Of course, providing an additional financial incentive in exchange for a worker's active participation in her own job's demise assumes a quality of commitment that may or may not materialize at the time of transition. Nevertheless, the offer should be made. One CIO compares management's request for staff involvement in the teaching of their replacements to asking people to dig their own graves before shooting them.[3] It is an excellent metaphor if overly dramatic.

- **Internal Reassignment.** Managers with oversight and operational responsibility of the offshored business processes must clear a path for internal reassignment of laid off workers. This tactic might require overcoming HR bureaucracy and complacency. Workers subject to layoff from offshoring are entitled to fast track hiring consideration, which means expediting the personnel department's pro forma screening process and any other obstacles that may exist between the laid off worker and the available job inside. Let workers know as early as possible in the offshoring timetable if they have a future in another job at the company. If not, at least they can prepare for an external job hunt early enough to minimize the time with no income between gigs.

- **Outplacement Resources.** Provide all the company resources available to help workers find gainful employment, and apportion a structured amount of company time for workers to engage in job search activities. What kind of informal job placement networking is HR prepared to prepare with the constellation of other companies the offshoring organization is in direct contact with? Suppliers, customers, joint venture partners, and so on.

ARGUMENT FOR A BIG RESPONSE

The rationale for a deep resource commitment to offshoring's inevitable outcomes is embedded in the idea that layoffs from offshoring, as opposed to layoffs from dire financial conditions, are completely divorced from considerations of the quality and contribution of the workers. Even in a layoff situation instigated by a recession or industry downturn some people are viewed as indispensable and will survive the axe. Some assessment about specific employee quality is made in separating the wheat from the chaff. This is clearly not the case in offshoring. Organizations will sacrifice great employees because of the perceived greater future value in offshoring the business processes for which they have responsibility. In offshoring, the layoff decision is concerned only with the processes moving overseas and who is involved with them. Even in the biggest business cycle layoff some people in business units or operational areas survive in recognition that someone has to stay if only to sustain the company as a going concern. In offshoring, an entire operational area or subset is cut loose because of the dictates of the goals involved. The other difference between standard lay-offs and those from offshoring is found in the fact that offshoring can occur when business conditions are far from dire. The company offshores simply to minimize its cost structure because offshoring provides the opportunity to do so and nothing else. Business might be great. For these reasons, an argument can be made that layoffs from offshoring require a somewhat differentiated response than traditional downturn layoffs. Individual companies will have to decide whether this argument is worth buying into.

If they do buy into this stance, it should be plainly clear that the not insignificant resource investment in the targeted workforce must be accounted for in a business case or cost/benefit analysis. Although some of the costs associated with a resource commitment might be difficult to quantify—the opportunity cost of work foregone as a laid off worker still on the payroll searches for new employment, for example—enough of the costs are concrete and transparent that the organization will understand quite well what percentage these resource commitments to offshored workers represent to the overall upfront cost profile from an offshoring initiative. This understanding will not necessarily stop the company from offshoring. The total expected value creation from the offshoring effort might minimize resource commitment costs, but those layoff commitment costs are likely to push the payback period or time to cash positive further out the value timeline, not unlike the situation with big iron, risky software investments. The fact that resource commitments to laid off staff just adds more burden to the upfront cost profile creates the pressure for senior management to minimize these commitments, particularly in a rough economic climate. There is no one right answer or proven template that can coach an organization toward the treatment of laid off workers from offshoring. This is a value judgment each organization will need to make for itself. The suggestions in these pages reach for the most humane approach possible under the circumstances.

OPERATIONAL-LEVEL READINESS

Assuming that the organization has built a strategic framework for offshoring decisions and implemented a workforce strategy that not only understands how offshore layoffs will be handled but also articulates internal resources committed to these events, it can build the infrastructure that comprises organizational readiness at an operational level. Operational readiness describes the governance procedures that plug into the offshoring strategic decision-making framework. Governance defines the people who constitute a body whose purpose is to administer something. Therefore, operational readiness for offshoring outlines what procedures and processes lead the organization to an offshoring decision and who is involved in these decisions. One way to understand operational readiness is to ask the pertinent questions that collectively create it.

OPERATIONAL-LEVEL READINESS: THE ELEMENTS

Who Has the Final Decision for Any Specific Offshoring Proposal?

If offshoring is viewed as strategic, certainly the CEO will wield significant power in arriving at a decision. Strategic offshoring is a board-level activity. Otherwise, the organization will leave the decision to the business unit or operational area under offshoring consideration with input from an operations chief and the CFO.

What Guidelines Provide an Operational Readiness Framework?

An offshoring charter and mission statement, which can include the operating principles for offshoring decision making. This document includes:

- A declaration that offshoring is a strategic-level decision involving the most senior people in the company.
- A declaration that offshoring ideas are encouraged from anywhere in the organization (although it is unlikely that lower-level employees will actively champion their own layoffs).
- A goal that the strategic framework into which managers analyze offshoring initiatives, if it exists, is transparent and understood by all C-level executives.
- A description of the players who compose an offshoring strategy committee. A permanent committee includes C-level executives, among them the CIO and legal. A revolving committee would comprise the business sponsor for a specific offshoring initiative if outside the permanent C-level strategy committee, as well as additional technical subject matter experts that the CIO believes are needed on a case-by-case basis. Insofar as IT supports a great many business processes, their input into the inevitable technical challenges of offloading IT assets to a service provider in situations, when this is part of the offshoring

package, is critical. The legal department offers invaluable advice across the entire range of regulatory and legal issues affecting the decision, including international and tax laws.

- A description of how an initial offshoring idea should be introduced into senior management and what form that initial introduction should take. A company can build a short template asking for the early relevant information supporting the idea. This jumpstarts the deeper exploration. An operational manager might be asked to submit the idea to an operations chief, who shares it with the CFO.

- A description of the frequency with which specific offshoring initiatives should be proposed. The organization might specify that it wants every operational area to identify the possible business processes that are good candidates for offshoring once or twice a year.

What Empirical Data Will the Company Rely on to Inform an Offshoring Decision and Who Provides It?

This will include an initial proposal followed later by a formal business case, which presents a full cost-benefit profile of the specific initiative. While the business sponsor will build the formal business case, the company might decide that finance must sign off on the findings. The business sponsor should feel free to consult with anyone on the permanent committee who could offer important information relevant to the specific business case.

How is Data Captured?

If offshoring is perceived to offer strategic importance, the organization should invest in the software infrastructure and tools constituting an analysis environment in which managers can enter important data and make calculations. The analysis environment should ideally span the entire Offshoring Value Delivery Framework. Therefore, such an environment is necessarily process-driven and iterative. As a new offshoring initiative unfolds, a series of templates on the company intranet, for example, could walk managers through each phase of the analysis from validating the specific strategic value of the initiative to business case development to contracting to ongoing management and performance tracking. The benefits of having a structured analysis and decision-making environment are manifest. If the environment is process-driven, managers' expertise in offshoring and its myriad issues grows through repetition, an analysis environment and the data it generates are a repository of wisdom that can be leveraged in exploring ideas, and, usually a favorite among senior management, there is the idea that an analysis environment offers one version of the truth, always important when many spoons dip from the decision-making barrel. As in-house application development projects go, an interactive offshoring decision making and analysis environment, perhaps leveraging the company Intranet, is not technically difficult to create. The first question the company might ask: If we are looking to build software, should we offshore the work?

How each step in operational decision-making governance plays out is less important than the need to have the elements in place. Should the business sponsor approach the CFO first or the chief operating officer? If an assistant manager in an operational area champions an offshoring idea is his manager obligated to forward the idea up the corporate hierarchy or is she given the authority to unilaterally shoot it down on the merits before anyone else knows of the idea's existence? Companies are aware of their unique culture and should not have difficulty in applying operational principles in a way that best suits their people, organizational structures, and business goals. There is no one right way to roll out operational principles. The idea is that optimal offshoring is best served when decision-making governance is supported by the elements described above.

WHEN THE OPERATIONAL FRAMEWORK FAILS

The chief criticism of this governance framework just might be that it is overly theoretical and in denial of the way things really work in corporations. The best response to this objection might come by way of a parable.

Let's take a high-tech gadget company that has experienced in the past few years good if not spectacular market success with a series of products, each innovative in its own way. The head of marketing and sales identifies some nascent preference or desire in a gadget's functionality that if the company could deliver it would translate into a significant boost in not only revenue but also the marketing chief's own reputation and influence. The marketing head is also aware that some of the best design work is coming out of offshore service provider organizations in Asia. Several offshore service providers have conducted the design work for the company's competitors, and the results have been hit products. Furthermore, the marketing chief is not all that thrilled with the internal design team. Their work has been adequate but uninspiring in her estimation, and the team has been undisciplined in controlling costs and delivering on time. At least one design was late which delayed a product launch. The marketing chief is ready to make her move.

She follows the company's mission statement and operational principles of offshoring and writes a several page memo evangelizing the concept of offshoring the design of the next big product, soon due out of the R&D lab, and circulates it to the divisional CFO and operations chief. After some informal soft sounding, a preliminary meeting is scheduled with all the important actors of this little drama, including the colleagues she first floated the idea by, the CEO and, of course, the head of design at the company. While consensus is reached that the company ought to move forward with a formal business case, the design head's superficial enthusiasm masks fear, resentment, and a seething desire to stick a wrench in the works before momentum for the idea moves beyond his ability to stop it. The design chief interprets the idea as an indictment of his organization to deliver the innovation value the company needs in its products and an indictment of his own abilities. Insult the team, and you are insulting the team chief. Should offshoring design for just one project succeed, other dangerous implications emerge. More design work might find its way to an offshore service provider, which might mean layoffs—even though none were proposed for this one project—and budget cuts to bring operational funding needs more in line with the reduced work load. Smaller staff and smaller budgets mean less influence. The strategic impact of this offshoring move are obvious and compelling. But none of those benefits accrue directly to the department under offshoring consideration.

Now begins the palace intrigue worthy of Louis XIV's Versaille. The design head rallies allies in R&D and in the finance organization and gets them to buy into the argument that offshoring design of anything represents surrender of strategic capabilities, core competencies, and intellectual capital, which, in this particular case, is not true. Some of these allies might not fully believe it, but they are good golf buddies of the design chief. The marketing chief knows better, having followed the offshore design market closely while discussing a vendor's capabilities with a colleague at a non-competitor. (Readers know better from a previous chapter—lots of design is moving overseas). In the end, the offshoring idea is abandoned because momentum can't be sustained and because of the design schedule demands that these activities kick into gear.

One aspect of the operational framework suggested in these pages is its seeming lack of preparedness for the scenario above: Can this governance structure work when the champion of an offshoring initiative is evangelizing offshoring business processes outside his or her purview and control? This kind of offshoring scenario might be viewed in the same way as a group of people watching a burning building with one suggesting that the person standing next to him go in to make sure that no one is trapped; everyone is great at volunteering others for the pain. In the context of offshoring, this kind of situation is more likely to occur when offshoring is analyzed from a perch in search of strategic value rather than from purely a tactical cost-cutting perspective. Good managers are expected to think holistically: How do all the pieces of the operational puzzle add up to the value creating whole? The marketing chief considered this offshoring project in exactly this way. She understood the revenue-creating possibilities in offshoring product design to one of several offshore design houses with a proven track record of delivering to other customers.

BELIEF IN EMPIRICISM IS THE ANSWER

The imperfect answer is that these kinds of decisions must be made on the merits, in the presence of good empirical data, which argue that although the risks are real, offshoring the design of a new product makes strategic sense. Management's attitude should mirror that of John Locke and Sir Francis Bacon, two giants of the Enlightenment and the Age of Reason. They believed, like good scientists, that empirical evidence and observation are the only basis on which to have an understanding of the world. In the same way, a thorough business case and the informed consultations of senior executives are the only basis on which companies can make valid decisions—about anything. It is amazing how many companies still apparently do not believe this, because they certainly do not practice it.

For those that do, a solid business case would have demonstrated the cost savings as well as the strategic potential in the relationship: quicker design turnaround and, assuming every other function stays on schedule, therefore, faster time to market, and higher-quality aesthetics in the design, which is becoming a competitive advantage in the cell phone market. If the CEO stands behind a strategic framework for offshoring decision making, it should prove itself immune to the most destructive kind of politicking that either completely sabotages or undermines the effectiveness of an offshoring idea. Although this example is apochryphal, this very scenario will play itself out in many companies—if it hasn't already—as design, once considered a sacred and coveted capability, is increasingly offshored to service providers who can do it at less cost and at least equal quality. The design function, once considered one of the most strategic activities in a company, is about to undergo a revolution. This offshore design marketplace is poised to explode over the next several years, and we should not be surprised if at least a few design chiefs respond in a predictable way. Will those organizations stand up to them?

A SHARED SERVICES PERSPECTIVE

Shared services is a model of business operations at least 10 years old. Many readers might have direct experience with a shared services initiative in their organizations. The proposition is simple enough: *shared services* describes the centralized management and administration of the business processes that deliver various services to many "customers" in the company—IT, HR, finance, and procurement to name several. The argued value in a Shared Services Model is, first, cost reductions. Companies that comprise many business units situated in locations across the planet can eliminate the process and capital expenditure redundancies in straightforward business tasks—invoicing, preparing payroll, procurement, and IT provisioning—that result from decentralized management structures where business units build processes and buy resources like autonomous nation-states. Because the services these processes deliver—IT capabilities, payroll, employee benefits help desk services, and self-service capability—touch the entire organization, why not centralize their management and delivery, and in this way, achieve economies of scale by spreading resource commitments across the entire organization? Bristol-Myers Squibb, for example, embarked on shared services nearly eight years ago, consolidating financial transactions business process delivery with the support of one global IT organization. Invoices, for example, are no longer processed at one of its more than 80 locations across the globe. The result is that Wal-Mart receives one invoice for all Bristol-Myers Squibb's product brands.[4] In another example, a European airline whose operations spanned 100 countries, rolled up accounting services into a Shared Service Delivery Model that eliminated such redundant functions as employees entering data into duplicate systems. The end result was 35% cost savings.[5]

Beyond cost savings, additional expected value from a shared service model is high-quality service delivery. The consolidation and central management paradigm is predicated upon the philosophy that if the organization is going to deliver business processes as a service, the organization must deliver at a consistently high quality level. Service quality becomes an operational goal monitored through the use and tracking metrics that have a value-oriented focus. In the case of IT, system uptime and application availability for customers are more important metrics than internally focused technical performance measures like CPU cycles and buffer activity. In HR, one of the most popular operational domains for a Shared Services Model, has the organization created a self-service environment that is both easy for employees to use and more efficient than having to call the help desk all the time? In finance, how satisfied are managers with a new service, which gives them greater visibility and ease of access to budget information? Since these kinds of questions are the focus of shared services, an organization focused on quality will work with business units to construct meaningful service level agreements (SLAs), no different in purpose than one between customer and an offshoring service provider, specifying the quality customers expect and that the organization can reasonably deliver. SLAs are an important feature of shared services.

Another fundamental element of shared services is the implementation of a quasi-market mechanism in which the shared services organization charges the customer departments for the services delivered in order to cover its cost of delivery. Some companies, however, do not abide by a disciplined chargeback approach, citing the administrative headache in managing it. Often, chargebacks processes are not even automated through integration with IT systems and must be handled manually, thereby detracting total value from the shared services model.[6]

Since shared services and offshoring have in common some basic principles around the focus on value and accountability, is the existence of a shared services model the optimal condition for organizational readiness in offshoring? Companies with experience in the shared services model are well positioned to apply hard-earned lessons to establishing a relationship with an offshore service provider. As difficult as some organizations have found constructing a workable SLA that balances the quality levels employees want with the service levels the delivery organization is capable of carrying off, it not only defines important contractual obligations of the internal "service provider" to its customer population but also reflects the minimum levels of service employees have concluded they need to do their jobs effectively. This mutual understanding serves as an effective baseline against which to determine a service provider's fitness to take over the daily management of business processes managed internally within a shared services regime. An internalized vendor/customer market habit of mind directs focus toward value captured from services delivered, which should serve organizations in selecting an offshoring partner.

Those organizations who have developed a workable shared services chargeback system will have a firm grasp of the costs involved in administering and delivering services from specific business processes. That level of understanding should prove enormously useful in negotiating with a service provider. An understanding of business process costs establishes another important baseline and benchmark against which to judge vendors and allows the organization to weigh and balance objectively various service price points that competing vendors charge against any differing service levels associated with those price points.

A substantial risk in establishing a smoothly executing shared services organization as a prerequisite to offshoring is the mixed message conveyed should the time for offshoring, in a captive or vendor scenario, arrive. Companies have had to overcome the suspicion from operational departments that underwent this transformation that in supporting business units they were viewed as "noncore" and somehow second class, when, in fact, this very transformation defines them as another business unit with P&L and service level accountability. The company made the effort to explain these service organizations' critical role in supporting lines of business to meet the demands of the marketplace. A shared services organization that now understands its role, accepts it, and has its collective self-esteem raised, suddenly discovers that its role is somewhat important but not as important as a 30% labor arbitrage the company is expected to enjoy offshoring these very business processes to the Philippines. It is unlikely that the company would articulate a set of offshoring principles that includes a shared services initiative as a first step to eventual offshoring. Buy-in from affected workers would probably be nonexistent, and big buy-in is a necessary ingredient to shared services execution. If a company sees the value in a shared services implementation as a first stage in offshoring, it is faced with explaining how such an initiative fits within the larger context of offshoring and risk resistance or confine its plans to the boardroom. A tough choice either way.

Organizations who do decide to build shared services first and use this operational paradigm as the basis for offshoring later find that, by consolidating services first, then offshoring, the company captures the double cost reduction impact of redundancy elimination and labor arbitrage, both of which can offset the costs of shared services implementation, which are not insignificant. Again, business context influences whether these multiple cost impacts are reachable. Depending on organizational size and scope of the initiative, implementation of a Shared Services Model can take two years or longer. For many organizations, establishing shared services first as a basis for an offshoring strategy is untenable when the speed of offshoring deployment is critical. A business unit head with a mandate to cut costs quickly or the company facing a product launch and the need to build logistical capability in a foreign market are unlikely to be persuaded that shared services are an excellent foundation for offshoring—which it often is. For these reasons, this text does not explicitly argue that shared services are a prerequisite for offshoring, because empirical evidence shows companies without a shared services capability successfully offshore anyway. But acquainting readers with the basics behind this management discipline demonstrates how well shared services and offshoring fit. For organizations with the luxury of time, shared services might emerge as an option to set the stage for strategic offshoring later on.

BUSINESS CASE

A formal business case is an argument for any capital and operational investment and has a long history in corporations as a decision-making tool. Regardless of whether the offshoring initiative is strategic or straightforward cost cutting, management will want to model all the costs, benefits, and risks in a structured, easily understood way. This model becomes a key component of a formal business case. Once someone has made the initial case for an offshoring iniative and validated its possibilities within a company's high-level strategic decision-making framework, and senior management has conferred over its merits, the sponsor can undertake constructing a formal business case comprising more detailed intelligence that further validates the soundness of the project.

Given the importance of a business case within offshoring strategy, this critical tool of decision making and management receives its own chapter, which is next.

CHAPTER TAKEAWAY

Here are some key concepts to leave this chapter with:

- A strategic offshoring framework is not optimized if it is not followed with an organizational readiness blueprint, which outlines the decision rights and power structure of decision making. Who has a say in offshoring, how big is their say, and how will inputs from business units and operational areas be used?

- An important organizational readiness strategy must include a communications plan, which provides a clear, consistent, and honest rationale for offshoring's new importance in the organization. Communication planning is not a follow-on tactical activity that occurs at layoff time.
- What obligations does the company have to its employees slated for layoff from an offshoring initiative? Does the fate of these workers deserve a differentiated response and deeper support commitment, particularly when the layoffs cannot be justified by deteriorating business conditions?
- Shared services are a potentially excellent base for offshoring because organizations will be well versed in structuring service levels to strike the right balance between pricing for services and quality it requires. Shared services also acts as a potent baseline and benchmark against which vendor capabilities can be assessed during the selection process.

NOTES

1. Interview David Wagner, CIO, and Allen Holt, director of manufacturing systems, ON Semiconductor, March 8, 2005.
2. Interview David Wagner, March 8, 2005.
3. Stephanie Overby, "Lost in Translation," *CIO Magazine*, July 15, 2004.
4. Elizabeth Ferrarini, "Shared Services," *ComputerWorld*, November 27, 2000.
5. "Success Through Shared Services," AT Kearney, no author cited, 2004, p. 8.
6. Ibid, p. 13.

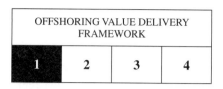
6

MAKING THE CASE

Offshoring should be viewed as an investment with all the requisite financial analysis that goes along with it. Therefore, business case and financial model construction, an old idea in age but not importance, is an Offshoring Value Framework Delivery activity conducted just before the selection process begins. Once the germ of an offshoring idea has been conceptually validated within the company's offshoring strategic framework (and we are assuming that this exists), the organization will want to build a specific business case that articulates to the best of the company's ability all the costs and benefits of the specific offshoring initiative. In fact, board-level involvement might require the submission of a business case if the proposal is to be taken seriously. A cost/benefit analysis serves as the foundation for determining the return on investment (ROI) or net present value (NPV) of the proposal, a baseline against which a future determination of value from the initiative is made. Since a cost/benefit model represents the foundation to initiate all the subsequent activities that hopefully lead to value creation from a business process offshoring effort, this element of decision making deserves its own chapter. Throughout the chapter the term business case and cost/benefit analysis will be used synonymously.

THE BUSINESS CASE LIVES

Full value of a business case is captured when the organization treats it as a living document subject to change, refinement, and revision as the organization travels through all the phases of the Offshoring Value Delivery Framework. Each phase of the framework represents a continuous process of cost and potential value discovery. While the purpose of a business case is to anticipate all the costs very early in the process so that they can be factored into planning and, indeed, can even influence whether the organization should proceed with the offshoring initiative at all, it must accommodate the unknown, particularly when a project is new to the organization. Such an accommodation gives the offshoring business case its protean quality. As new costs and benefits are revealed iteratively through decision making and discussion in each phase, the company wants to document adjustments to any financial numerical value and add new costs and benefits to the total analysis as the organization moves to the launch of an offshoring initiative with a service provider. Exhibit 6.1 represents this process of discovery.

The first three phases in the exhibit constitute all the decision-making and management activity that takes the organization to the water's edge at

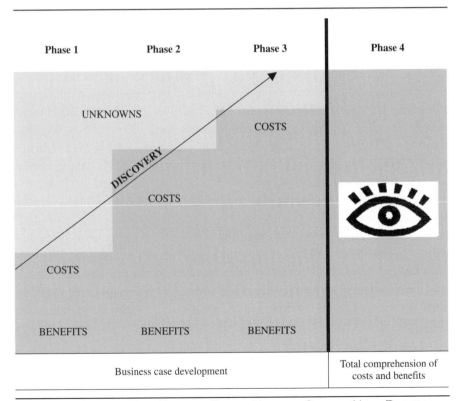

EXHIBIT 6.1   COST AND VALUE DISCOVERY PROCESS USING THE OFFSHORE VALUE DELIVERY FRAMEWORK

the beginning of Phase 4, when the initiative is actually launched. The true costs of the offshoring scenario will not be fully known until the organization has reached steady state because additional costs might only emerge as the company transitions its business processes and the assets that support them to the service provider. Steady state describes that condition in which the business processes have been fully transitioned to the service provider and the offshoring company is well into its management of the relationship. Many costs in the early part of Phase 4 will be known, but surprises can emerge if the transition, for example, does not run as smoothly as anticipated. Other Phase 4 cost surprises can include the unexpected need to provision additional IT assets to run the business processes because initial resources proved inadequate. The organization might not reach an "eyes wide open" state of total cost/benefit comprehension until several months into the relationship. It is unlikely to happen at the beginning of Phase 4, except for the simplest of offshoring projects.

PROCESS OF DISCOVERY

To see how this process of discovery unfolds, consider vendor pricing. Early in the selection process, Phase 2, the offshoring organization might scan the market to get some sense of what service providers are likely to charge for services that becomes, in turn, a key cost data point for a cost/benefit analysis. Yet the organization will not have a completely accurate figure until it has chosen a provider and entered into a contract. During price negotiations the company might discover that final pricing might fluctuate depending on varying service levels. A 15-minute service provider callback service level to acknowledge a critical failure in an IT system might be priced significantly higher than a 1-hour or 90-minute guaranteed callback level. Although the service provider cannot guarantee when systems operation will resume, it can guarantee how much time will transpire before acting on the problem. And that time lag will impact the total time to resumption of steady state, which has cost avoidance implications for the company. Contract signing time is the only point when the organization will have complete visibility into vendor costs because some elements are highly negotiable.

Discovery can unfold around issues of software licensing transfer or when senior management makes a late decision to have an operational manager make regularly scheduled trips for the first few months of the relationship to ensure the initiative launches smoothly. Or, that assignment decision can pop up in Phase 4 if it indeed turns out that the relationship is off to a bumpy start and management believes that the on site presence of a project manager will expedite the achievement of steady state. Either these specific data points were not part of the early business case development because they were unanticipated or they were included as a cost item but no dollar value was assigned because the organization wasn't sure early on that these cost-incurring activities would actually emerge. But now that these costs are proven real, they are populated into the cost/benefit analysis. By contract signing, which signifies the official launch of the offshoring initiative, all the *forecasted* costs are known to the organization. But again, additional costs can emerge even after the initiative has begun, and these must find their way into the business case if the organization sees the value in using it as an economic value discovery and tracking mechanism.

While Exhibit 6.1 depicts the revelation over time of both costs and benefits, the discovery of new costs over the phases of the Offshoring Value Delivery Framework is more likely than the discovery of some hidden benefits. The reason for this: Benefits from offshoring are pretty well-known and understood even if the total extent or financial value of the benefits are not. This is so because most offshoring today is concerned with cost reductions and this single metric becomes almost a binary goal; either a company reduces its business process operating costs below those that it incurs in-house by hitching up with a service provider or it does not. In less strategic offshoring the benefit(s) become a single data point: pure cost reductions. There just isn't much else to reveal on the benefit side over the course of executing Phases 1 through 3 of the delivery framework. However, pure cost reduction propositions do not constitute the entirety of offshoring, which is made clear at plenty of points throughout this text. Some are highly strategic, involving new market penetration and revenue. In these rare cases, various points of benefit manifest themselves over the course of laying the groundwork for the initiative and so the image reflects this possibility.

CAPTIVE VERSUS SERVICE PROVIDER BUSINESS CASE

The analysis in this chapter concerns itself with offshoring involving a service provider, but the exploration of costs and benefits is virtually the same in a captive scenario. The process of discovery is similarly revealed as each phase of the delivery framework unfolds, although since costs are completely within the control of the organization some might prove more predictable. The obvious difference between captive and service provider cost profiling is in the nature of the costs. In a captive scenario, the company is faced with potential recruitment and retention issues if it turns out that additional staff to augment business process administration is required. Tax and working capital issues that are less of a concern in a service provider scenario are quite relevant when the company is offshoring internally to an office in a foreign country. Canada, for instance, burdens foreign companies with a capital deposit requirement that it does not demand of its domestic insurers.[1] This certainly affects the cost-benefit analysis which supports a business case. And while the organization no longer faces service provider fees as a monthly or quarterly cost item, this fact alone demonstrates an additional difference around the respective business cases: in a captive scenario the process of value auditing is in some instances more difficult and arguably more critical for the following reasons.

A value audit is a Phase 4 activity—explained in detail in Chapter 12—in which the organization validates that the measurable goals from the offshoring initiative reflected in a fully loaded cost/benefit analysis actually came true. As already mentioned, in service provider offshoring where the goals are significant cost cutting, these objectives were either achieved or they were not. Or the cost savings goals were achieved but not to the degree the organization had hoped. Validating achievement of objectives is a fairly clean exercise. This may or may not be so in a captive scenario. The organization is fully accountable for cost savings results because the labor and capital allocation decisions placed into the hands of the service provider are back in the lap of company management. Since all offshoring decisions are in the control of the organization, the results might not be packaged as neatly as a single monthly service provider fee. Some cost savings will be clear, but the total of the cost savings impact might be more diffuse, spread out between the target offshoring operation and the location from which business processes were moved. Diffusion of benefits means the investigation of value might require digging data out of multiple parts of an IT system supporting those processes.

TOTAL VALUE OF A BUSINESS CASE

Beyond a thorough comprehension of the costs and benefits of an offshoring initiative, other points of value from a business case exist. They include:

- Allegiance to a thorough cost analysis ensures that the true cost implications of offshoring business processes emerge before the organization commits to the initiative, even if all costs cannot be fully predicted. This is because as new costs emerge through all phases of the Offshoring Value Delivery Framework, managers will formally document them. Because business case owners should be continually on the prowl for new costs as they emerge, completeness is injected into the cost analysis.

- A business case is a single version of the truth. It acts as a narrative guide to the telling of the offshoring value story while preventing storytellers from straying or embellishing it. A single version of the truth does not mean that consensus about future courses of action will be arrived at more efficiently, because data can be interpreted multiple ways. It does means that the facts themselves out of which decisions are made are not in dispute. Were the facts in dispute, decision making would be impossible.

- A business case represents a baseline against which additional costs will be added. Capturing a footprint of initial cost/benefit forecasts against its evolution allows the organization to build a powerful learning capability into offshoring management, which can only improve the likelihood of future value capture from other offshoring initiatives if the organization takes the process of learning seriously: What costs were unexpected? Why were those costs unexpected? What issues required deeper exploration? Would deeper exploration have manifested those costs earlier in the process? Is organizational governance adequate to ensure a full understanding of all the financial implications of offshoring?

HOW TO REPRESENT COSTS

For the purposes of this analysis, costs are categorized as startup and ongoing rather than fixed and variable. The reason for this is that in the context of building and updating a business case, thinking about costs chronologically and within a narrative rather than in terms of the laws of budgeting is easier and more analytically useful, since costs revolve around services rather than manufacturing. In the manufacturing world fixed costs have real meaning. If a company wants to build a product, there is no way around the need for plant and equipment—unless the company subcontracts the work to an outsider. With services, fixed costs are not as conceptually relevant. People are a fixed cost in a services business to a certain degree, but it is a matter of degree. They are fixed until layoff time. Alternatively, the textbook definition of variable costs is those influenced by sales. A salient definition perhaps in an offshoring call center environment where the launch of a new product in an electronics category is almost invariably followed by a spike in calls to a customer service rep who walks callers through issues on how to use the thing. More people are assigned to the account to handle the call volume spike, and the customer is charged incrementally more in response to this temporary situation. Categorizing costs as variable is less relevant, however, when a company offshores its employee benefits help desk or payroll.

Startup and ongoing costs, however, are quite relevant: What are all the costs to ramp up an offshoring initiative? And, what are the recurring costs beyond just the service provider fee to make the offshoring relationship work? Exploring costs in this light is far more probative. If need be, managers can transpose these costs into the lingo of budgeting as necessary.

OFFSHORING COST/BENEFIT MODEL

Exhibit 6.2 represents a basic cost benefit construct managers have likely seen many times before. Quantifiable costs plus quantifiable benefits adjusted for the risks from offshoring equals value. Quantification of each of these categories poses challenges. Offshoring costs are mostly measurable, but some might prove unpredictable. Some benefits might be hard to measure: How does a company quantify efficiencies captured from consolidating global and diffused business processes in one foreign office? Do those benefits manifest themselves in a measurable way? Risks might prove both unpredictable and difficult to assign probabilities to. Later chapters demonstrate that the risks of offshoring are extensive, touching on operations and execution, as well as the economic, regulatory, and legal environment of the target country. Achieving a confidence level that all risks have been made visible and assigned an accurate probability of occurrence requires both a completeness and rigorousness of risk analysis. Only on a risk-adjusted basis will the organization have a true understanding of the real value of an offshoring initiative.

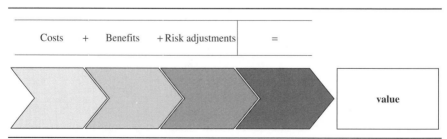

| Costs | + | Benefits | + Risk adjustments | = | |

value

EXHIBIT 6.2 SIMPLE MATH IN REACHING VALUE

MAPPING COSTS ANALYSIS TO THE OFFSHORING VALUE DELIVERY FRAMEWORK

An effective way to understand the cost side of a cost/benefit analysis is to document the most common of them companies incur through offshoring. This is accomplished by mapping costs to the Offshoring Delivery Framework, depicted in Exhibit 6.3. Startup and ongoing costs do not map precisely to the delivery framework in Phase 4, since some activity here, such as transition work, is really not an ongoing cost but a crucial Phase 4 startup cost required to place the service provider in a position to begin managing business processes on the customer's behalf. For this reason, both startup and ongoing cost categories appear in this phase.

COST EXPLORATION

The costs represented in Exhibit 6.3 are representative and indicative of many offshoring initiatives but are not absolute. Some organizations will benchmark, with the help of a consultant, current service levels to deliver services internally; others will either already have this data or decide that the effort is not worth the investment. Some organizations will incur significant layoff costs if labor arbitrage is the key reason for the offshoring move, while others won't lay off any employees. The extent and the nature of the costs facing the organization are determined both by the nature of the offshoring initiative and why it is being undertaken, as well as by the extent to which the company is committed to thoroughness and completeness of the management principles reflected in the Offshoring Value Delivery Framework.

The following brief sections explores some of the less obvious costs found in each of the delivery framework phases.

Phase 1

Chapter 5 argued strongly that adoption of offshoring as an ongoing objective requires a management platform on which all activities can be analyzed and documented and the cost of development and maintenance requires inclusion in a business case, although the cost is amortized over its useful life for all future offshoring projects. Organizations must also factor in the cost of new staff dedicated to long-term offshoring management and spread those costs out accordingly.

Phase 1	Phase 2	Phase 3	Phase 4
Initiative startup costs			Startup and Ongoing costs
			Startup
Consultants	Consultants	Consultants	Transition project management—dedicated temp assignment
New permanent staffing	Purchased business intelligence data	Software asset transfer, licensing costs	
Building web-based offshoring management work environment	Benchmarking	Connectivity—dedicated data pipe	Knowledge transfer and training, also documentation creation and publishing
	Travel costs		
Maintaining web-based offshore management work environment	Layoffs—severance, outplacement resources	Additional IT—hardware, security technology	
		Pilot project	
			Ongoing
			Vendor fee
			SLA adjustments up—vendor fee increase
			Balance sheet—book value (if assets are transferred)
			Temporary executive assignment on site
			Travel costs
			Vendor to monitor legal environment
			Tax
			Regulatory compliance
			Phone/online meetings
			Additional IT over time

EXHIBIT 6.3   MAPPING SPECIFIC COSTS OF OFFSHORING TO THE OFFSHORING VALUE DELIVERY FRAMEWORK

Phase 2

Research and business intelligence purchased to support offshoring decision making is not cheap, which is why its cost should be documented. The organization might want to purchase vendor analysis data from a research house that tracks the market as a way to get a rough idea of what the service provider's fee structure will look like. Or it might be interested in information that profiles the financial condition of privately run vendors. Readers will see in Chapter 7 which covers vendor selection, that the financial health of the service provider is an important selection criterion. Travel costs emerge when management visits the operations of final candidates.

Phase 3

Software license transfer in those cases where necessary present a cost surprise to the organization when not properly planned for. Companies who view this issue as an afterthought are in for some nasty surprises, such as when the software vendor's salesperson finds out about the company's offshoring plans accidentally and the organization has not developed any negotiating strategy to wrestle out of a restricted license that will not allow transfer to the service provider. The salesperson sees this as an opportunity to stick up the customer and force the purchase of a new license specifically for the offshoring initiative.[2] Had the organization prepared for negotiations with the software vendor, it might have secured a much better deal. Some software vendors flat out do not allow licensing privileges to service providers to administer a customer's business processes.[3] If IT assets are scheduled for transfer to the service provider, then review under what conditions that change in ownership is possible and the cost implications.

As far as data connectivity costs are concerned, they are rarely a major issue in low-scope, low-complexity cost-driven offshoring projects, but loom large in those cases where, in the name of collaboration, large amounts of data needs to be transferred back and forth between the customer and the service provider. Offshoring product design might be one instance where high-bandwidth, dedicated connectivity is needed. Who pays for this connectivity and how are the costs allocated between customer and service provider?

Security issues suddenly receive heightened awareness in an offshoring relationship because important business processes are no longer under organizational control. A heightened awareness might translate into a need to tighten security at the domestic data center that the offshore service provider will regularly access to manage business processes. Security strategy is explored in detail in Chapter 9.

Phase 4

Ongoing costs suggest predictability and consistency. This is true—to a point. Organizations will discover that the service level agreements, which define the level of quality the customer can expect from the service provider, are subject to refinement and renegotiation over time as the needs of the business change. If new service levels mean an upward vendor fee adjustment, then the customer's ongoing costs have just risen. So much for predictability.

Perhaps the most unpredictable set of costs in offshoring for unexperienced organizations surround transition activities when companies undertake those activities to prepare the service provider for steady state management of business processes. The single biggest cost can derive from the organization's misestimation of the time it will take to execute the transition. As the book demonstrates in Chapter 12, knowledge transfer is a critical transition activity, which involves the training of service provider staff to bring them up to speed on the specific expertise needed to manage business processes successfully. Transition delays not only bump the time to payback or the time to cost savings but also introduces higher costs early in the relationship because the contract might specify a hard start date for the service provider. Service fees are now live, but the knowledge transfer has yet to be completed. Vendor work quality might suffer, which raises the issue of missed service levels; can the service provider really be penalized when the customer could not fulfill its transition obligation to adequately train service provider staff within the prescribed time frame? Bad transition execution can really create a mess for everyone.

Another area of potential cost is incremental information technology required to either service the relationship or run other operations. Does the transfer of IT assets to the service provider leave the organization under-provisioned for all the other work it does? Or, does the organization require additional IT specifically for the success of the offshoring relationship? Analyzing IT capacity from a workload perspective provides the organization a measurable way to monitor infrastructure's ability to keep up with the demands of an offshoring relationship while meeting ongoing internal needs: in mainframes the measurement is million of instructions per second, in connectivity the measurement is gigabytes of data transfer, in IT help desk the measurement is volume of calls. Organizations with a clear understanding of its future needs a service provider might fulfill will be in a strong position to anticipate future IT infrastructure needs.

COST BENCHMARKING

As data emerges it might be in the interest of organizations to collect benchmarking information that reveals what the typical up front and ongoing cost profiles look like for the particular class of business processes the organization is intent on offshoring—payroll, inbound/outbound call center, logistics, finance, and so forth. Even small-in-scope offshoring projects, such as help desk offshoring, can represent several months worth of operating costs. How does one company's cost profile look in comparison to a population of companies offshoring like business processes? Startup and ongoing cost baselines help the organization establish expenditure boundaries as they embark on an initiative. Large variances in one company's costs is a potential signal that its offshoring execution is flawed and requires reexamination.

SUBJECT OF CHANGE

The idea of change should have been added to the saying that the only certainties in life are death and taxes. Change is an immutable reality to corporations and impacts every corner of their operations: changes in staff, in leadership, in technology, in innovation, in the management techniques available to better run a business, in laws and regulations, in the competitive landscape, in marketshare, in customers. Change frequently introduces costs at an operational level. That is, by virtue of some change, new costs emerge that are causally linked to that change. Change is an equally useful cost analysis concept in offshoring. Exhibit 6.4 shows why.

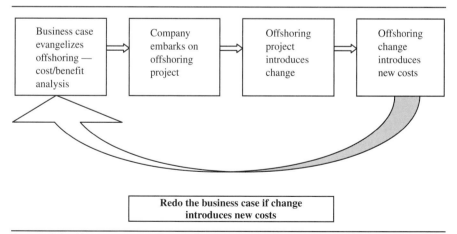

EXHIBIT 6.4 UNDERSTANDING CHANGE INTRODUCED BY OFFSHORING AND ITS IMPACT ON COST

Understanding the cost implications from a change perspective is simply another way of arguing the need to update the business case as new costs emerge during offshoring execution. However, many organizations do not consciously or explicitly analyze costs from a change context. Looking at offshoring costs from a slightly different angle might help managers identify and anticipate costs that otherwise would have been overlooked. The concept of change itself seems very broad and analytically vague. Therefore, organizations might want to drill down into offshoring change along four dimensions:

1. **People.** What changes regarding the organization's workforce will occur that are causally linked to the offshoring initiative and will those people changes introduce costs? The obvious derive from layoffs and the hiring of new permanent staff. But considering cost impacts from the perspective of change is more interested in the less obvious cost implications. If some existing staff will assume new roles and responsibilities what might be the training and skills development costs that ensue? Again, the idea is to pin down the cost implications of people change arising directly out of the offshoring initiative.

2. **Processes.** What cost impact could emerge from business process offshoring for all the business processes that remain under the control of the organization? If the company offshores HR help desk, how does this change HR work flows that remain behind? The business process change might be negligible but managers can conclude this only if they bother to ask the question this way.

3. **Organization.** Will the offshoring initiative introduce changes in organizational structure now that business processes have left the company? What are the costs of organizational realignment or new reporting structures that result? Have the paths of communication been optimized in response to a new organizational reality?

4. **Technology.** Because IT is the life blood of every organization, it is worthwhile to explore IT infrastructure change implications because more IT certainly means additional costs. As was already mentioned in the last section, aligning the new business condition after offshoring begins with IT capabilities helps the organization plan for the future.

CHAPTER TAKEAWAY

Here are some key concepts to leave this chapter with:

- The offshoring business case and cost/benefit analysis—is the organization's sacred text, which reveals truth about the real value it can expect from an offshoring initiative. Clarity in comprehension of costs and benefits provides the organization a clear decision-making path.

- The business case is a living document subject to update and refinement through the evolution of offshoring execution when all the costs cannot be anticipated up front. Avoid the trap of creating the business case once and then throwing it into the proverbial drawer. Diminished business case awareness as the initiative moves forward decreases the focus on the end result, which can lead to poor decision making. Frequent updates as necessary keep everyone's eyes on the offshoring goals.

- A business case is as important in a captive offshoring situation as it is in a service provider scenario. Because all decision making in a captive situation is under the control of the organization, the scope of costs might be greater and their measurability more challenging. The organization truly concerned with understanding the measurable value of captive offshoring will need a solid grasp of baseline costs to deliver services as a meaningful baseline against which future value can be depicted.

- All offshoring represents change both obvious and not so obvious. Analyzing offshoring cost implications from a change perspective can be a powerful approach to comprehension.

- A true cost benefit analysis must adjust for the risks involved in offshoring.

- In a service provider offshoring scenario, single-minded focus on what the service provider will charge for business process management misses the overall cost profile the organization actually faces. Vendor fees represent only one component of the overall cost profile associated with offshoring.

NOTES

1. Interview with Jim Maloney of Corillian, April 19, 2005.
2. Nick Huber, "Avoid License Pitfalls in Outsourcing Contracts," *Computer-Weekly*, November 16, 2004.
3. Ibid.

Phase 2

Selection Process: Plan

Now that the strategic and operational foundations for offshoring have been set, the organization would like a selection framework for choosing a service provider that offers the right fit for the organization. The first step is to develop a selection criteria framework that helps an organization arrive at a set of vendor requirements the organization seeks to fulfill for any business process offshoring initiative. Then, the organization embarks on an initial search to establish vendor candidates who fulfill those criteria. Vendors that make that first cut are then subjected to an additional winnowing process in which the company performs due diligence around criteria that are universally important, no matter the nature of the offshoring initiative, such as the financial health of the vendor. Vendors who survive that second cut are then asked to respond to a request for proposal (RFP). The organization will next visit the vendors left standing after RFPs have been analyzed and a final decision is made. Think of the process as a funnel, illustrated in Exhibit 7.1 on page 112. A number of vendor candidates enter at the top but only one emerges at the other end as each step is executed. Although this approach is explicitly designed for service provider selection, organizations can apply this thinking to an in-house arrangement.

7

SO MANY CHOICES

SELECTION CRITERIA DEVELOPMENT

There are probably as many ways to establish vendor criteria as there are vendors. One of the most effective approaches is to begin the selection process with this question: What are the desired outcomes from the relationship? Desired outcomes can be categorized into three broad groups. They are: (1) basic services, steady state kinds of business processes such as inbound call centers or application maintenance, (2) enabling services in which the idea is to gain a new capability or productivity improvement from the relationship, and (3) strategic services. Here, the offshore service provider is a company's business partner. You can see that the business processes under offshoring consideration help define the three outcome categories. For instance, there is little strategic value expected in offshoring application maintenance. Alternatively, hiring a service provider to manage processes around new product development and launch can hardly be considered providing basic services. This work is highly strategic and value-added. When the business processes candidates for offshoring are tied to the business value sought in the arrangement and the strategic flavor of the relationship emerges, a company is in a far better position to determine whether a specific service provider is equipped with the necessary ingredients to deliver the various levels of outcome value embedded in each category. Next up is a deeper explanation of the three outcomes-based service categories. More examples of each are then provided after that.

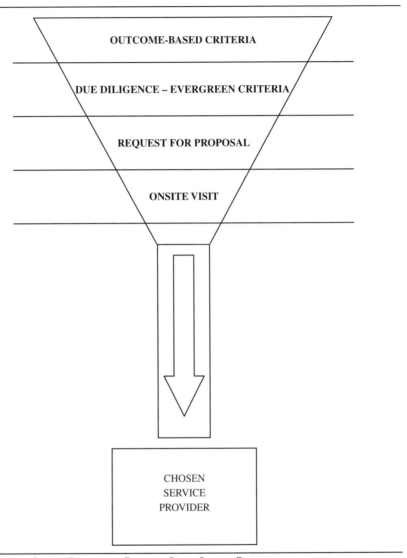

EXHIBIT 7.1   SIFTING PROCESS TO FIND THE RIGHT SERVICE PROVIDER

Defining Criteria by Outcomes Sought

Basic Services Relationship.   These are plain vanilla functions highly mature in business process offshoring today. In the context of IT, basic services provisioned are "lights on" kinds of business processes such as hardware and software maintenance, upgrades, bug fixes, and other traditional IT tasks. Companies that run IT as a utility service are proud that their budget might represent 1% of sales and that this proportion is fixed and immutable. It seeks little else from the offshore service provider in moving these processes out of the organization. Check or bill processing represent another type of basic offshoring services. In these relationships cost is far and away the biggest consideration. Companies are searching for 30%+ cost reductions. Are these the kinds of outcomes the company seeks in the relationship with the service provider?

Enabling and Enhancement Services Relationship. In this kind of relationship, a company seeks greater value in the form of either an enhancement of existing business processes or a new capability. We have seen how some organizations such as Intel seek to build relationships internationally to tap into high-quality technical talent to enhance the scope of their research work. Or how a startup relied on foreign sources of programming talent to build a software product that could not have been created using domestic labor sources given the wage costs involved. In this way the startup sought a service provider who could build the application to its specifications; the service provider essentially became the company's product development team. Cost is important—the software startup couldn't launch a product in the United States unless it retained foreign programming talent but the issue is cost plus a more strategic capability because there is some expected future value involved. In this startup's case, revenue from sale of the software application. Are these the kinds of outcomes the company seeks in the relationship with the service provider?

Strategic Service Relationship. In this highly strategic kind of relationship, the goal is innovation or new market entry. The growing amount of design work moving overseas is evidence of the pursuit of innovation goals from offshoring. The pharmaceutical industry, as we saw, is aggressively offshoring key elements of drug development to China, either through in-house facilities or through third-party R&D operations. Cost reductions are always an attraction in any offshoring move, particularly with young companies that stretch precious investment dollars in scientifically validating the viability of a new drug between venture capital funding rounds. Yet service pricing is not a top priority in motivating many of these arrangements. One Chinese offshore drug development service provider offers late stage development services as part of a larger deal in which it obtains Asian licensing rights from its customers to market these new products.[1] Joint ventures and arrangements that focus on future value and not just current cost reductions typify this category of service provider-customer relation-ship. Are these the kinds of outcomes the company seeks in the relationship with the service provider?

Managers should discover a couple of things from this framework. As the outcomes sought from offshoring business processes move from prima-rily cost reductions to the future value impact from the relationship, pricing and cost alone become lower priorities for the customer. Thinking about vendor selection from a desired goal perspective is useful for in-house off-shore projects as well. Even if the organization has few choices in the num-ber of internal locations where business processes can actually be offshored, by starting the thought processes around outcomes, managers possessing a deep understanding of the internal operational capabilities can validate whether the target offshoring location is equipped to deliver on the outcomes, be they cost-driven or more strategic.

Map Outcome Categories to Specific Vendor Criteria

After a company determines which category best describes the flavor of the offshoring proposal on the table, it can then establish a list of additional cri-teria, specific and unique to each category type, and apply those outcome-specific criteria to vendors. Again, the idea is to develop criteria that factor in a mix of outcomes sought and the business processes under offshoring review that drive those outcomes. These criteria will help the organization determine whether there is a reasonable expectation that the service pro-vider can deliver the outcomes sought given the goals in play. Notice that the criteria are not vendor-specific but rather relationship/outcome cate-gory-specific. Exhibits 7.2, 7.3, and 7.4 represent grids an organization could construct for the three types of outcomes-driven categories, into which spe-cific service provider information would be populated.

Outcome Driven Criteria	Vendor 1	Vendor 2	Vendor 3
—	—	—	—
—	—	—	—
—	—	—	—
—	—	—	—
—	—	—	—
—	—	—	—
—	—	—	—
—	—	—	—

EXHIBIT 7.2   OUTCOME CATEGORY: BASIC SERVICES

Outcome Driven Criteria	Vendor 1	Vendor 2	Vendor 3
—	—	—	—
—	—	—	—
—	—	—	—
—	—	—	—
—	—	—	—
—	—	—	—
—	—	—	—
—	—	—	—

EXHIBIT 7.3 OUTCOME CATEGORY: ENABLING AND ENHANCEMENT SERVICES

Outcome Driven Criteria	Vendor 1	Vendor 2	Vendor 3
—	—	—	—
—	—	—	—
—	—	—	—
—	—	—	—
—	—	—	—
—	—	—	—
—	—	—	—
—	—	—	—

EXHIBIT 7.4 OUTCOME CATEGORY: STRATEGIC SERVICES

Listed within each of the three grids in the left column would be the specific category criteria that a company will investigate for any service provider emerging as a vendor candidate. For illustrative purposes three vendors are used. A company might investigate three or fewer or six or more vendors.

Now that we have our grids set up, we will analyze theoretical service providers for three types of offshoring initiatives. One initiative is highly cost savings driven. The outcomes sought from the relationship are basic services. A second initiative is higher value-added. Cost cutting is not the only outcome sought. A third initiative is highly strategic. Outcomes include revenue or marketshare enhancements. As you will see, some criteria are applicable to more than one relationship type, other criteria are unique.

Two additional points require emphasis here: one, the idea is not to bog down the selection process by seeking to drill to the center of the Earth on each and every criteria. Clearly, some are more important than others. And while offshoring is a new kind of business arrangement it certainly is not the only kind of arrangement that companies have embarked upon. The intensity of the due diligence in the selection process will be influenced by many factors, including the reputation of the service provider, its financial position, the complexity of the processes under offshoring consideration, and the sophistication and experience of the company itself in establishing international business relationships. For these reasons some criteria might require more attention and some less. Two, the whole purpose of arranging vendor criteria this way is to lead the organization back to one fundamental question: What business value and what outcomes out of business process offshoring does it seek in forging a relationship with a service provider and does the service provider measure up based on the criteria that are indicative of the outcomes sought?

Basic Services Criteria Scenario

An IT organization seeks to offshore its application maintenance work because management has informed the CIO its next fiscal year budget is going to be drastically curtailed. The CIO is well aware that this type of business process offshoring is popular, a number of vendors operate in the space and the processes themselves are mature and well established. Cutting costs is priority one here. Given the outcomes the CIO expects from the offshoring initiative, predictable IT services at a much lower cost structure than the organization can deliver with in-house resources, what kind of vendor criteria might the CIO develop? The following sections describe the basic services outcomes vendor criteria.

CRITERIA: Cost Savings Proposition.   Cost is a big deal. A company wants a clear understanding of what the monthly or quarterly payment will be. Cost comparisons are easy to make in basic service outcome relationships because many vendors compete for business and comparisons will be made against consistent service level frameworks. So, even though final vendor quotes may vary, prices are generated across vendors from a common baseline of service expectations. Cost should never be a sovereign condition for offshoring, but it is still awfully important, which is why it appears at the top of the criteria list for this outcome category.

CRITERIA: SLA Adherence.   This criteria attempts to determine with what frequency service providers do not meet SLA performance levels. SLAs are the centerpiece of cost-centric basic services relationships and the business processes protected in them are well defined and suitable for metrics. Consider the call center. There exist dozens of key performance indicators across all its operational dimensions. Call center IT infrastructures are efficient at collecting performance data suitable for crunching to arrive at metric values. For this reason service providers will know precisely the frequency with which some element of an SLA has been breached with customers. This criteria reveals a couple of things: one, a frequency of SLA noncompliance far higher than average suggests the service provider's resources—people and IT—are overextended; two, it overpromises in order to get the engagement. Customers want to know if either conditions are true. Whether vendors will share this data is another matter, but ask for it anyway.

CRITERIA: Specific Business Process Focus. How much faith can a company have in a prospective service provider if it has little experience in the management and execution of the very business processes it seeks to offshore? A sales guy for a vendor with a medical transcription focus might try to convince a manager it is well equipped to handle its claims processing work. Caveat emptor. How much of a service provider's work in either revenue or number of clients should consist of the processes the organization seeks to offshore? A third? Half? No rule of thumb exists, but if possible, plug into any available thought leadership to determine if a pattern of proportionality is emerging for specific business process domains. While a client number percentage will provide a sense of the depth of process domain expertise— call centers, IT, HR, and so forth—the percentage revenue total in that domain will indicate the heft of the responsibility and customer commitment.

CRITERIA: Average Time to Steady State. As readers will see in Chapter 12, which confronts transition planning, steady state defines that business condition when the business processes have been completely forklifted out of the organization and into the managerial control of the service provider. While the time it takes to reach steady state will differ with the size of engagement—the number of employees involved—and its relative complexity—transitioning out maintenance of a dozen mainframe applications is harder than transitioning to an offshore legal transcription service— managers would do well to get a sense of how long it takes from the start of the transition to reach this condition. Time to steady state is heavily dependent on the customer. If planning is not thorough, it is likely to bungle some phase of it and delay the vendor's full assumption of business process management. For this reason, organizations should be careful not to misjudge the vendor. However, the service provider also influences the time to steady state; the maturity of its administrative processes and managerial experience in facilitating customer transitioning will affect transition effectiveness. Although this measure is influenced by many fathers, it is worth getting a handle on the performance measure, particularly when delays can materially affect the offshoring investment's payback period.

CRITERIA: Average Age of Engagements in Process Area.   The length of engagements in a process domain indicates the amount of experience the service has in managing the processes the organization seeks to offshore. This is also a rough proxy for customer satisfaction. A three-year relationship is a likely indication that the customer is satisfied with the vendor's service delivery.

CRITERIA: Percentage Labor Turnover Rate in Specific Process Management Area.   Attrition is a growing problem in certain sectors of the offshoring market, approaching 50 to 75% in India,[2] What is happening is in some offshoring relationships, the Indian labor team is sent to the U.S. company's operation during the transition phase. This experience becomes a valuable element on a worker's resume, which translates into his or her departure for a better deal at another service provider once he or she returns home. Organizations should seek as stable a workforce environment as possible. High turnover can be very disruptive to the overall effectiveness of offshoring if service provider managers are constantly acquainting themselves with new staff and coaching them about the subtleties of the work involved as new hires ramp up their understanding of the business processes they are assigned to.

CRITERIA: Training Commitment and Effectiveness.   How much resources in time and money is the service provider investing in skills development? Is the service provider's philosophy to provide formal training up front for new hires only or is skills development across all business processes it manages imbedded in its culture? What kind of partnerships has the service provider forged with institutions of higher learning? Accent neutralization, for example, is a focus of service provider training for call center or help support work involving heavy customer interaction.

What metrics are relevant for this selection criteria? It does not lend itself to easy quantification. Input performance indicators—amount of money spent on training as a percentage of a service provider's operating budget, number of people trained—are not necessarily leading indicators of outcomes success. The organization should focus more on training effectiveness in helping service provider employees achieve at a performance level that delivers the value the offshoring customer seeks. Looked at this way, the level and quality of worker training can have a direct bearing on the outcomes from offshoring. In one BenchmarkPortal survey exploring the United States' reaction to call center experiences with offshore reps, while a small percentage of customers found it difficult to communicate with heavily accented reps, the greatest source of dissatisfaction was found in the inability of the rep to resolve the problem.[3] Clearly, reps were not adequately trained in some aspect of product or service support, resulting in low first-time resolution performance. The offshore customer would want to explore call center service provider customer satisfaction results and particularly the problem resolution metric as a rough proxy of effectiveness of training resources it has in place.

Once managers have conducted their investigations and have collected all relevant data, they will populate these outcomes-based vendor criteria in the selection grid, illustrated in Exhibit 7.5. The power of this approach is the intensity of focus managers have on outcomes, a focus injects clarity into the vendor criteria essential to achieving them. Focusing on outcomes first, then backing into relevant criteria should crystallize for managers all the process and resource requirements of the vendor to do the offshoring job. Do they demonstrate a readiness for the organization's offshoring goals given the performance in these criteria areas? Well-understood requirements mean unambiguous contracts, SLAs, statements of work and RFPs. Clarity in all these documents, as we shall see, is critical to offshoring success.

Outcome Driven Criteria	Vendor 1	Vendor 2	Vendor 3
Cost savings proposition	30% off current cost	42% off current cost	48% off current cost
SLA adherence	High	Low	Average
Specific business process focus	High	High	Low
Average time to steady state	4 months	7 months	6 months
Average age of engagements in process area	2 years	3 years	1.5 years
Percentage labor turnover rate in specific process management area	30%	22%	63%
Training commitment and effectiveness	High	Low	Medium

EXHIBIT 7.5 OUTCOMES CATEGORY: BASIC SERVICES

In addition to outcome-specific criteria, management is interested in a number of evergreen criteria for which vendors should have a baseline competency. These criteria will be explained in more detail in the section entitled "Evergreen Selection Criteria."

Enabling and Enhancement Services Criteria Scenario

Just as a basic services relationship drives some specific criteria to choose vendors, so does an offshoring initiative, which presents a new capability for the organization to reveal relevant vendor criteria dictated by expected goals. Here is an example.

A large health insurer anticipated a flood of paper-based claims as new Health Insurance Portability and Accountability Act (HIPAA) regulations were going into effect. The outcomes the company sought were twofold: to minimize overtime costs in its claims processing unit and to establish a condition of "future preparedness" in the event that a sudden large spike in claims processing materialized when the laws went into effect. In addition to legal compliance, the company wanted to achieve operational quality performance levels in claims processing to ensure customer satisfaction.[4] Therefore, the goals were: additional capacity to handle a raw increase in claims in addition to minimizing claims handling-error rates. In this scenario the company essentially seeks to enhance claim-handling business processes through a service provider relationship. Given the cost-effectiveness, capacity handling, and quality goals what kinds of vendor criteria might managers at this healthcare company apply?

The next sections discuss the enabling services outcomes vendor criteria.

CRITERIA: Cost Savings Proposition.   Cost savings are important but are a goal that coexists with other expectations. Within a disciplined cost structure, a health insurer wants to equip itself with a new capability to handle an increase in claims, while simultaneously reducing error rates in those claims handling processes. If the insurer could accept more errors proportional to the new amount of claims it would need to process, then the value proposition would be limited to additional handling. However, a concomitant decrease in errors at the new volume processing level means not just a capacity increase but also a capacity increase at higher quality. Certainly, the company is seeking a new capability. Furthermore, the company seeks the new capability at a cost no greater than what it could fetch in-house, but the real value will reside in how quickly the service provider can deploy the new capability because the organization is facing regulatory deadlines. The company might conclude that provisioning service at breakeven to its internal cost is still worth it because of the time element involved. This point of value—time criticality—is as important as pure cost, which is why this scenario is an enabling-outcomes type offshoring initiative.

CRITERIA: SLA Adherence.   Effectiveness in meeting SLA guidelines remains an important consideration considering the company is seeking quality improvements. If the customer seeks specific claims handling error rates codified in an SLA, understanding the vendor's compliance here in relation to other customers is critical.

CRITERIA: Specific Business Process Focus.   This criteria only grows in importance when the outcomes are enabling and not just steady-state. The capture of a new capability from offshoring implies that the offshore service provider is demonstrably better at the business processes under consideration at a lower cost, or why wouldn't the organization undertake the work itself? This is likely true only if the vendor has developed very deep expertise in the specific business process domain, in this case working with insurance carriers and their industry-specific processes. Among several service providers, which one emerges as having a clear advantage here relative to the others?

CRITERIA: Training Commitment and Effectiveness.   Training is often more important in enabling relationships, since the stakes are higher than in a basic services scenario; the company wants to capture measurable outcomes from enabling a new capacity through the service provider. The offshore customer should also realize that industry and process specialization and domain expertise only grow in importance. Clearly, a service provider with little insurance industry and claims-processing experience will have a more difficult time delivering value—if it ever can. This reality reminds managers that the domain focus selection criteria can directly affect the service provider's ability to train workers in the processes designed to deliver a new capability. Because an enabling capability scenario is highly contextual, requiring specific knowledge, the service provider might not have all the relevant expertise to conduct the necessary training. Therefore, the focus on training as a selection criteria shifts from resource commitments to the service provider's ability to support the training and knowledge transfer efforts (training and knowledge transfer are synonymous) of the offshoring customer, since the customer is placed by default into the role of educator. A relevant metric in this case might be average time to competency across customers. This metric takes on added urgency, since the insurance company faced a deadline date on which it needed all the offshoring pieces in place. Also, what kind of track record does the service provider have in supporting efficient and effective process specific training delivered by the customer? Is it used to this role? Does the service provider offer an efficient and effective train-the-trainer training model in which the customer brings service provider supervisors up to speed on the process requirements and, in turn, the supervisor assumes responsibility for training workers adminstering the processes with some support from the offshoring customer? In enabling scenarios proper training is hugely important, the criteria focus, however, shifts.

CRITERIA: Integration and Development Domain Expertise.   Enabling relationships often require the transfer of complex supporting information technology. What is the vendor's track record in successfully integrating the customer's applications and the hardware necessary to manage the business processes?

CRITERIA: Time to Value.   In a basic services relationship, managers are interested in how long it takes the service provider to assist the organization in reaching steady state. In an enabling relationship, the measurement is time to enabling and new capability value. Explore the kinds of new capabilities it has delivered to customers and the time involved in doing so.

In the same way that these data points are populated into a decision grid in a basic services scenario, managers can construct an enabling services outcome grid and input relevant information particular to each vendor along these criteria dimensions.

Strategic Services Criteria Scenario

Back to the offshore drug development scenario. Suppose that a U.S. pharmaceutical company sought to reduce the cycle time involved in drug development. In its search for relevant service providers, it might discover that an Asian company offered a way not only to accelerate late stage development processes but also the means to penetrate the Asian market with this new drug. Its web of contacts and marketing expertise in the region proposes a deeper and quicker market penetration than the domestic drug company can achieve on its own. In exchange for regional licensing rights, the service provider proposed bringing the product to market quicker, while generating revenue for the U.S. customer. In light of these service provider capabilities and the outcomes the pharmaceutical company seeks in the relationship, what outcomes-specific vendor criteria might managers construct? One note: this scenario assumes the existence of multiple vendors who offer a similar package of services that deliver the value a customer seeks. Should an organization find that few service providers exist to meet its unique combination of strategic needs, these selection criteria lose their comparison value but not their probative value. They remain points of discussion with the offshoring partner and determinants of the suitability of a strategic offshoring relationship even if the criteria cannot be compared against other service providers. The following sections describe the strategic services outcomes criteria.

CRITERIA: Cost Savings Proposition.   Beyond validating that any upfront costs are not so prohibitive as to make the partnership proposition untenable, the customer is going to focus far less on these particular criteria than it is the elements of future value. Cost is universally a consideration but given far less weight in a selection decision framework if market entrance possibilities and future revenue is on the table.

CRITERIA: SLA Adherence.   Service level agreements are important to the extent that they serve as a gut check that the service provider is going to uphold some minimal standards to ensure that the strategic value proposition is reachable and that the terms of the relationship are maintained at an acceptable level.

CRITERIA: Training Commitment and Effectiveness.   It is debatable the extent to which training is an important feature in highly strategic relationships, which resemble joint ventures as much as offshoring. Training might take the form of high-level consultation rather than process-specific, hands-on vocational teaching. Given how unique these arrangements can be, the customer will soon discover in discussions with the service provider the required scope of knowledge transfer and "training" that must occur for its partner to embark on the work and, therefore, whether this dimension is even relevant as a selection criteria.

CRITERIA: Time to Value.   This is the same criterion that is applied in an enabling relationship. In this specific case a couple of events determine time to value in context of the outcomes sought from the relationship. One, time to product regulatory approval is a key milestone given how byzantine and time-consuming such approval is for a new drug. Time to market ramp up might also emerge as an important time to value indicator in this instance.

CRITERIA: Value Achievement Record.   If the offshore development company has a track record sheparding late stage development, what is it and for whom? Different drugs involve varying development times so an apples-to-apples comparison to a particular drug company's product might be impossible—and not relevant. A track record of successful development, market launch, and revenue across a number of pharmaceutical products is a good indication of its scientific skill as well as its ability to market a range of products across a range of diseases. It all gets down to this: What kind of hard dollars has it generated on behalf of other customers? What percentage of other customers' annual revenue over the life of those offshore relationships does specific revenue totals in the service provider's market represent?

CRITERIA: Cultural Alignment.   Difficult to measure quantifiably but the offshoring customer must know if organizational culture differences are poised to foment mistrust and misunderstanding. Cultural friction can doom a partnership that is much about trust as it is contractual obligations. How new is the *customer* to this kind of offshoring arrangement? How structured are the relationship management processes of the service provider? The service provider's marketing and sales organization might be a fast cat—lean, hungry, and inured to administration and bureaucratic follow through. The customer is, however, a basset hound—persistent, steady, competent at what it does but slightly plodding and wedded to meetings and consensus building. Culture clashes have submerged the biggest and most publicized mergers and acquisitions, forget offshoring deals that are puny in comparison. The existence of competing cultures should not deter forging the offshoring relationship except to say that the differences should be documented up front and these specific concerns articulated and addressed.

CRITERIA: Vision and Values Alignment.   Does the service provider understand the core functionality of the product and the set of comprehensive market opportunities such a product offers? Are the customer's strategic goals for the product clearly understood by the service provider? Is the customer's strict code of ethics, which exceeds government regulation standards and that sets the behavior of marketing and salespeople, completely understood by the service provider? Customers will have to decide the merits of working with a service provider knowing that after every meeting, managers feel like taking a shower.

In the same way that managers can construct an outcome-based criteria grid in a basic or enabling services scenario, qualitative and quantitative criteria results around a more strategic relationship can be summarized in the same manner.

Strategic Selection Criteria and Measurability

The more strategic the outcomes in this selection criteria framework, the less quantifiable and measurable some of those specific criteria. In the basic service outcomes category, criteria are highly measurable. Whatever parameters the organization establishes for those criteria will deliver hard numbers it can work with in the selection process—percentage of customers in specific business domain or percentage SLA misses, for example. Benchmark or consulting data might tell the company that the lack of SLA adherence beyond a certain percentage is a cause for alarm; that is, in a calendar year if a service provider has breached specific service levels that, in total, represent more than a certain percentage of all service levels outlined in the contract, this should give the company pause. It was already mentioned that the amount of a vendor's business process focus by revenue percentages or total number of customers is a subjective judgment, but it is measurable, and industry benchmark data might exist for this criteria that give the company an objective, external industry-level baseline from which to compare service provider performance, as opposed to relying on the limitations of a relative comparison only between vendor candidates.

It is much tougher to measure cultural fit and alignment of vision. These determinations exist within the realm of business judgment. But managers are called on to use business judgment often in the absence of hard data. The inability to arrive at objective measures does not mean these criteria are less important. Not only may more intangible criteria prove more important in the context of the outcomes sought, but there may be less opportunity to make comparative judgments if few service providers play in a strategic offshoring space. Or, there might exist several vendors but few existing customer references that fit the company's unique service needs, making an apples-to-apples comparison to the experience of any other customer quite difficult.

EVERGREEN SELECTION CRITERIA

Which of three outcome-based categories any offshoring initiative fall into will determine what criteria are important in the selection process. However, some vendor selection criteria are evergreen—universally relevant no matter the size, scope, or strategic impact of the offshoring initiative. These considerations have existed as long as outsourcing, so they are likely familiar to managers with outsourcing experience. Managers who are not aggressive in exploring these evergreen criteria might find themselves, as one small company looking to offshore did, partnering with service providers possessing the following attributes: one 40-employee company was actually a family-based business working out of an attic, a technology chief didn't graduate from Oxford but rather a far less prestigious state university, and the CEO of another company was facing fraud charges.[5] If nothing else, these investigations can be fun and full of surprises.

Financial Health

An offshore service provider offers little future value if its very survivial is in question. Companies must capture important data that indicates the service provider's ability to deliver on the terms of the relationship for the life of that offshoring relationship. Some service providers are publicly traded today, so a profile of financial health is not difficult to build. At a minimum, the organization should request unaudited and audited financial statements of nonpublic service providers, their credit history, and information about their capital structure. The last data point is simply another way of determining the service provider's debt load. In exchange for agreeing to a nondisclosure, the searching company should ask for a letter from the CFO or CEO declaring that the financial information provided represents the true condition of the service provider at the time. If this investigation sews any doubts, talk with the service provider's bank. Or find another candidate.

IP Protection

This issue alone spooks companies out of even considering offshoring. Can the customer really have complete assurance that the ideas in a strategic and innovative product are not going to be lifted by a service provider's employees and pirated by a competitor? The answer is no. A U.S. maker of labeling software for the printing industry had source code to an important product boosted by a software engineer at its offshore development facility in Mumbai. Apparently she used a Yahoo! email account to attach and send out the intellectual property. Keep in mind that this did not even involve a service provider. It took place in the company's captive R&D center.[6]

At an infrastructure level, companies are just as concerned with IP protections should someone breach data stores housing it. Not a few news stories have emerged over the past several years in which either a service provider employee or an outside perpetrator hacked into a vendor's IS system and stole profile information of the offshoring customer's customers or the offshoring organization's employees. Often the culprit is not applying simple fixes like configuring software correctly. But the only way to ensure minimal risk of the compromising or theft of intellectual property or other key information assets is to establish a thorough security strategy internally, then apply these standards and procedures to the service provider. Vendors unwilling or unable to meet internal security standards should be eliminated from consideration. Establishing the proper security standards and protocols is covered extensively in the pages exploring Phase 3 activities.

But beyond theft at an operational or infrastructure level, other IP issues can emerge. Consider a financial services company that decides to outsource its lending operation to a service provider.[7] The deal took the form of a divestiture—which many outsourcing or offshoring scenarios are, even though they are not regarded as such by the media or managers.[8] In divestitures, a company cuts costs by transferring assets—people, intellectual property, and IT—to a service provider. The financial services company outsourced its workforce and IT in return for certain service levels. But the managers who structured the deal failed to realize that the terms arrangement precluded the company's developing a new lending product. The contract expressly prohibited the development of new forms of lending. The company inked a bad deal, and to make matters worse the service provider wasn't capable of developing it on the customer's behalf either. A lose-lose situation.

Managers conceive of outsourcing, and by extension offshoring, as an arrangement that allows the recovery of all the company's assets at the end of the relationship.[9] Therefore, before IP is explored from a security perspective, it must be considered from an *ownership* perspective. What is the IP? Is it real intellectual property such as patents and copyrights or the trade secrets and know-how that are nevertheless important sources of value but not intellectual property in the formal sense? What IP requires transfer of ownership to the service provider for the relationship to work?

- **Recognition of United States as the Jurisdiction for Legal Issues.**
  As already mentioned in the section on intellectual property, will an
  offshore service provider explicitly recognize the United States as the
  jurisdiction in which legal disputes will be resolved, if sadly, it comes
  to that? Overlooking this can present some hair-raising possibilities.
  A large U.S. drug company decides to bring a lawsuit against its offshoring service provider based in Prague, Czech Republic (an increasingly popular place to secure offshore talent) near the company's U.S.
  heaquarters. It discovers that under Czech law all disputes involving
  Czech companies must be litigated in that country unless the contracting parties expressed otherwise in a contract. The company has to
  scramble to find suitable counsel in the Czech Republic and must also
  budget for a costly litigation in Eastern Europe.[12]
- **Customer Participation in Staff Selection.** Will the service provider
  allow the organization to actively participate in choosing the staff that
  will manage the offshored business processes? This element of vendor selection becomes more critical if the next dimension of operational completeness is fulfilled.
- **Dedicated Work Staff.** Can the service provider assure the customer
  that a dedicated staff will be assigned to the customer's offshored
  business processes, at least for a minimum period of time? Service
  providers will have little control over the labor market conditions that
  result in high attrition rates. They might guarantee the customer, however, that absent attrition, a specifically identified team will work the
  customer's business processes for some time period after steady state
  has been established, if for no other reason than to provide the customer time to get comfortable managing this new relationship. Although
  this selection element moves the customer awfully close to telling the
  service provider how to get the work done rather than focusing on
  outcomes of that work—which is precisely *not* how to go about establishing an offshore relationship—the organization must weigh what
  might be perceived as micromanagement against a legitimate desire
  for continuity. More than once this text has emphasized the importance of worker knowledge in operational excellence and the real
  risks of losing it from offshoring. Even the simplest, least cognitively
  demanding processes involve some degree of experiential knowledge
  for maximum worker effectiveness. How can workers achieve this
  knowledge if they are constantly moved around among different assign-
  ments involving different processes?

Security

As already mentioned, security describes the comprehensive set of measures that an organization implements to protect the integrity of its entire information systems infrastructure—hardware, software, networks, and data—from external or internal compromise. It is one of the most important selection criteria in the vendor search.

Outcomes Criteria + Evergreen Criteria = Criteria Completeness

Once the organization has developed a comprehensive criteria framework, it can begin populating grids with the results it has collected. Exhibit 7.6 demonstrates this for the Basic Services scenario. In this illustration, the evergreen criteria boxes have been deliberately left blank since it is a simple matter of populating those criteria in the left column of the scoring grid and the specific vendor's performance results appropriately. Also, Enabling and Strategic Outcomes scenarios were not included because the principles

Outcome Driven Criteria	Vendor 1	Vendor 2	Vendor 3
—	—	—	—
Cost savings proposition	30% off current cost	42% off current cost	48% off current cost
SLA adherence	High	Low	Average
Specific business process focus	High	High	Low
Average time to steady state in process area	4 months	7 months	6 months
Average age of engagements in process area	2 years	3 years	1.5 years
Percentage labor turnover rate in specific process management area	30%	22%	63%
Evergreen criteria	—	—	—
Financial Health	—	—	—
IP Protection	—	—	—
Legal	—	—	—
Managerial Quality	—	—	—
Operational Procedures Completeness	—	—	—
Security and privacy			

EXHIBIT 7.6 OUTCOMES CATEGORY: BASIC SERVICES

of populating data for the relevant criteria for those specific grids are exactly the same as in the case of the Basic Services scenario.

This selection criteria framework should be considered just that—a framework. A company might make a determination that some outcome-driven or evergreen criteria are not important in the selection process and will discard them. Or, it might identify a criteria unique to its own business needs that requires inclusion in the framework, not currently presented. Organizations should use those criteria that senior management has made a judgment are relevant and probative. The specific business need context into which offshoring is placed for consideration will also have management assigning weights to specific criteria. The company might decide that although average time-to-steady-state is a criteria worth including in the selection framework, it deserves less weight and importance than the vendor's specific-business-process-focus criteria because the organization has made a determination that there is little immediate urgency in offshoring nonstrategic business processes.

Readers will also discover that the same measurability challenge presents itself here as in the context of outcome-based criteria; not all criteria metrics necessarily lend themselves to a hard number, rather some lend themselves to more qualitative judgments, unless, of course, decision makers decide to set hard minimums for certain critiria that suddenly make them measurable and quantifiable. For example, managerial quality as a descriptive phrase evokes qualitative assessments of the service provider management team's fitness to deliver, based on years of relevant experience, educational background, or professional certification. The customer might decide to sharpen the criteria to no less than 10 years experience in the business process area for any senior manager on the service provider team. Cast this way, the criteria immediately results in discarding a number of service provider candidates because the metric is quantitative. Or in the case of a service provider's financial health, the customer might decide to eliminate vendors who surpass a certain debt-to-revenue limit, fearful that too much debt could compromise the service provider's ability to fulfill the company's offshoring expectations. The vendor might cut corners to improve margins at the expense of the customer or it is simply too distracted on its survival to devote the attention to the level of service expected. In either case, the decision team's job is easier because hard criteria lead to efficient conclusions.

Given the range of offshore scenarios emerging today across so many operational and strategic functions, however, managers should be aware that they need to benchmark these criteria for themselves. No hard-and-fast rule exists that tells managers that the best offshore service provider management teams are composed of personnel with a minimum of 10 years experience in a business process domain. Best practices data is available in less strategic and popular offshoring plays—IT, call centers—but scarcer in processes that represent a small percentage of business process offshoring, such as HR. Which is why the organization might want to keep certain criteria subjective so that certain reputable vendor candidates aren't immediately purged from consideration. It might just be that a service provider relatively light on managerial experience has an excellent track record with customers. Some organizations discard any subjective criteria or hard-to-quantify benefits altogether in moving ahead with IT investment, a not surprising policy given how outrageously disappointing some big iron technology investments have proven historically. This tack might be unrealistic in offshoring, however, given the breadth of criteria involved which lead to fully informed decision making.

Request for Proposal

You learned in Chapter 2 that cheap connectivity and web technology lower transaction and search costs for businesses, making it possible to outsource processes today unimaginable 30 years ago. Would that this were true in selecting an offshore service provider. There is no getting around the laborious drudgery of constructing a request for proposal—an important element in the total vendor selection effort. Any detailed mention of the RFP process was saved, deliberately, for here because managers with experience in building these documents understand that the RFP, as a vehicle for information gathering and vendor profiling, can be introduced in a number of places in the selection process. The Offshoring Value Delivery Framework argues that the introduction of RFPs is best done at this point, since many, if not all, the specific criteria that the organization determines are important can end up as specific response items in the RFP. The organization might obtain its answers to a number of outcomes-specific and evergreen criteria for a particular vendor before the vendor ever responds to an RFP, but certainly management is better equipped to prepare one when all the criteria and vendor issues are explicit and universally understood and agreed upon by the management team members who have a voice in the selection decision making.

Whether the organization conducts a request for information as a prelude or moves straight to the RFP to finalize its selection, one of the most valuable activities management can conduct as an RFP is built is a final validation that the business processes it seeks to offshore are completely understood by the decision-making team. If management makes incorrect assumptions about what it is exactly the company seeks to offshore, the RFP will suffer from an incorrect design, and much of the information the vendor provides will prove misaligned with real needs and some of it will be irrelevant. Much as when dancing, the organization leads and the service provider follows; it is taking its cues from the organization. If managers don't understand the nature of the processes being offshored, neither will the vendor.

Consider these elements in constructing an RFP as a comprehensive selection process vehicle:

- A very detailed description of the exact business processes that will be offshored. If process maps are available, provide them.
- A very detailed description of all the business outcomes sought from offshoring these business processes. Make it clear that if the goals are mostly around cost reductions that they are subject to negotiation based on feasible service levels, any unique customer demands of the relationship, and any differentiated services the service provider might offer that are especially attractive to the customer.
- A detailed request that the service provider explain what performance measures it will use to define success based on the business outcomes sought by the customer. The response will indicate to what extent the service provider understands the customer's vision and expectations. Also, how will success indicators be calculated and where will the data come from to make these calculations?
- All selection criteria both outcome-driven and evergreen. What is the service provider's profile and standard operating procedure around all these criteria? Where applicable, ask for hard measures to support the responses.
- Explicit and clear procedures for a Q&A, RFP clarification process. The customer should anticipate that vendors will have questions as they prepare responses, particularly if the RFP is detailed and complex, and if this situation materializes, the customer must figure out before RFP distribution how much time to build into this specific process within the total RFP distribution-collection time frame, and what administrative procedures are in place to collect questions and respond to them.

- Explicit instructions to potential vendors that they reply to elements within the RFP mapped exactly to customer specifications. Consistent presentation of RFP responses makes it much easier to compare and contrast the contents of each response. Organizations might consider including a provision in which failure to respond within the precise structure it outlines is cause for elimination from the selection process. Government contracting RFPs routinely include this provision.

- Establish a normalization process. Requiring vendors to respond using a certain presentation format is one step toward normalization, but because the contents of each RFP response will differ, the organization will need to establish a basis for apples-to-apples comparison of all vendor offers. This might require clarifications or additional data from the service provider candidate.

Selection Process Summary

The vendor selection process is flexible enough for an organization to discard, modify, or rearrange its order to suit unique preferences or its experience and comfort level in choosing service providers with whom to work. The selection process within the Offshoring Value Delivery Framework is equally suited to outsourcing, and many organizations have deep experience in this regard, so they will modify this approach. To summarize the Offshoring Value Delivery Framework approach in specific order:

1. Scan the offshore service provider marketplace. Use any of the selection criteria to arrive at a first cut of possible vendors.

2. Document a complete understanding of the outcomes the organization seeks from offshoring business processes. Through considered business judgment, identify what kind of outcomes-based scenario the company faces and categorize it as such.

3. Construct relevant quantitative and qualitative outcome-driven selection criteria. Use any and all criteria that have a direct bearing on outcomes. Build the metrics that will drive the organization to an understanding of the suitability of candidate service providers to deliver the outcomes sought. Seek out best practices and benchmark data where available and relevant to get a handle on where candidate vendors fall for any specific performance measure.

4. Add evergreen criteria, those that are universally important to any kind of offshoring scenario. Seek out relevant and available benchmark data

to provide baseline understanding of service provider performance. Assign weights to all criteria.

5. Build a formal business case and economic model for the offshoring proposal. Because some sense of service provider charges are required to build the cost profile, distribute a request for information from vendors chosen from an initial market scan to obtain basic pricing information based on the specific business processes and goals for which the organization seeks a service provider. Business case construction can begin contemporaneously with the start of the selection process but will be held up until service provider pricing information emerges from an RFI. If the organization is comfortable with it, third-party sources, IT research houses, or other business data repositories might offer an expeditious substitute for data submitted by the vendor.

6. Distribute RFPs and include all relevant selection criteria as the basis for response information. Tabulate results for each vendor. Arrive at finalists.

7. Visit service providers' facilities. This specific issue wasn't addressed directly in the selection framework section because there is not much to add, except to say that, for the talk of offshoring processes and building distance relationships, what drives business yesterday, today, and tomorrow is the human touch. Does the management team that visits the service provider's headquarters get a good vibe from the visit? What impressions of the management team and the facilities emerge? There is no framework or methodology that will answer this question. Managers will just know intuitively. Human nature dictates that face-to-face interaction is a prerequisite for any kind of business deal, offshoring included.

8. Make the final decision, explore a pilot project option. The issue of pilot projects is considered in Phase 3 of the delivery framework, although if the results of a pilot bear directly on whether a company finalizes a long-term relationship with an offshore service provider, this consideration belongs here in the selection process framework. If the pilot turns out badly—and they can—the organization moves to the next vendor finalist.

The Speed of the Selection Process

The Offshoring Value Delivery Framework specifies the most rigorous and detailed kind of selection process. Others exist, however, and they are worth exploring briefly before the subject is concluded. The Offshoring Value Delivery Framework assumes that time is available in enough abundance for the organization to make a fully informed, fully considered decision. Of course, this is the ideal. Whether the goal is predominantly cost savings or highly strategic such as new market entry, the organization will have a specific tolerance for the time it takes to reach a selection decision, and this tolerance can dictate how thorough the selection process is and, therefore, what kind of selection methodology is used. Exhibit 7.7 illustrates the correlation between the level of information completeness needed to make an offshoring decision and the time commitment required to reach that decision. Between these correlated issues are mapped the various selection approaches that attempt to make acceptable tradeoffs between the two. The value of these various selection approaches is that they are designed to expedite vendor selection but not at the expense of having enough information to make an informed decision.

One vendor. This approach certainly cuts the time to decision making, but it deprives the organization of any meaningful cost comparison from competing service providers. If cost is the primary consideration, this is not the optimal approach even though it saves a significant amount of time. The single-vendor selection option is generally reserved for situations where

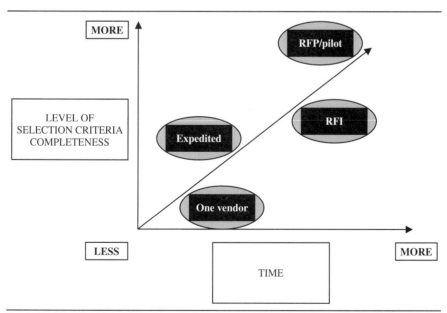

EXHIBIT 7.7 SELECTION APPROACHES: TRADEOFF BETWEEN SELECTION RIGOR AND TIME INVESTMENT

the organization already has a business process relationship with a large service provider organization that can extend offshore management to the additional processes.

Expedited. This approach can work when the organization makes a unilateral decision up front to limit its market scan to two or three vendors at most and decides to minimize the intensity and scope of selection steps found in more deliberative offshoring decisions. A comprehensive RFP is jettisoned in favor of a more streamlined scope of work document on the journey toward contract signing. The company will benefit from price competition, but the approach is designed only when the business processes and the expected outcomes are very well understood. The reason for this is the RFI/RFP process can often clarify an organization's thinking about the offshoring value proposition because vendor response information addresses issues in more detail than the organization considered or raises issues the organization overlooked. And while pricing options are more transparent, they are limited, because this approach assumes, as in the one-vendor approach, that the organization is willing to forego cost savings in exchange for accelerating the offshoring ramp-up.

RFI/extended. If an organization takes seriously the need to build a formal business case arguing the merits of offshoring, and a service provider is the only sourcing option—going captive is not a choice—then the cost profile for the class of business processes being offshored has to come from somewhere. The RFI is one vehicle that can assist in extracting this critical information. Organizations comfortable bypassing a formal business case early in the offshoring decision-making process will simply forego visibility into vendor pricing until far further down the selection process path. Using this vehicle, of course, takes considerably more time.

RFP. At the risk of drowning or suffocating in data, the RFP approach provides a breadth and granularity of information—and hopefully wisdom—that no other selection methodology can. Readers should be familiar with the comprehensive vendor selection approach because it is the foundation of Phase 2 of the Offshoring Value Delivery Framework. The explicit correlation of time versus alternative selection approaches is closely associated with the total volume of vendors identified as selection candidates. The more time critical the organization perceives the need to reach vendor selection the fewer candidates are scrutinized. This should not be taken to mean that there is a direct positive correlation between the selection approach and the outcomes category of offshoring under consideration. Basic services offshoring is not automatically better suited to a one vendor approach, while a revenue-generating, high strategic impact offshoring initiative is not, by default, best suited for an RFP approach. In fact, the reverse could be true. So many basic services vendors are selling their wares that the organization might decide to go slow given how overwhelming the choices. Alternatively, a highly strategic offshoring scenario lends itself to a fast-track decision because few service providers fill the specific niche.

Any type of offshoring initiative can run the spectrum of selection approaches simply because business context will influence the selection process eventually chosen. A company in a stable business environment experiencing healthy financial performance might decide to take its sweet time all the way up to the RFI process in choosing a service provider to administer and manage basic services IT. A growth-oriented, resource-constrained company that is more risk tolerant by nature might use a two-vendor approach and pit them against each other to extract the best service pricing, while at the same time expediting the selection process because of its need to enter a market quickly that the vendor can provide access to. In another scenario, a company seeking out a joint-venture-style relationship might discover that only one vendor is the best fit for its needs yet engages in a several-month RFP-oriented selection process with all the selection process work entailed, as demonstrated in this text's delivery framework. This detailed vetting process gets the customer comfortable for a type of relationship it is unaccustomed to, while minimizing risks around the decision to partner—a long courtship before marriage. Again, vendor availability, business context, and senior management's judgment are levers that direct the organization to a specific vendor selection approach. The Offshoring Value Delivery Framework is the ideal; some organizations will decide they cannot afford that.

CHAPTER TAKEAWAY

Here are some key concepts to leave this chapter with:

- One approach to vendor selection begins with an understanding of outcomes the organization seeks from the offshoring business processes. Once the company characterizes the nature of the offshoring as basic, enhanced, or strategic services, it is in a position to build criteria relevant to those outcome categories.
- The criteria outlined within the three outcome categories is not law. Companies can decide to discard some criteria or include criteria

from another category or devise a criteria unique to their own situation. Whatever optimizes the selection process is what organizations must strive for.

- Some criteria are highly measurable, others are not. Difficulty in quantifying a criteria does not mean that it is less important to the selection process, unless the organization makes a conscious decision to include only those criteria that are quantifiable and measurable. This approach, however, might overlook service provider characteristics that are still probative.

- While many criteria are suited to the outcomes the organization seeks, other measures are universally important no matter the type of relationship or outcomes sought. These evergreen criteria must be included in the overall vendor funneling or weeding-out process.

- The act of data gathering to score vendor candidates is time-consuming and subject to gaps. The organization is relying on the service provider itself to share much of the data. If rigorous selection is the company's chosen path, it might consider supplementing vendor information with industry benchmark data where it exists.

- The request for proposal is the primary vehicle through which criteria information specific to each vendor is collected. The RFP must be as unambiguous as possible to ensure information quality and accuracy while not dragging down the offshoring timetable.

- Some organizations might decide to shortcut the entire selection process by limiting the number of possible vendors under review to three or less. Organizations will have to consider the tradeoffs that such a fast-track approach necessitates: faster offshoring launch versus information incompleteness or faster offshoring launch versus assumption of higher risks to any criteria because criteria are not investigated as thoroughly. An expedited vendor selection process raises the importance of existing customer referrals and recommendations.

NOTES

1. Laura Santini, "Drug Companies Look to China for Cheap R&D," *Wall Street Journal*, November 22, 2004.
2. Noam Scheiber, "As a Center for Outsourcing, India Could be Losing Its Edge," *New York Times*, May 2, 2004.
3. Dr. Jon Anton, "The American Consumer Reacts to the Call Center Experience and the Offshoring of Service Calls" in *BenchmarkPortal*, Chapter 4, p. 29.

4. This scenario is a slight reworking of a Keane client case study entitled, "A Large Health Payer Organization." In this client example, the health-care company had already contracted with Keane to provide claims-handling business process offshoring in India. The chapter scenario, however, does not assume that a preexisting relationship between customer and service provider already exists.

5. Basil Tesler, "Choosing Your Outsource Service Provider," Intetics Web Space Station, webspacestation.com, no date.

6. "Source Code Stolen from US Software Company in India," IDG news service, as reported in *ITworld*, August 8, 2004.

7. Although the example provided is characterized as outsourcing, it offers relevancy for offshoring as well.

8. David Craig and Paul Wilmott, "Outsourcing Grows Up," *McKinsey on Finance*, 2005.

9. Ibid.

10. Ralph Pais, Fenwick & West, attys, "Be Smart About Intellectual Property," *Optimize Magazine*, September 2004.

11. Ibid.

12. Jon F. Doyle, atty, "Avoiding Outsourcing Pitfalls," Outsourcingoffshore.com, no date.

8

LOCATION IS EVERYTHING

A wholly different perspective into the selection process involves a focus on location. Where are the places in the world where offshoring is an attractive option? In many instances, offshoring seeks to exploit geographic advantages in labor costs and market proximity for the provisioning of services at an equal level of quality already in place. So, it stands to reason that if several locations offer offshoring opportunities, an organization would use a criteria-based methodology which, through a series of decisions, directs it to the optimal location choice.

SITE SELECTION

Location Criteria in the Selection Mix

As a selection methodology, location issues are as important as other decision drivers for some organizations. In 2000, Agilent hired The Hackett Group to benchmark finance organization performance against manufacturing competitors.[1] The results showed the company the road it would need to travel in order to transform finance services into world-class status. This benchmark work was the basis for a global captive offshoring strategy in finance that included location decision drivers in the mix. The company has a large global presence with some kind of operation in more than 30 countries, across businesses, which include test and measurement equipment, semiconductors, and life sciences products, so it had a number of location factors to consider. Agilent established a phased approach for finance function consolidation and rollup in which the goal would be that 80% of all finance business processes would be conducted in one or two locations.

In the first phase, Agilent established an offshoring framework for finance business processes, which involved the creation of three business process organizational entities: global hubs, geographic centers of expertise, and in-country units. Geographic considerations influenced both the design of the offshoring framework and where, globally, these entities would be located. Agilent chose a location outside New Delhi, India, for its hub. It offered cost efficiencies as well as a well-trained workforce to manage and execute business processes such as data entry, accounts reconciliation, internal help desk, and other administrative functions that could be rolled up and performed from one location.

In addition to identifying a business process hub, Agilent chose four locations for what it called its geographic centers of expertise: Colorado Springs, Barcelona, Singapore, and Penang, Malaysia. The geographic criteria used in deciding these locations revolved around the need for physical proximity of specific finance services to outside business partners and other stakeholders (manufacturing, operations, etc.) within the company. In-country location criteria included finance work requiring local language skills or where physical presence in performing tasks was required. Geography-driven criteria directed various finance business processes to locations in which Agilent had a presence.

Keeping its sights set on reaching benchmark goals required further consolidation of finance processes. This represented the next phase. In framing the issue of where to target for further consolidation, it classified countries in which the company performed some finance operations into three groups using location-specific criteria. One group was composed of countries where Agilent earned little revenue and had a small employee population base to begin with. Finance employees here would be completely eliminated. A second group was composed of countries in which Agilent earned relatively more revenue and had a relatively moderately sized employee population. A small group of finance workers would remain here. A third group was composed of countries where Agilent earned significant revenue and had a significant number of employees and amount of manufacturing activity. Here, Agilent decided to keep the finance staff small and instead tie most of the workers to lines of business. In addition to identifying countries where finance operations were ripe for consolidation, it established a centralized reporting structure in which all in-country finance activities would report to the controller. By 2006, Agilent hopes to have transitioned 80% of finance employees into hubs, with the remaining ones divided between its geographic centers of excellence and the various other company locations. Most finance functions, including procure-to-pay, accounting-to-reporting, quote-to-cash, and customer service business processes will be centralized at a hub location.

Business process consolidation into one or two primary in-house locations is a common offshoring move for organizations with globally dispersed operations who have the luxury of choosing among many countries to balance resources and obtain an optimal operational condition. Geographically driven selection criteria are naturally part of the mix because location plays an important role in influencing operational costs—mainly people—and the creation of value—proximity to important internal staff, business partners, and customers. Many criteria were factored into Agilent's decision, but those geography-driven considerations played an important role in both where and how offshoring consolidation took place.

Site Selection Framework Oriented around Location-based Criteria

If a company with a global footprint decided to use location in the selection mix, it could consider the specific and unique business context criteria that are important, as in the case of Agilent, and then yoke those customized context-driven criteria to a higher-level filtering process that drills down in another direction, into a number of location-specific issues universally applicable to any offshoring where the idea of location is important. Companies offshoring to a service provider might also find a country-specific selection framework useful in those instances where the service provider has an international footprint and there actually exists a choice for the organization as to where to offshore business processes. In many offshoring scenarios involving a service provider, however, the where issue is off the table simply because the vendor's presence is geographically predefined. Nevertheless, the framework clarifies either captive or vendor-based offshoring decision making because the results of a country-specific analysis can be leveraged in a risk analysis. Even if the company has no choice in the selection of the offshoring target country, it can use a country-level analysis to inform a formal business case in those instances where the country-based risks to offshoring are as relevant as the costs and benefits. A conscious decision was made to place a country-specific criteria framework here because of its explicit selection criteria applicability. Recasting it around risk analysis and business case development gives it a different use and puts it in a different place within the Offshoring Value Delivery Framework, but does not diminish its potential probative value.

Top Candidates from the Economist Intelligence Unit

Exhibit 8.1 illustrates some of the top offshoring country targets today as ranked by the Economist Intelligence Unit (EIU), a sister company to *Economist* magazine. EIU ranked 60 nations total across a number of country-level site selection criteria, including labor costs and regulations, political risks, the tax environment, and the quality of physical infrastructure. The overall results should hardly come as a surprise even to those least acquainted with offshoring. China's conspicuous placement at number two in the rankings, however, might raise a few eyebrows among companies acutely aware of the country's glaring weaknesses in intellectual property protection owing to cultural attitudes as well as a weak legal system, and its higher language barriers than other locations for customer-facing activities. Nevertheless, China appears near the top because EIU's scoring included manufacturing activity where, because of an abundant labor supply, improving

	Score	Rank
India	7.76	1
China	7.34	2
Czech Republic	7.26	3
Singapore	7.25	4
Poland	7.24	5
Canada	7.23	6
Hong Kong	7.19	7
Hungary	7.17	8
Philippines	7.17	9
Thailand	7.16	10
Malaysia	7.13	11
Slovakia	7.12	12
Bulgaria	7.09	13
Romania	7.08	14
Chile	7.08	15
United States of America	6.91	20
United Kingdom	6.60	29

EXHIBIT 8.1   OFFSHORING COUNTRY ENVIRONMENT RANKINGS

SOURCE: Gareth Lofthouse Adapted from "CEO Briefing, Priorities for 2005," Economist Intelligence Unit, January 2005, page 14.

infrastructure, and proximity to Taiwan and Hong Kong, the country is booming.[2] Other notable results is the strong presence of Eastern Europe. Freed from communism, Poland, Slovakia, Bulgaria, and other former Soviet satellites are proving their mettle as offshoring locations for a number of business process functions because of their relatively low labor costs, physical proximity to Western Europe, and cultural ties to it. Many Eastern Europeans are bilingual as well. Four million Romanians speak French and 2 million, German.[3]

MERCER FRAMEWORK

Jay Doherty, a partner at Mercer Human Resources Consulting, has generously offered the firm's site selection framework for this book.[4] It is depicted in Exhibit 8.2. Each of the selection categories—labor market,

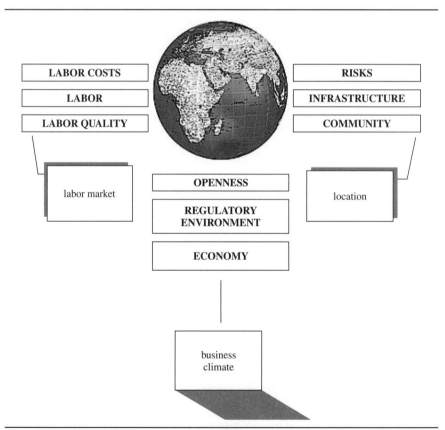

EXHIBIT 8.2 LOCATION SITE SELECTION FRAMEWORK

location, and business climate—are composed of specific dimensions that companies might want to explore in using the concept of location as a selection criteria subject for offshoring. We will explore each of the nine criteria within the three categories outlined. Labor-related costs are often the largest and most variable factor when looking at options to expand or (re)locate. Yet understanding alternative labor markets requires more than sizing up labor costs alone. Organizations need to gauge external factors such as overall competitiveness, labor demand in the region, future labor supply, and related costs such as real estate. Productivity, quality, customer impact, brand, employee satisfaction, and retention differences across location choices will also inform the location-specific offshoring decision.

Labor Market

Costs.   This is the sine qua non of offshoring. How do fully burdened labor costs measure up comparatively? Obtaining precise labor cost information might be more relevant in captive scenarios where organizations will obviously know what they will need to pay workers in a local market. In a service provider scenario, labor costs are likely buried in the price for total business process service delivery—unless the vendor is willing to share detailed cost structure, pricing, and margin information. The flip side, of course, is that captive offshoring requires much more labor data collection and analysis efforts because the company will bear directly these labor costs instead of indirectly through a service provider.

For the captive offshoring scenario, a comprehensive understanding of a fully burdened recurring labor cost should break out wages into compensation, benefits, and taxes. An organization might also explore the composition of total wages—base pay, bonus, overtime, and benefits. In one country a larger percentage of total employment costs might reside in benefits masking true cost differences if wages are considered alone. For example, in India it is common for benefits and perks to exceed base salary. The organization will also want an understanding of nonrecurring labor costs, such as recruitment, training, and termination costs. (Part of recruitment costs is tied to labor availability, explored next). Watch to see if these costs rise in dynamic offshoring locations such as India, where a healthy economy offers plentiful job opportunities for workers resulting in the need for increased recruitment resources to keep up. Termination flexibility is another nonrecurring cost. How easy is it to terminate employment for cause? Spain, for example, has relatively lower labor costs versus the rest of Western Europe, but laws make it far more costly to lay someone off, according to Doherty.

Managers researching site selection issues will discover the inherent tradeoff in labor costs for the kinds of work a country has developed strengths in, which simply follows the rules of economics. As a country develops a reputation for higher-value-added kinds of business process offshoring, the labor arbitrage diminishes. India is a terrific place for IT and call center operations and some business process offshoring, but more highly skilled functions are still more at home in a highly developed economy like Singapore, which is proving itself as an offshoring destination for equity research, bond pricing, supply chain coordination, and direct procurement. Because Singapore is low-risk and business-friendly, wages are substantially higher relative to other offshore destinations.

Labor Availability. What is the size and quality of the labor pool in the offshoring target country? Consultants will advise companies that countries with high unemployment rates are attractive labor markets for this geographic selection criteria (though not so high as to represent a crime risk—a range of 8 to 14% is considered desirable). Regions with very low unemployment experience rising wages and increases in employee turnover as workers seek new job opportunities. Key metrics to investigate in this selection category are growth in labor supply in the specific occupations the company will need to fill, as well as the number of graduates in an occupation that local or regional universities are producing every year. Other factors include employment rates, proximity of competitive employers, and work schedule issues—in Brazil it is customary to provide a month long paid vacation each year, while in certain other countries there are restrictions on women doing shift work.

Availability has proven not only an important selection criteria but a motivation to offshore. Companies will look increasingly overseas when domestic labor markets do not provide either the volume or quality of workers a company needs. Labor arbitrage is still the most important location selection criteria in an offshoring decision framework, but the availability of high-quality labor is a high priority for organizations whose future domestic recruitment looks grim. One client of Mercer's, a medical equipment manufacturer seeking skilled labor for a laboratory environment decided to place labor availability at the top of its selection priorities. We already saw how companies like Intel establish a presence in Russia to take advantage of its excellent pool of technical talent.

Labor Quality. In any labor-driven offshoring scenario, it is universally assumed that cost reductions will not materialize at the expense of quality, however the company defines it. There is little value to offshoring a call center or payroll processing if for that 30% total labor cost reduction workers are ill-prepared to perform the work and errors, delays, and customer dissatisfaction rise. When managers pursue big labor cost reductions, they do so in the context of comparable labor quality even when this element is not explicitly articulated. From a geographic perspective, important metrics to investigate to validate quality include productivity rates, educational levels, the number of annual university graduates as a percentage of the working-age population versus other offshoring target locations and the size of the bilingual workforce.

Business Climate

Economy. The Business Climate criteria refers both to the economic climate into which companies will invest in offshoring and the country's use of specific incentives to encourage that investment.

In terms of business climate, other criteria to probe include the country's GDP growth trend and its inflation rate. A few companies may wish to take a contrarian strategy and brave locations that are in decline. Also, consider whether your business wants to locate in an area where tax base for infrastructure costs most be borne by a diminishing number of businesses. At a more tactical level, what economic incentives does the government offer to a company who offshores? Incentives might include the availability of import duty exemptions, tax holidays, and subsidized land and power. Does the government offer any tax incentives for training or job creation? Mercer says that in many locales tax incentives are almost a case-by-case proposition and subject to negotiation. Often organizations wait until a site has been selected before engaging with bureaucracies to secure tax credits. Mercer says that this is too late in the process not only because they lose some negotiating power but also because of the time it takes to secure the tax credits when working with plodding government agencies.

In a move designed to solidify its place as the go-to location for offshoring, India waived its 35% tax on corporate profits for organizations that offshore back-office and IT work to the country.[5] This was a response to similar moves by the Philippines. Ironically, the consulting firm McKinsey surveyed 30 companies that offshored work to India and discovered that economic incentives were the least important criteria in their location decisions. Far more important to executives were the quality of the country's infrastructure to move people and goods in and out, labor force skills, and the size and growth of the country's domestic market. McKinsey pointed out that if all else were equal, companies might commit to the country with favorable incentives, but criteria are never equal in offshoring. Managers are faced with a complex array of issues that do not receive equal weight. Economic incentives offer a very attractive reduction in quantifiable offshoring costs but for many organizations will not provide enough of an inducement to compensate for other more important criteria.

Openness.   How open is a country to immigration? What are the rules around securing work permits and visas? How long does it take to secure permits and licenses necessary to do business? These are all proxies for how hospitable the business environment is generally.

Regulatory Environment.   Regulation runs the gamut from private property and intellectual property protection, direct foreign investment laws—especially relevant for a company investing in new facilities as part of an offshoring effort. Consider the ease of import and export flows. Does there exist a relative low or high level of red tape to get stuff in and out of the country? This criteria also includes a tax profile—corporate tax rates as well as tariffs. Companies who offshore in Europe, for example, are well aware of the Acquired Rights Directive (ARD), which, among other things, spells out workers' rights if their job is transferred from an employer to an outsourcing company. The ARD transfers workers' employment terms and conditions from the current employer to the new one, while also making certain terminations unlawful.[6] The law has proven particularly controversial in outsourcing relationships, and several cases have ended up in the European Court of Justice.

Location

Risks.   What are the constellation of risks that a country exposes an offshoring organization to? They fall within a number of categories:

- **Political.** How stable is the country's government? Political stability translates into some degree of regulatory predictability. Companies are not blindsided by potential changes in the law that materially affect business operations arising out of frequent changes in leadership. Neither is a country a better offshoring environment because it is democratic. China is hardly a democracy in the Western sense of the word, yet it is one of the fastest-growing offshoring target locations today.

- **Natural Disaster Risk.** As rare as tsunamis on the scale of the devastation wrought on Asia just after Christmas 2004 are, the risk of natural disaster striking is real. The Philippines are hit with an average of 20 typhoons a year.[7] Locations will vary dramatically as to the amount of lost workdays or interruption of the supply chain. The risk consideration might not be so much the probability of occurance but rather that the extent of the damage, should a natural disaster occur, is potentially far higher in some countries both because of a lack of preparedness and the fact that buildings are structurally weaker than in the United States. Building codes and laws that spell out construction specifications in the case of natural disasters such as an earthquake are not as rigorous in the developing world as the United States. Inclusion of natural disaster risk is an important part of business continuity planning and should merit consideration in a site selection framework.

- **Operational Risks.** This issue is tied closely to the quality of a country's physical infrastructure. This dimension is particularly important to manufacturers. Are the roads of questionable quality and raise real concerns about the ability of suppliers to get raw materials to your manufacturing site? The same question applies with ports. How efficient are the ports at moving goods in and out of country? Do particular goods face any unusual delays?

- **Currency Risk.** What impact will currency fluctuations have on costs of operation? A falling dollar relative to other currencies is great for U.S. companies selling abroad but not so good for an offshore manufacturer looking to the U.S. market for sales, because imports—and offshored labor—become more expensive. Companies use sophisticated hedging mechanisms to manage this risk, but it is a risk nevertheless that can have a material impact on the total value of offshoring.

Infrastructure.   What is the quality of telecom infrastructure? Quality is defined as telephone system reliability—frequency of clogged circuits, dropped calls, and bad connections. What is the country's broadband penetration by household and business? Just as important is the reliability of the power grid. Is the power clean, a power supply that does not spike or frequently stop for brief periods? As attractive as India is on a number of criteria, many companies will not locate there a data center supporting business processes for data protection reasons but also because of real concerns about the reliability of power supplies. Even the shortest of outages, if frequent enough, create a lot of headaches for businesses running power-hungry IT systems that are the central nervous system of any business process offshoring.

Quality of the transportation infrastructure is also an important data point within the economic development criteria. Companies operating a 24 by 7 facility should confirm the existence of adequate night transportation for workers.

Community.   This criteria looks at the cost of living in the offshoring region as well as the quality of life—worker safety, good schools, low crime, proximity of cultural institutions. It is the only criteria in this site selection framework that explicitly has the worker's interests in mind. One useful measure to compare different sites is the relative buying power of wages. This considers the after-tax buying power to maintain the same quality of living for employees in different family status. While a criteria with less relevance in a service provider relationship, these attributes are actually quite important to some organizations opening a captive offshoring operation that requires the relocation of part of its workforce. Organizations have a vested interest in placing employees in environments where their personal lives can thrive, particularly if they have families.

Experiencing a Site Up Close and Personal

Just like U.S. intelligence agencies, who conceded that a lack of human intelligence resources on the ground in the Middle East and Asia weakened their ability to have any true understanding of the scope of the terrorist threat against the United States, managers should know that country analyses conducted from an office somewhere in the United States are useful starts but not necessarily comprehensive. There is something to be said for looking at a country's offshoring attributes "on the ground" like a good CIA agent. Take India. Managers who interact with locals will discover not only the yin and yang of prosperity in constant contact with unspeakable squalor but also the unique indigenous cultural forces at work which will influence offshoring. While much of India's middle class is "Americanizing" many still do not grasp simple concepts such as ATMs, interest rates, credit cards, or mortgage refinancing—all financial services business process functions—because the country's economy is still maturing.[8] These folks can certainly be taught such concepts, but managers should not take U.S. ideas and habits of mind for granted in the developing world. Because these financial concepts are so alien to many locals, a company exploring a financial customer service call center will be better prepared knowing that it must approach worker training in a way that recognizes the different realities in which people live in other parts of the world. The most effective way to learn about the offshoring target country is to visit it.

Overlapping Criteria in Site Selection

Documenting and analyzing selection criteria with a focus on location is fluid and fungible. Some experts might place currency risk in a criteria category called "macroeconomic stability." Some might look at the level of government corruption as a regulatory issue while others place it in a risk category. It is not as important where these issues are placed categorically as that these issues are raised at all and reviewed thoroughly within the total selection framework. If you can't manage what you can't measure, you certainly can't manage that which is unknown to the organization.

CHAPTER TAKEAWAY

Some key concepts to leave this chapter with:

- Where a company is going to offshore is almost as important as to whom the organization is going to offshore. In a captive offshoring scenario, the organization faced with several country choices will factor location issues into the mix of strategic and operational considerations specific to the goals the company hopes to achieve.

- In an offshoring scenario in which the service provider has a limited footprint, the offshoring organization will have little if any choice as to where offshoring will occur. In this case, location is not a selection criteria but a subject for equally important risk analysis; what are the location-specific risks in offshoring with the chosen service provider and how do these risks change the value profile in a business case?

- While cheap labor at comparable quality to U.S. workers drives the location decision train, many managers are equally concerned with the quality of the country's infrastructure–roads, sewers, and power grid.

- While political risks are not at the top of managers' concerns, how much would they rise in importance were social instability to manifest itself more visibly? In recent years, radical Islam has taken its grievances to the streets in India with terrorist attacks against the Hindu majority population there. What would a few terrorist-style bombings in the country's urban centers where offshoring is concentrated do to managers' enthusiasm to relocate business processes there?

NOTES

1. The Agilent story is based on background material provided by Gary Baker, communications director for The Hackett Group. This background material was part of a presentation that Agilent executives delivered at a business process outsourcing conference sponsored by The Hackett Group in Atlanta, October 21, 2004.
2. Gareth Lofthouse, "CEO Briefing, Priorities for 2005," Economist Intelligence Unit, January 2005, p. 15.
3. Ibid, p. 16.
4. Thanks to Jay Doherty of Mercer Human Resource Consulting. Background for this site selection framework took the form of PowerPoint presentations as well as interviews in January through March of 2005.
5. "The Truth About Foreign Direct Investment in Emerging Markets," *McKinsey Quarterly*, Number 1, 2004.
6. "Select Committee on European Communities Twenty-Second Report," from the U.K. Parliament House of Lords website, 1998. www.publications.parliament.uk/pa/ld199798/ldselect/ldeucom/098/ec2203.htm
7. Scott Warren, "Eye on Offshoring: Lessons from the Tsunami," *Computerworld* through International News Service, February 21, 2005.
8. "Offshoring? The World Can Be Your Oyster—or Clam," Knowledge@Wharton as reproduced at techtarget.com, April 28, 2004.

Phase 3

RELATIONSHIP BUILDING

The organization has endured a grueling set of decisions that attempts to cast offshoring in a strategic framework. It has built a formal business case, including a cost benefit analysis, it has soul searched the control issues involved in offshoring, and it has run several vendors through a decision framework that considers the outcomes the organization seeks and chosen those that provide the best fit. After a detailed and rigorous request for proposal (RFP) process, it visited the site of one vendor and walked away convinced that it was the best service provider for the company's needs. But it wants to make sure. Welcome to the pilot project, just the first in a number of important and sometimes complex activities managers confront as the relationship with a service provider takes flight. Successful planning and execution of Phase 3 activities can mean the difference between soaring or crashing.

9

AN ALLIANCE IS FORGED

PILOT PROJECT

A pilot project is a useful risk mitigation tool. Can this outfit we plan on offshoring our processes to really do the job? A pilot reveals a service provider's strengths and weaknesses before the organization has made a full commitment to entrusting those processes to the vendor's daily administration and management.

Consider the software vendor, who, finding itself in desperate need of web-skilled developers and unable to fulfill its labor needs, contracted with a Mumbai, India service provider for software coding and testing. The first problem, which emerged right away, was that vendor employees were sharing access codes on its network. One access code was in use for 18 hours a day. The vendor's immediate fear was that someone was exporting intellectual property. False alarm. This crisis passed only to be surpassed by others. Email communication between the software maker's California office and India proved less than effective. The time zone difference delayed responses from either party for at least a day, which contributed to the worst problem—the poor quality of coding and testing work. The company was getting back software with 80% error rates.[1]

Had the company started the relationship with a pilot project, these problems would have manifested themselves just as quickly but with fewer disruptions to operations because of a pilot's natural limited scope. Instead the company engaged a service provider to conduct important business processes that satisfied product development plans and dove head first into a contract with the service provider. Had the organization validated the vendor's ability to do the work, the company might have been saved the disruption at first, discovering that the wheels were falling off what it thought was the answer to a labor shortage and two, having to spend more money and time to fix the problems that made matters worse than they might have been. In fairness to the company, its labor shortage emerged during the e-boom and bust of the 2000 time frame. Desperate for workers, offshoring seemed the silver bullet. That it wasn't simply reinforces the idea that offshoring quickly to meet some immediate pressing need may be worse than not offshoring at all. While the vendor can't be blamed for taking the risk given its specific business environment the results are a cautionary tale.

This story will also remind managers that a pilot project is more than a pro forma due diligence exercise and that such a project might very well reveal the vendor is not what the organization expected. Organizations that opt for a pilot ought to take it seriously enough to understand that one of their worst nightmares might be realized. Yet this kind of "hot stove test"— touch it and get burned—might be the only way for some organizations to grasp the nuances and complexities of offshoring.

Take Life Time Fitness, a fast-growing fitness and nutrition company.[2] The company engaged an Indian service provider the company had already had an outsourcing relationship with to execute IT systems development work. The early pilot went well, even though in that project the developers worked at its Eden Prarie, Minnesota, headquarters. The company felt confident enough to sign a contract for development of a mission critical application from the vendor's India location. It was botched.

The first malfunction arose out of a fundamental misunderstanding from the service provider's team about the company's user needs, the basis for the application, and the definition of a successful project.[3] All this hindered system requirement documentation. The budget ballooned when a Life Time Fitness technical writer had to be brought in to save the documentation, which extended the process two weeks. A few months later deliverables started rolling in. The data model for the program was as ugly as a hog in mud. Documenting all the errors and defects took more than the week budgeted for the entire data model sign-off process. Quality assurance testing produced blank screens and lost data. A completely unusable application. Life Time Fitness brought the work back in house.

Though they can seem as expensive as an Ivy League education, pilot projects that fail are about lessons learned and the deliberate application of those lessons to the next offshoring project. The lesson learned here is the critical importance of knowledge transfer during the transition of business process management to the service provider. Knowledge transfer is covered extensively in the Phase 4 section of this book.

Another important consideration in pilot projects is the fact that the promise of future business does not necessarily mean the vendor will deliver the goods in alignment with the company's business objectives. One organization contracted with a well-known software vendor to pilot the construction of a messaging application that would fit into its group collaboration efforts. Despite an understanding that if the pilot was successful the service provider would win the work, it did not build a test application but rather one that was designed for an enterprise-wide scale instead of the customer's test environment. The system did not work, and the project was jettisoned altogether.[4] What would have mitigated this misalignment is a service level agreement (SLA) that spelled out in detail not only the service levels in managing the project—timetables, milestones, and deliverables—but the services the application would be expected to perform within the 40-seat test spec the customer outlined. SLAs can be an important risk mitigation and expectation alignment tool not only in full-fledged offshoring contracts but also in pilot project scenarios as well. SLAs are covered in detail later in Chapter 10.

For companies committed to a pilot project in anticipation of formalizing business process offshoring with a chosen vendor, they should consider these qualitative criteria in determining the suitability of a pilot project for business process offshoring:

Alignment of Project Scope to Business Goals

One school says that pilot projects should be big enough to adequately verify the service provider's capabilities but not so big that managers are consumed with managing the pilot on an almost daily basis. Pilots should not disrupt daily operations. However, an alternative philosophy argues that perhaps it is better to align the pilot to the ambitions of the organization. Some organizations might want to reach for a project of slightly bigger scope to get a quick win from the offshoring concept, while building internal momentum and acceptance of the idea that offshoring is here to stay in the organization. Although the size of the pilot project, measured in cost, time to completion, and other resource demands—people, technology, and time—is always an important consideration in developing a pilot, equally important is ensuring that the pilot scope aligns well with the goals of the organization.

SMALL OFFSHORING SCOPE IF PROCESSES ARE NOT PROJECT-BASED

Unlike information technology deliverables, which are uniquely suited to a project orientation, the offshoring of HR or finance business processes does not lend itself to a pilot in the strict sense, because the processes do not have a beginning and end time frame that sets the parameters for any kind of project-oriented pilot work. Therefore, many companies contemplating large offshoring efforts in non-project-oriented initiatives will start small and build out. Offshoring well-defined subsets of business processes, such as help desk or payroll in HR or billing or accounts receivables in finance, is the next best thing to a formal pilot project when an actual pilot is impractical.

Level of Interaction

Projects that do not require intensive communication and constant interaction are more suitable for a pilot. See the "Intensity of Knowledge Transfer" later in this chapter. Having less documented and explicitly available knowledge during pilot transition will guarantee very high company/vendor interaction, which is exactly what many organizations seek to avoid during a pilot project.

Low Integration

A pilot project is one that does not require a high level of integration from a technology perspective. A lot of non-IT offshoring has been fueled by the adoption of enterprise resource planning (ERP) systems, which support many business process functions, particularly in finance and HR. Does the vendor have the same platform already in place to execute the work or would the pilot require an IT asset transfer? A pilot should not require the company invest in any additional hardware or software and ideally the project should have a minimal impact on software license costs.

Intensity of Knowledge Transfer

As we saw in the experience of Life Time Fitness, poor knowledge transfer can doom offshoring before it really begins. Piloting business processes that require minimal knowledge transfer to the vendor organization increases the likelihood of a quick win. Needing less knowledge transfer drives the project into pilot mode more quickly and lessens the risk that a company was insufficient in adequately training vendor staff. One indication of knowledge transfer readiness is the extent to which the pilot processes are formally documented and easily accessible by vendor staff. That is, can service provider staff tap into an extensive, well-arranged knowledge base on the offshoring company's intranet or does the pilot require creating documentation from scratch?

Pilot Team Size and Scope

Does the internal team that supports various aspects of a pilot possess the domain expertise necessary to pull it off? Ideally, the team overseeing the pilot consists of the same employees who will have important roles should the relationship gel and the processes be formally offshored. Executing a pilot project with the same personnel who would manage the offshoring relationship builds operational continuity and provides the opportunity for acquisition of "lessons learned"—one of the primary benefits of conducting a pilot, even if not one of the primary motivations. Organizations should not have to go through a second knowledge transfer exercise with a new population of service provider staff if the relationship evolves into a formal contract after a successful pilot project.

A pilot project should be managed in the same way as business processes that are formally offshored, that is, if the organization adopts the Offshare Value Delivery Framework, then all the elements composing the four phases should be put in place, including critical elements that haven't been covered yet—SLAs, contract negotiation points, a full security plan, a well-defined relationship model, transition plan, and value auditing and performance tracking. Because the scope of the pilot is limited, not all elements will require the intensity of analysis and management as if undertaking formal offshoring. But managers should discover that a successful pilot is a kind of dress rehearsal for formal offshoring. Following the tenets of the delivery framework raises the organization's preparedness for the real thing, while also putting into place early on in the relationship elements that would otherwise require resources and attention anyway had the offshoring organization skipped a pilot and moved straight to a full business process offshoring deal.

As hokey as it might sound, managers should keep a journal of their experiences during the pilot project, particularly if the organization is new to outsourcing and offshoring. It needn't be formal or even compliant with proper grammar. The purpose is, rather, to capture an accurate assessment of impressions during the pilot project's lifecycle. What was surprising or unexpected during any phase of the project? Were vendor project managers easy to get along with? How were their English skills? How efficient was communication via email between these great distances? What was the most difficult activity necessary to bring the project off? What activities seemed like a waste of time? Committing thoughts to paper reinforces experiential memory and might prove invaluable should the organization march ahead with the vendor upon pilot completion. Notes are also useful talking points during meetings meant to gather feedback from the internal offshoring team. This activity can actually be formalized into the delivery framework with the construction of a couple of templates in the offshoring management environment that captures this data. The information is the basis for lessons learned and informs a decision to move forward with a long-term offshoring relationship.

SECURITY FRAMEWORK

A comprehensive security framework helps the organization plan for the specific information security and privacy procedures that it seeks from a service provider who will administer business processes on a daily basis. The framework is introduced here only because it is assumed that most corporations already have in place such an enterprise security and privacy plan whose standards and service levels can be implemented by the service provider in preparation for the start of an offshoring relationship. The organization might conclude by virtue of offshoring discussions that it wants to revisit and upgrade the company's complete enterprise security strategy, given the vulnerabilities that emerge in even thinking about turning over business process management to an outsider. In this case, the security framework here becomes a Phase 1 strategic activity. The company will execute a new security strategy and use this as a basis for selecting a service provider who can meet or exceed its internal security standards.

Should the organization decide to revisit its entire security strategy it might consider mapping it to the Offshoring Value Delivery Framework. Each phase of the delivery framework comprises discrete activities requiring execution as the organization journeys toward the ultimate goal— measurable value from offshoring initiatives. In the same way, each phase of an offshore security strategy is composed of a set of well-defined activities that contribute to a comprehensive and well-conceived security and privacy infrastructure that the service provider will be required to model in its organization. Exhibit 9.1 illustrates the alignment of a security framework to the Offshoring Value Delivery Framework, regardless of which phase a comprehensive security strategy is introduced.

OFFSHORING VALUE DELIVERY FRAMEWORK

Strategy Development	⇑	Selection Process	⇑	Relationship Building	⇑	Sustained Management
1 Think		2 Plan		3 Negotiate		4 Execute & Manage

□ Strategy/Goals Alignment
□ In-House or Out of House
□ Organizational Readiness
□ Strategic—Workforce Plan
□ Operational—Decision-Making Governance
□ Business Case
		□ Develop Selection Criteria
		□ Selection Process
		□ RFP
		□ Site Selection
				□ Pilot Project
				□ Security Framework
				□ Revise Business Case
				□ Contracting
				□ Relationship Model
				□ Exit Strategy
						□ Transition Strategy
						□ Performance Tracking
						□ Internal Governance
						  □ Strategic
						  □ Operational
						  □ Just-in-Time

OFFSHORING SECURITY FRAMEWORK

Strategy Development	⇑	Selection Process	⇑	Relationship Building	⇑	Sustained Management
1 Think about Security Policy		2 Plan Vendor security and Privacy		3 Negotiate Security Terms		4 Execute & Manage Security Policies and Procedures
□ Objectives & Definitions: Security, Privacy □ U.S. Regulatory Issues □ Company Readiness to Execute and Abide by Enterprise Security Policies		□ Service Provider Readiness to Execute and Abide by Enterprise Security Policies □ Review Country-Specific Security and Privacy Risks		□ Security Dispute Framework □ Jurisdiction □ Validate Vendor Security Framework Alignment with Company		□ Security Auditing Framework □ Auditing Project Management and Reporting □ Monitor Technical Innovations which Improve Security □ Monitor Changes in Law in Country and in U.S. Materially Affecting Security Strategy

EXHIBIT 9.1 MAPPING AN OFFSHORING SECURITY FRAMEWORK TO THE OFFSHORING VALUE DELIVERY FRAMEWORK

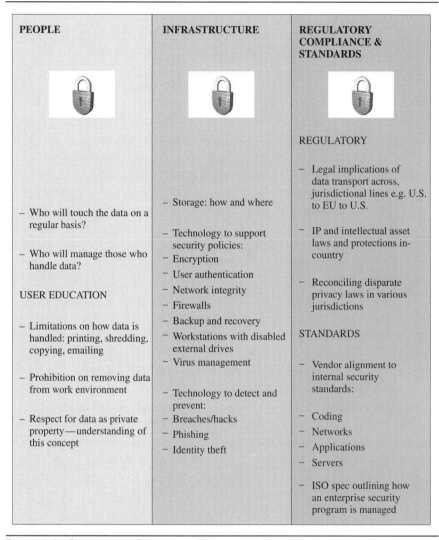

PEOPLE	INFRASTRUCTURE	REGULATORY COMPLIANCE & STANDARDS
		REGULATORY
		– Legal implications of data transport across, jurisdictional lines e.g. U.S. to EU to U.S.
– Who will touch the data on a regular basis?	– Storage: how and where	
	– Technology to support security policies:	– IP and intellectual asset laws and protections in-country
– Who will manage those who handle data?	– Encryption	
	– User authentication	– Reconciling disparate privacy laws in various jurisdictions
USER EDUCATION	– Network integrity	
	– Firewalls	
– Limitations on how data is handled: printing, shredding, copying, emailing	– Backup and recovery	**STANDARDS**
	– Workstations with disabled external drives	
	– Virus management	– Vendor alignment to internal security standards:
– Prohibition on removing data from work environment	– Technology to detect and prevent:	
	– Breaches/hacks	– Coding
– Respect for data as private property—understanding of this concept	– Phishing	– Networks
	– Identity theft	– Applications
		– Servers
		– ISO spec outlining how an enterprise security program is managed

EXHIBIT 9.2 SECURITY AND OFFSHORING: FRAMING THE ISSUES

As your organization delves into security and privacy, consider the conceptualization in Exhibit 9.2, which can aid in building a comprehensive strategy. Fundamentally, security and privacy depend on an understanding of three interrelated issues—people, infrastructure, and regulatory compliance—on top of which sit the operational guidelines and processes required to fulfill security goals found within these perspectives. Operational security issues include such areas as configuration management and control, application lockdown procedures, data access procedures, and standards setting and adherence for coding and IT infrastructure maintenance—networks, applications, and servers.

Phase 1 Security Issues

Security and Privacy Objectives. Whether the company has a comprehensive information security and privacy strategy already in place, it will want to revisit what its objectives actually are. Articulating this clearly creates the baseline against which the service provider will be measured. Security objectives could include the maintenance of information integrity and confidentiality as well as auditability and availability. Privacy objectives would include the protection and confidentiality of customer, partner, and employee information.

The company must also clarify its definition of intellectual property (IP), which has a specific definition in U.S. law. IP consists of patents, copyrights, logos, trademarks, and servicemarks. Trade secrets and other unique capabilities and know-how are not intellectual property but rather intellectual capital, which may be protected under the law if stolen and compromised, but are formally different than real intellectual property. The larger point is that organizations use the term intellectual property as a catchall for its closely guarded information assets and the fact is that IP, from a taxonomy perspective, leaves out a lot of those assets that the organization might believe important enough to merit special handling by the service provider. In the security world, "key information assets" is a common term used to describe both intellectual property and intellectual capital as well as customer, partner, and employee information.

Regulatory Issues. An organization's security strategy should include a reaffirmation that all U.S. laws will be complied with when the offshoring deal is consummated. Sarbanes-Oxley and the USA Patriot Act are just two complex sets of laws that an organization might review to affirm that business process and operational designs are not in conflict. Many organizations will establish information management workarounds if there is any concern at all that the offshoring initiative might run afoul of the law. For example, companies might strip a data store of sensitive information and simply provide a subset of that data for offshore employees. Sensitive database fields are either randomized or eliminated altogether.[5]

Sarbanes-Oxley is poised to focus managers' minds like no other pain. For instance, one section of the legislation, Section 404, which outlines internal control policies over financial reporting, might encourage publicly traded organizations to step up Statement on Auditing Standards 70 (SAS 70) audit activity. SAS 70 is a standard for auditing service organizations established by the American Institute of Certified Public Accountants (AICPA). A SAS 70 audit ensures that outsourcing service providers have adequate financial reporting controls in their operations when working with a customer's information.[6] Section 404 of Sarbanes-Oxley ensures the offshoring organization has in place its own financial controls for financial reporting and that management is accountable for the reporting structures in place.[7] You can see how an organization might conflate these distinct but related legal provisions. Since the offshoring organization must account for the establishment of controls in its financial reporting under Sarbanes-Oxley, it might feel compelled to include frequent SAS 70 audits of the vendor to ensure vendor financial controls compliance as a way to demonstrate the U.S. offshoring company's Sarbanes-Oxley good faith compliance.

SAS 70 audits require an independent onsite examination from an accounting firm and they can be expensive. Many questions arise: Who pays for it? How extensive is the audit required to be? How frequently must they be performed? Will Sarbanes-Oxley encourage more rigorous internal controls in the service provider organization because of U.S. customers' desire arising out of that legislation to audit them? These are just a few of the questions introduced by the new legislation (Sarbanes-Oxley was passed in 2002, but 2005 will be the first year of compliance for many companies[8]). A grasp of the nexus between U.S. law and offshore service provider relationships is critical for the relationship to proceed smoothly.

Company Readiness. While security and privacy are key concerns in organizations, the perceived need for a heightened level of preparedness rises, sometimes dramatically, because all of a sudden a third party will manage key company information. The company is offshoring and an outsider is now involved. Trusting an outsider with some of an organization's most coveted assets escalates the urgency that the vendor treat security and privacy issues to the same standard as the offshoring customer.

One way to gut check the company's preparedness is to undergo the same security and privacy self-assessment that the organization will subject a service provider to. Corillian, a Portland, Oregon–based maker of Internet banking software, has created a self-assessment for vendors to complete during the partnering or vendor selection process that is highly applicable to offshoring initiatives. Jim Maloney, Corillian's chief security executive, graciously provided this self-assessment, which his company uses in partnership relationships; it is equally useful for the company engaging an offshoring vendor. That self-assessment is provided in the next phase, under "Vendor Readiness."

Phase 2 Security Issues

Vendor Readiness.   Vendor readiness for a security and privacy regime that meets the offshoring company's needs is a key selection criterion as well as an operational imperative at the time the relationship is forged. As mentioned earlier, Corillian requires a vendor to submit a security self-assessment on the heels of signing a service contract. Although this self-assessment is meant to meet the security and privacy needs of companies explicitly in the financial services vertical, the principles are applicable to any company in any industry. Corillian's approach is arguably a good baseline and benchmarks because the financial services industry has some of the most stringent rules going.

In addition to the self-assessment, Corillian routinely requests the following documents in its vendor security due diligence: security policies, security organization and reporting relationships, business continuity plan and/or disaster recovery plan, network diagram for production processing facility, and SAS 70 reports.

Here are some representative questions an organization can ask of a vendor in a security self-assessment:

Security and Privacy Self Assessment

- Does your company have documented information security policies? If so, describe them. Address policies, procedures, security awareness and training, information classification, and your security organization.

- Describe how our company information, company client information, and end user customer information is protected from unauthorized access or disclosure during processing, transmission, or storage.

- How is the integrity of company information, company client information, and end user customer information maintained (e.g., automated error checking, input/output validation, and file size verification)?

- How is the availability of company information, company client information, and end-user customer information ensured?

- How is company information, company client information, and end user customer information protected in the event of a system failure or disaster?

- In the event that a security incident occurs that affects company information, company client information, and/or end user customer information, describe your company's incident response and escalation procedures (including notification and involvement of company or a company client).

- Describe the following technical controls used to support this service or application: user access management, separation of duties, network architecture, system redundancy, and patch-level management. Attach a network diagram of the systems and surrounding components where company information, company client information, and end user customer information may be gathered, processed, transmitted, or stored.

- What policies, procedures, and processes are in place for user identification and authentication (e.g., user ID, password, and encryption)?

- Describe your hiring procedures for individuals who may have access to company information, company client information, and end user customer information (e.g., background checks).

- How is antivirus or other antimalicious code software configured and managed throughout your enterprise?

- How is your change-control process performed for product development, testing, and production?

- What physical security provisions are in place to ensure that information, systems, and operations are adequately protected?

- Describe your auditing and monitoring procedures for networks and systems where company information, company client information, and end user customer information may be gathered, processed, transmitted, or stored (including audited events and logging, log protection, log review, and log retention).

- Describe your company's process for complying with applicable regulatory requirements for end user customer privacy (e.g., Gramm-Leach-Bliley Act[9]).

- Describe the type of company information, company client information, and end user customer information gathered, processed, transmitted, or stored by your product(s) or service(s) (e.g., personally identifying information, corporate information, passwords, or PINs, and other sensitive information).

Review Country-Specific Security and Privacy Risks. If this security strategy action item did not emerge because the organization did not conduct a formal site selection analysis, now is the time to review country-specific security and privacy risks to offshoring. Disregard for the idea that intellectual property is held as a property right of its owner no different from a chicken or mule owned by a farmer has not stopped China from going on a tear as one of the hottest offshoring markets in the world. Companies should review their comfort level with the security and privacy risks introduced by offshoring business processes to a specific country.

Phase 3 Security Issues

Security Dispute Framework. A mechanism for the offshoring company to formally raise concerns about the service provider's security provisions after a contract has been signed needs to be in place. If the company finds weaknesses in the vendor's security policies in the future, say through an audit, a formal vehicle to air and resolve these specific concerns quickly and to the mutual satisfaction of both parties is more effective than ad hoc debates with various points of contact in the service provider's organization. The company wants to identify a go-to manager in the vendor organization to whose attention these issues can be brought, while establishing a path to resolution that includes timetables, procedures, and an explanation of how a security dispute resolution framework will fit into a general dispute resolution framework covering any disagreement that arises in the course of the contract.

Validate Vendor Security Framework Alignment with Company. The offshoring organization will want to see a comprehensive security strategy document from the vendor reflecting the implementation of all the security and privacy provisions at contract signing time. This confirmation of readiness will document every category of security and privacy issues raised by the customer and an acknowledgment that all measures and resources for effective security management are in place. If the organization adopts the ISO standard for security management, one way to accomplish this verification objective is to map the vendor's security strategy in place against the standard.

Phase 4 Security Issues

Security Auditing Framework. There are two kinds of security audits a company can perform on a service provider. At the technical level a company can perform penetration testing against the service provider's infra-structure in an attempt to hack into its environment or otherwise find possi-ble weaknesses in IT infrastructure that poses real security and privacy vulnerabilities. The service provider authorizes the offshoring customer to probe its system, discover weaknesses where technical improvements can be made and report back.

The other technique involves site checks and onsite interviews with ser-vice provider personnel to determine, first, if the security and privacy strat-egy is executed adequately and, second, to determine if security practices are well publicized and understood by the staff. The organization will want to see explicit evidence of review and sign-off on policies and procedures. This can be as simple as the service provider posting the entire set of poli-cies and procedures, do's and don'ts, of its security strategy on its intranet for all employees to print the last page and sign. Every signature is placed in the employee's HR file.

Auditing Project Management and Reporting.   Regular security audi-ting should be looked at as a discrete project requiring planning and timeta-bles and the use of project management software (or a custom web-based offshoring management program argued for in Phase 1 of the Offshoring Value Delivery Framework). How frequently will audits be performed? Who will supervise and report the results in the offshoring company? What direct vendor cooperation and manpower is required when audits are performed?

Monitor Technical Innovations That Improve Security.   Over time the offshoring company discovers the availability of innovations in security technology. If the organization seeks to enhance service provider security and privacy, how can the company ensure vendor adoption? Who will pay for new security technologies?

Monitor Legal Changes In-Country and in the United States Materi-ally Affecting Security Strategy.   There are so many laws both domestic and international that can touch the issues of security and privacy that unless the organization is of sufficient size that it has a big legal department to do the job it might want to outsource (offshore?) this function to an experi-enced law firm who, as a matter of business, regularly follows trends in the legal marketplace and can advise the company about laws that might require a change in security and privacy policy.

REVISE BUSINESS CASE

The only comment needed here is that Phase 3 of the Offshoring Value Delivery Framework is the point in time when the organization has a strong grasp of all the upfront costs involved in offshoring because pricing has been negotiated. As the organization reaches the point of contract signing with the vendor the cost implications are more transparent, if not complete. (The transition still looms.) Companies who take business cases seriously will want to revise the early cost/benefit justification for the initiative to reflect cost revisions as well as the introduction of new costs.

CHAPTER TAKEAWAY

Here are some key concepts to leave this chapter with:

- Pilot projects represent a potentially effective risk mitigation tool. For organizations with limited offshoring experience, a pilot will heighten the awareness of critical offshoring issues such as its overall preparedness for a long-term relationship as well as vendor weaknesses.

- Not all business processes lend themselves to a pilot because they do not have a project orientation. HR and finance, for instance, represent ongoing processes not bookended with a hard start and stop date like application development. A viable stand in for a pure pilot is the idea of offshoring discrete subsets of overall business process categories— maybe payables or receivables in finance or payroll in HR.

- An aggressive focus on cost savings may not be the first priority of a pilot project but rather a deeper understanding of all the implications of offshoring. Organizations might even want to consider a pilot as a loss leader where little if any cost savings accrue. The value is rather in the lessons learned from the experience as a predicate for a long-term relationship with the service provider. The organization will have to make a value judgment as to whether the acquisition of this wisdom is worth the cost of a no-savings pilot project.

- Security strategy is a critical element of offshoring that emerges here because the pilot might represent the first time the organization will work with an offshore service provider. A pilot as predicate for long-term offshoring represents the opportunity to revist the organization's security strategy, ratchet up its standards if needed, and require the service provider to adopt them. The vendor is not likely to make large IT investments for the enhancements of security standards on the basis of a pilot project but might be willing to upgrade if the pilot is a success and a long-term relationship is forged as a result.

- Security—strategy is an evergreen issue, a critical operational imperative whether the organization offshores or not. Again, security strategy was introduced in Phase 3 of the Offshoring Value Delivery Framework because a company's search for an outsider to manage business processes provokes a full review of current security policies and procedures. The delivery framework is meant to be flexible and organizations might want to introduce security strategy review during the selection process or as far back as Phase 1 when enterprise strategy is formulated.

NOTES

1. See Roy Harris, "Making It Work," one article in a special offshoring issue of *CFO Magazine*, June 1, 2004.
2. Stephanie Overby, "Lost in Translation," *CFO Magazine*, July 15, 2004.
3. Ibid.
4. lana Varon, "Getting the Best From Your Vendors," *CIO Magazine*, November 1, 2003.
5. "Security and Privacy Best Practices in Offshoring," NeoIT, issue 12, September 2003, p. 3.
6. About SAS 70," SAS70.com, 2004.
7. "SEC Implements Internal Control Provisions of Sarbanes-Oxley Act," Securities and Exchange Commission press release, May 27, 2003.
8. Beth Ellyn Rosenthal, "New Outsourcing Risks in 2005 and How to Mitigate Them," outsourcingoffshore.com, no date.
9. The Gramm-Leach-Bliley Act is also known as the Financial Modernization Act of 1999. The law outlines procedures for the handling of consumer's personal financial information held by financial institutions. The act is comprised of many privacy provisions, including personal information disclosure and safeguarding and protection of that information. More can be found at www.ftc.gov/privacy/glbact.

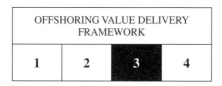

10

LET'S MAKE A DEAL

If offshoring is a kind of marriage, contracting is the exchange of vows and rings. Each party enters the relationship with perceived mutual understanding and high expectations. Just as prenuptial agreements remind everyone that a marriage contains contractual and legal obligations, companies should not lose sight in the good feeling and excitement of embarking on a new relationship that an offshoring contract is primarily a risk mitigation tool. Include those provisions a company believes are essential to future value into legally binding language and they will likely be honored. Leave them out and suffer the consequences.

CONTRACTING

While the precise contents of individual contracts are as numerous and varied as the number of offshoring relationships that are established, some universal guidance does exist for structuring offshoring service contracts. Bill Bierce, a principal in the New York City law firm of Bierce & Kenerson, which publishes the outsourcing-law.com website, offers advice on specific offshoring contracting clauses requiring thorough review. These discussion points are arranged in alphabetical order and do not represent an order of importance in negotiation. Readers should also recognize that many of these topics were covered already, in the context of vendor selection. When organizations search for a service provider a request for proposal (RFP) and discussions will reveal the service provider's willingness to agree to the sought-after terms. This section simply reinforces the idea that now it is time for vendors to prove that willingness by signing a contract containing these elements.

Audits

Audits come in three flavors: security and privacy, billing, and performance. Each is explored here in the context of contracting:

1. **Security.** The offshoring company will want a contract clause that spells out the need for periodic security audits which includes both onsite investigations of vendor's ongoing security and privacy practices and penetration audits, both discussed in Chapter 9. The clause should spell out timetables for audit activity, reporting results, and taking action should the effort turn up any problems. As already mentioned in the section concerning security frameworks in Chapter 9, the organization wants to establish an explicit dispute resolution framework, which spells out the procedures by which both sides resolve deficiencies.

2. **Billing.** While the organization will get in the habit of paying the service provider's bill, the more flexible and fluctuating the fees (think of shared risk/reward versus fixed fee) the more bills bear regular scrutiny. What contractual process exists by which the organization recoups money it overpays the service provider? Attorney Bierce cites one example where a technology supply company overpaid a million dollars for telecom services. He also had a client discover overbilling after two years, as much a reflection of the customer's negligent relationship management as the service provider's misreading of the scope of work and related pricing provisions. In billing arrangements where payment is made before services are rendered, the customer might want a provision that provides for invoice review with the service provider before services start.

3. **Performance.** Offshoring companies will want to confirm that the service levels detailed in a service level agreement (SLA) have actually been consistently met. This might require access to transaction data within the vendor's IT platform used in managing the customer's business processes. The internal reporting tools that come with most enterprise software that run business processes is usually sufficient to make these calculations. A clause that outlines timetables, frequency, and the support of the vendor organization is essential if audits are

going to be efficient and effective. Performance auditing is covered in more detail in Phase 4 of the Offshoring Value Delivery Framework in the audit section.

Exit Strategy

While building an exit strategy is an offshoring management function, the final contract must include provisions to ease this challenging process. A contract should specify the processes and procedures the service provider will support and fulfill should the organization at the end of the contract decide not to renew but move the work to another service provider or back in-house. Exit strategy issues are covered in more detail later in Chapter 11.

The more alarming question is how does the organization get into a 45 turn out of a nosediving offshoring initiative? A failed relationship is potentially embarrassing to both sides. The most common reason for a premature end is a contractual breach from either side, and this possibility is routinely acknowledged in outsourcing or offshoring contracts as grounds for ending the relationship.

Innovation Capture

What happens if new technical capability emerges driving business process improvements, but the vendor is not inclined to invest in it? The customer could insist on investment, and the service provider would be happy to oblige if the customer wants to pay for it. How innovations are going to be treated needs attention in the contract. It's in the interest of the customer to seek out service providers with a fairly extensive business process track record over a large customer base because the vendor is more likely to make the investment; provisioning this innovation pleases a large number of customers and its cost can be amortized more quickly. The customer should look for ways to motivate the service provider to encourage innovation investments. In a simple example, suppose that new HR self-service tools cut down on the number of help desk calls. Structure contracts in such a way that rewards the service provider with a portion of the savings won.[1]

The innovation issue is a simple reminder of the need for flexibility in offshoring contracts. The very concept of innovation means change. Both sides must recognize that while the goal is stability and consistency in business process offshoring management, all the world changes around them.

Technology changes (hopefully for the better), the law changes, and the goals of the organization change. What contracting elements need to build in the possibility of change over the life of the offshoring relationship?

Hiring Policy and Procedures

As was discussed in the section addressing service provider selection criteria in Chapter 7, while the organization is not interested in micromanaging the service provider's hiring practices, two considerations exist. One, does the organization seek hiring rights over service provider staff assigned to the account? This issue is more clear cut in an Offshore Development Center scenario, where the vendor dedicates specific resources to manage the organization's ongoing offshoring project needs. The organization might want direct involvement in staffing issues when the relationship is mature and deep. However, if the scope of the project or business process management is small or the relationship is new, the service provider might want the flexibility to move around lower-level staff to best manage its business. The service provider and organization will need to come to terms with the importance of stable staff working on the ground particularly if, as time passes, vendor employees build unique, company-specific experiential knowledge that improves their performance. Lots of staff change disrupts this accumulation of expertise and potential service value. Consider contract language that specifies a limit to the number of people staffed to lower level positions in any contract year, with the exception of cases of employee departure from the service provider.

The second issue is: Does the organization seek hiring rights over key personnel, such as the manager with direct management oversight of the account? Supposing that manager is juggling several accounts and the organization believes it is not getting the proper attention and focus? The customer wants to include provisions having a direct say in who is hired or assigned internally to the account. This clause might include provisions specifying a minimum time of assignment to the account to ensure staff stability.

Price Adjustments

At some point in the relationship, companies might discover through a market scan that the service provider competition is offering the same offshoring services at lower cost or offering improved technology at the same price, which means that the organization is overpaying. Can the organization build in contractual language that speaks to vendor price adjustments should these circumstances occur? The example just cited is a simple, clear-cut example where price adjustments are practical. The difficulty in most situations is making apples-to-apples service package comparisons between what the company receives and what other vendors are offering, at seemingly reduced cost. Upon deeper examination, that generous 15% price discount is not so attractive when the organization analyzes all the service details. Nevertheless, if organizations are intent on continuously benchmarking market pricing, the contract ought to address how pricing can be adjusted where an accurate comparison with market conditions is possible.

Subcontractor Arrangements

The law does not care that subcontractors might be the source of vendor nonperformance. If the United States is the established legal jurisdiction, the service provider has responsibility over the subcontractor's work. The potentially bigger risk is the knowledge and trade secret leakage that could occur. The customer and service provider develop business process know-how over time which, through the course of work, is obtained by the subcontractor assigned to the customer's account. This knowledge could then wind up in the hands of a customer's competitor should the subcontractor build a relationship with the competitor directly or through other service providers who have the relationship with the original customer's competitors. Limiting subcontracting ensures higher service provider accountability and service quality.

Transition Planning

Ironically, a common pressure point during business process transition arises when the offshoring relationship hasn't even really begun. Lots can go wrong in the transition phase of offshoring, as has been alluded to earlier and that will be made clearer in Chapter 12. The service provider could fall down in executing timely knowledge capture; the offshoring company could fall down in providing proper knowledge documentation. Technical glitches could arise during technology asset transfer, which could be either party's fault. Unless specific work deliverables, milestones, and timetables are spelled out for the transition, any delays could easily end in acrimony and bad blood before the relationship has had a chance to mature. The good news is that the transition phase is very project-driven and, therefore, should be managed and executed like a project.

Terms and Conditions

Fifty or more provisions can compose the terms and conditions clause of an offshoring contract. The following are some of the most important sub-clauses to consider:

- **A Dispute Resolution Framework.** If a dispute over any aspect of the offshoring contract arises, what mechanisms and procedures will the organization and service provider mutually create in writing to attempt to resolve differences amicably and avoid costly litigation? A dispute resolution framework might include provisions that spell out the first point of contact either side would reach out to in initially raising a point of dispute. It could also include the path of escalation the dispute takes if successive levels of executives on each side cannot resolve the issue, including all the way to the CEOs. A dispute framework should also include timetables for important milestones along that problem escalation path.

- **Legal Jurisdiction.** Most service providers will go along with the wishes of the offshoring company, which means that the United States will act as the legal jurisdiction should problems requiring court intervention arise during the relationship. Although rare, the parties might mutually decide on New York State as the specific jurisdiction. New York allows civil actions in its jurisdiction if the disputed value is $500,000 or $1,000,000 more, depending upon the claim, even if neither party conducts business there.

- **Intellectual Property Ownership.** The parties will need to determine who owns any intellectual property (IP) created directly out of the relationship. For example, in the name of business process improvements the service provider creates new capabilities to the customer's existing IT environment. These new capabilities are actually new IP. The service provider will likely seek an understanding that it will own that IP. The organization might argue for joint ownership.

SERVICE LEVEL AGREEMENTS

SLAs are one of the most important contractual documents in an offshoring relationship. Fundamentally an SLA describes the levels of service the organization expects from business process delivery from the service provider across a number of dimensions of the entire service package. Using the language of metrics and key performance indicators this contractually binding document commits the vendor to measurable levels of execution and service delivery. The number of SLA scenarios is limited only by the imaginations of managers and the number of companies offshoring today. While SLAs have in common with snowflakes the fact that there are no two exactly alike, some broad principles in how to structure them have emerged over the past several years, fueled by IT outsourcing and the shared services craze. Those principles are introduced here.

In the broadest sense, SLAs define service levels for three primary functions within the offshoring relationship: the actual execution of business processes themselves, technology performance, and the support mechanisms in place that ensure minimal disruption in the administration of processes should an IT operations problem manifest itself in the course of doing business. Exhibit 10.1 illustrates the three interrelated silos of service level focus. You can see that although the three service level perspectives are siloed there is a high degree of interdependence among them. Business process service levels that meet or exceed internal performance are not going to be achieved if adequate service levels are not established, defining either the performance for the IT hosting the business process applications (ERP, inventory, and so on) or the speed at which people intervene to correct problems when technology malfunctions.

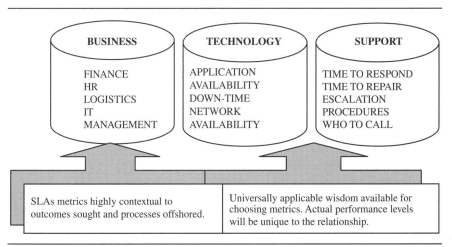

EXHIBIT 10.1 SERVICE LEVEL METRICS FOCUS

Three Broad Metrics Perspectives

Because SLA metrics in the technology and support categories are common, mature, and universally applicable to any offshoring scenario, we will begin with them.

Technology. Any offshored business processes will rely on partial or complete information technology automation, so it is obviously important that the service provider commit to guarantees of technology performance that influence the effectiveness of business process delivery. Technology-oriented SLAs are very common both because of IS organization attempts to measure and deliver service quality internally over the years and because of the extent of IT oursourcing that U.S. companies have experience with today. Such metrics as application availability and uptime as well as the amount of scheduled downtime are familiar service level provisions for many managers. "Five nines" or 99.999% of availability is pretty much a universal standard, which translates into availability for all but a couple hours a month. Asking for 100% availability is unrealistic because any IT pro will tell you that there isn't a piece of software in the world that doesn't have bugs in it. Establishing 100% application availability is possible, but it might effectively double the amount of resources needed to ensure this service level. Technology service level metrics are fairly universal across the offshoring landscape. The difference is not in the metrics themselves—availability and uptime—but the precise performance specifications within the metric. For one company, a time to respond of 2 hours is deemed adequate, while another organization would find it intolerable if the service provider did not respond to a problem within 30 minutes. The metrics are universal, the performance specs within them are highly contextual and driven by such elements as service provider track record and future capabilities, offshoring company culture (risk tolerance) and its willingness to pay more for increasing service level guarantees.

Support. Any business processes relying on IT for effective delivery will require the inclusion in SLAs of the terms which outline vendor service activities should a problem develop with the system. Metrics such as time to respond and time to repair are common performance indicators. Time to respond describes the amount of time that elapses from vendor notification that a problem has emerged to the time that a vendor employee notifies the offshoring organization that a problem actually exists. A company might seek an eight-hour time to respond service level for a less critical failure, such as a malfunction confined to one workstation and then escalate response times characterized by increasing degrees of urgency—serious failure, severe failure, and critical stop, which means that the entire platform on which the business processes are executed is not functioning. The organization and service provider will need to work on the definitions of the various failure levels and assign metrics accordingly. For example, is a batch job failure considered serious or severe? It is also important the offshoring organization does not allow extreme time zone differences to interfere with these service level metrics. Time to respond must encompass the service provider's 24-hour work day.

Business Processes.   Business process service levels are fairly new to the SLA game because business process offshoring is a maturing management discipline, although this type of service level has been put to use in shared services strategies. In the broadest sense, service level metrics revolving around processes are tied to the outcomes the company seeks. What is the quality of service we, as the offshoring organization, have historically delivered to our internal customers, and what kinds of service level metrics will define and ensure a comparable or better delivery of these business processes to customers, internal or external? A fully informed answer to this question is only possible if the organization has benchmarked internally its service delivery. From here, the organization has a useful baseline against which to set service provider process delivery expectations.

Some business process metrics can appear very different depending on whether the SLA is in HR, finance, IT, or call centers. To understand what business process metrics defining service levels might look like, consider the case of a car company that enters into an offshoring relationship with a logistics service provider for service parts help. Service parts logistics defines the warehousing, transportation, repair, and physical handling of parts for many different industries, including office equipment, computer storage, and autos, trucks, and machinery, to name a few.

The company offshoring these important business processes would be interested in such outcome-based metrics as time to respond by a technician once the logistics service provider is in possession of a faulty part, or time to repair, which describes the maximum amount of time allowed for the repair of the item—a cycle that may or may not include the amount of time it takes for the customer to receive physical possession of the repaired part. If the logistics provider is in physical proximity to the customer, a separate service level metric might specify the time to return the part to the customer after it has been fixed because the service provider might have control over this aspect of service, as opposed to shipping the part, a piece of the total service package over which it does not exert complete control. The SLA might also spell out specific service turnarounds on holidays and weekends. The idea behind service level metrics around business processes is to map service goals to performance measures directly tied to the processes themselves.

Operational Principles of SLAs

While specific business process service levels are tailored to the processes being offshored and the goals of the organization, a number of high-level principles exist that can guide the organization in SLA construction.

Win-Win. Philosophically, an SLA should not focus exclusively on penalties for vendor breach of service levels. An SLA that focuses exclusively on what the service provider loses should it not meet a specific service level metric undermines the spirit of mutual value creation both sides are entitled to out of the relationship. Monetary penalties for a vendor's failure to reach agreed-on service levels is a common feature of SLAs but also should be matched by rewards. If a vendor exceeds a certain service level for some specified amount of time, it might be compensated above and beyond contracted pricing. This issue is addressed in Chapter 12 when relationship models are explored, but needs mention in the SLA section because focusing on penalties alone establishes a potentially adverserial stance between the two parties, and this is the last thing the offshoring organization should desire.

While a belief that the service provider is entitled to rewards as well as being subject to penalties has merit, this philosophical approach might be best suited for more strategic kinds of relationships in which revenue or customer impacts are part of the service delivery. Rewards are less applicable for exceeding application uptime or batch file performance service levels because these results are expected of the service provider in exchange for winning the contract.

Penalty Structure. Penalties for missed service levels can be structured in a couple of ways. One approach is called "second chance," whereby the service provider is not assessed a financial penalty for a missed service level as long as the miss does not deviate more than a few percentage points from the target and it demonstrates continuous improvement in the service

Deviation from Target	Penalty Assessment
2% or less	8%
5% or less	17%
10% or less	25%
20% or less	50%
30% or less	75%
More than 30%	100%

EXHIBIT 10.2 SLA DOLLAR AMOUNT PENALTY APPROACH

delivery area. Another angle on this approach is the "earn-back," whereby penalties are assessed but not collected until the service provider has time to earn them back. If the service provider exceeds service levels for a specified amount of time—monthly or quarterly—the penalties disappear.[2]

If penalties are actually assessed, the organization can consider the three approaches, illustrated in Exhibits 10.2 through 10.4.

In a straight dollar penalty structure, the service provider would be assessed a varying penalty amount depending on the size of the service level miss. As the percentage size of the miss and, therefore the deviation from the service level target, increases, the percentage penalty assessed also becomes larger, because it is likely that the size of the impact on the business will increase as the deviation from the target increases. In a feathered penalty approach, service level penalties are tied to the rising degrees of business disruption caused by increasing service level misses. This approach is not interested in the degree of deviation so much as that the service level target was missed at all. Missing a payroll service level metric would warrant a

Service Level Miss	Penalty Assessment
One Miss	35%
Two Misses	65%
Three or More Misses	100%

EXHIBIT 10.3 SLA FEATHERED PENALTY APPROACH

Service Level Miss	Deviation from Target	Penalty Assessment
One Miss	10% or less	12.5%
One Miss	20% or less	25%
One Miss	More than 20%	50%
Two Misses	10% or less	25%
Two Misses	20% or less	50%
Two Misses	More than 20%	100%

EXHIBIT 10.4   COMBINATION PENALTY APPROACH

penalty at one percentage, a subsequent miss of the metric or a miss of several metrics means another increasing penalty level, and so on. You can see that the penalty for just one miss is high here, more than four times the penalty for a 2% deviation miss in the first penalty approach. Organizations might assign a high penalty assessment for service level metrics in the business processes category, while assigning much lower percentages for misses in technology and support. While all three categories of metrics are important, it is business processes that the organization is offshoring, in which it expects a minimal amount of disruption. The relative higher weighting of importance of metrics in the business processes service level category versus the technology or support categories acknowledges the priority treatment that this service level category deserves.

In the combination approach, there might be several metrics in an outcome or deliverable category, each of which is assigned a different service level. Take a service level category "application performance." Two measures are uptime and batch-file-processing time. If uptime is missed $X\%$ one penalty is assessed. If uptime and batch-processing time were both off by some percentage, another penalty would kick in. So, if uptime were off 20% or less, the service provider would be assessed a 25% penalty. If both uptime and batch-processing time were off 10% or less the penalty would be the same. The service provider is given some leeway in missing the service levels in this approach because a penalty does not kick in until some threshold is reached.

What are the specific dollar implications of these penalties? Every service level contract has an at-risk feature. The at-risk amount is the limit to the total number of dollars that a service provider can be penalized, and it might constitute 10 to 20% of the entire contract. Therefore, a 35% penalty speaks to that percentage of the total at-risk percentage. If the total contract is valued at $1 million, the total at-risk dollar amount across the entire SLA is that percentage of the value of the contract. Let's say the agreed upon at-risk dollar value is 15% of $1 million, or $150,000. A 35% penalty for one miss in the feathered approach means a loss of $52,500, which is applied against the organization's future service fee liability. This construct applies to all penalty percentages in Exhibits 10.2 through 10.4.

The other issue the offshoring company needs to decide is whether the total at-risk amount should be allocated to the three categories of service levels and how that allocation should look. It was just argued that the business process service level category is the most critical out of three—admittedly they are all very interdependent—so, the organization might want to assign a 50%, 25%, 25% weighting regime across the three categories. Therefore, in a $1 million contract, $75,000 of at-risk money is assigned to the business processes category, and $37,500 of at-risk money is assigned equally to the other two service level categories—technology and support.

The next related question concerns how category at-risk dollars are assigned to specific metrics. Supposing for simplicity sake that the business processes service level category contains a few service level metrics. Does the organization allocate the $75,000 category dollars equally across all metrics within the category? Or, does one metric cry out for preferential treatment? The company who offshored its service parts repair activities might decide that a time-to-repair performance indicator is slightly more important that a time-to-respond metric, even though both metrics are part of the business processes service level category. Therefore, time-to-repair is assigned $40,000 at-risk dollars, and the remaining $35,000 is distributed equally across the rest of the metrics in the category.

The organization might decide not to allocate at-risk dollars across metric at all and will simply allocate them across the three service level categories upon discovering that allocating at-risk dollars at such a granular level dilutes the impact of the penalties. Say that the service provider missed a service level one time and faced a 35% penalty. If the at-risk dollars were allocated at the metric level the penalty would apply to the amount of dollars actually allocated to the specific metric and not the category. If time-to-repair was allocated $40,000 out of the $75,000 and the other metrics in the category split the difference, the penalty for a missed time-to-repair service level would amount to 35% of $40,000 rather than $75,000. The company might want to structure the penalty clauses in such a way that whatever penalty approach is used, the specific penalty percentage is tied to the at-risk dollars for the *entire* service level category and not specific metrics within it. In this way, using the example above, the $1 million contract comprised of 15% at-risk dollars is allocated as follows: 35% of $75,000 for any business process service level misses, and 35% of $37,500 or any service misses in either the technology or support service level categories.

There are any number of ways for an organization to structure service level penalties. What approach the organization chooses depends on its trust in the service provider, service provider receptivity to various approaches, organizational tolerance for risk, criticality of the business processes the company is offshoring, and perhaps many other considerations.

Avoid Overproceduralizing.   An SLA is doomed if it spells out in detail how the service provider is expected to make every move in delivering to service levels. It is one thing for a car company to secure a parts logistics service level that specifies how much time elapses before a technician jumps on repairing a bad part but quite another to spell out how the work is going to be accomplished. The whole idea of offshoring is to capture cost savings and other value because the service provider conducts the processes at least as well as the organization. Stay focused on outcomes, not on process. The company cares when the train arrives, not which set of tracks the conductor decides to take to get there.

Flexibility.   The idea of flexibility has been alluded to several times in this book. In the context of SLAs, flexibility speaks to the ability of both organization and service provider to adapt service levels to the changing goals of the organization. In the service parts logistics example, the car company is poised to win a big fleet contract for its trucks but only if it can improve service parts repair times by 20%. The car company turns to its service provider and discusses the feasibility of restructuring its SLA to secure a 20% time improvement in this critical service level metric. Can the service provider deliver?

Flexibility is a nice idea but difficult to realize because often changes in service levels will mean change to the vendor's cost structure, and it needs to know, rightfully, how the new resources which support the service level change are going to be paid for. "You want a 20% improvement in the cycle time of service parts repair? Show me the money to pay for the additional staff and equipment it requires," says the service provider. Changes in service levels, particularly those changes to the business processes themselves, as opposed to technology or support, are significant enough to cause a review of the scope of work and the contract itself. Therefore, the concept of change and how it influences service levels and the agreements that specify them will be explored in greater depth.

Change and Contingency Planning. The idea of flexibility also speaks to the capacity to respond to change and the abstract concept of change in offshoring relationships has a larger context than just service levels. However, the SLA might be the optimal place to consider it within the context of the entire offshoring relationship because any kind of meaningful change is likely to manifest itself in the service levels the organization seeks and the vendor is attempting to achieve. To see this, think of change coming from three directions for both the customer and service provider: the external environment, the service provider's internal environment, and the customer's internal environment. Change in any one or more of these areas might mean the need for a change in the relationship and, therefore, a change in the service levels. Here are plausible examples.

The service provider's government is implementing a new tax that will raise its costs and make profit margins razor thin. Can the service provider raise its rates 5%? If not, it will be impossible for the service provider to deliver at the high service levels established in the contract. They will require adjustment. The car company's external environment changes because an existing customer is threatening to take its fleet business elsewhere unless the company can improve by 10% the parts repair turnaround time. Can the vendor adjust the service levels? The vendor's internal environment changes when employee turnover accelerates rapidly because of increased market competition. (Actually there are some external environment influences bearing on this internal change.) In order for the service provider to manage the customer's account to the service levels specified, it needs to bump pay by 10% to retain workers and maintain continuity and build experiential knowledge accumulation that ensures that service levels are met. Can the vendor pass along half this wage cost increase to the customer? The customer's internal environment changes when, on the heels of an acquisition, it asks the service provider handling direct deposit payroll whether it can add, over the next few months, paper check production services for the new employees who are not used to direct deposit. The acquiring company wants to transition these employees over to direct deposit after an education program has been conducted. A new service level is required. How is it structured?

In every one of these examples, some force changed the service provider or customer's existing reality, a force that caused a change in service and, therefore, a change in service levels. This is precisely how the need for flexibility is likely to manifest itself in an offshoring relationship, even if the probability is low that any one of these specific scenarios will occur. Probability is less important here than the idea that managers on both sides must be forced into thinking about the future, how the complexion of that future is likely to look, and the fact that the kinds of change which can materially affect the SLA must be acknowledged in the SLA. Anticipating change cries out for SLA contingency planning where change impacts service levels. Therefore, it is critical that the SLA portion of the offshoring contract build in language around the need for flexibility and change with additional provisions addressing continuous improvements of service levels.

Management Is Key.   Service Level Management (SLM) is as important as the agreement. SLM defines activities and oversight of the SLA, which include: one, tracking the service so performance auditing can be accomplished; two, service reporting for the same reason; three, a formal SLA review process no different in principle than an audit which reviews security procedures. The contract should include language which outlines the procedures for service level management—timetables for auditing and reporting and a formal review process where the customer and service provider discuss service level performance issues and plan for any changes to the agreement which loom on the horizon.

In consideration of timetables, two issues emerge: frequency of reporting and frequency of assessment. Both of these issues circle around the nature of the service level. For example, an organization might want performance data reported monthly or quarterly but will assess semiannually. This might be the case with technology performance service levels such as availability. The business processes, however, might call for the same reporting frequency but far more frequent assessment because of the highest priority of these service levels versus technology and support. Reporting and assessment frequency will also be influenced by the penalty structure in place. How often are penalties assessed, according to the contract, for each service level? More frequent penalty assessment means more frequent reporting and performance assessment.

CHAPTER TAKEAWAY

Some key concepts to leave this chapter with:

- Contracting is where the offshoring rubber meets the road and this road is strewn with possible potholes across many operational considerations. If the organization's legal team has little experience negotiating offshoring deals hire a lawyer who has. Contracting is a generic legal activity but contracting specifically in offshoring is highly specific and requires deep experience to negotiate effectively.

- Service Level Agreements might be the most important contractually binding document in the total offshoring contract. The SLA represents the assurances of quality in business process delivery from the service provider. The organization should approach SLA construction by building service levels within three categories that define the service relationship: business processes, technology performance, and support protocols.

- Establishing effective service level metrics means that the organization has a complete understanding of the business processes being offshored as well as a baseline of existing business process service delivery in the organization. Defining the terms of the SLA demands that the organization has a strong grasp of the service quality it wants from the vendor and this is best achieved if internal service levels have already been benchmarked. An absence of this understanding runs the risk of establishing offshoring service levels that do not meet existing performance levels. What organization wants less quality from a service provider than it already achieves in-house?

- The organization's attitude should look at SLAs as a win-win for both parties and not just focus on penalties and punishment. Is there a way to structure the SLA with a mix of both penalties and rewards?

- The penalty framework is very flexible with a number of approaches available to structure them. Once the at-risk amount in the contract is defined, the organization can determine how much at-risk dollars should be allocated across the three service level categories. How this allocation is arrived at is highly contextual to business need and biases.

- Change is a concept that exists throughout the entire offshoring relationship but often manifests itself in the need to revise service level metrics. The organization and service provider should anticipate to the fullest extent possible all the drivers of change and how each side will respond to change over the course of the relationship.

NOTES

1. R. Matlus, W. Maurer and L. Scardino, "Include Clauses That Allay Risks in Outsourcing Contracts," *Gartner Research Note*, August 24, 2004.
2. Barbara Beech, "Getting the Most Out of Your SLAs," part II, Cutter Consortium, 2003.

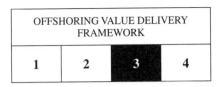

11

OTHER RELATIONSHIP DETAILS

Relationship issues with a service provider possess both strategic and tactical elements. At the strategic level the organization should figure out how it plans to deal with the entire collection of service provider relationships for all offshoring initiatives in such a way that is operationally and process consistent, but also flexible enough to accommodate the various objectives, people, and service provider practices that might be unique to each individual initiative. At a tactical level, the organization will seek to ensure that operational elements are in place to manage the specific initiative effectively. These brass tack issues include identifying the main points of contact in the service provider organization, establishing regular meeting schedules (particularly important in light of big time zone differences), and understanding the modes of communication that work best to support the relationship—phone, email, instant messaging, online meeting environments, and so forth. The following sections outline the important offshoring relationship issues.

CHIEF OUTSOURCING/OFFSHORING OFFICER

An old joke says that the best way to avoid losing your job to offshoring is to become the lead who manages all the offshoring in the organization. So when will we see the emergence of COO, chief outsourcing or offshoring officer? The increasing number of offshoring relationships a company has developed, increasing value at stake in offshoring relationships and an acknowledgment that these relationships require on going management all seem to argue for a dedicated executive who can direct an organization's offshoring initiatives.

What would the job look like? Ideally the COO's role would consist of a mix of consultative and operational responsibilities:

- Seek out offshoring opportunities across the enterprise through regular consultation with operational executives.
- Gatekeep offshoring proposals bubbling up from operational areas. All proposals flow through the COO for further consultation with finance and other senior executives.
- Act as a business sponsor's best friend. The COO would help the sponsor develop buy-in for an offshoring initiative. This might include proposal and business case development before an executive board.
- Coordinate the entire Offshoring Value Delivery Framework process from an operational level. The COO would serve as an important support lead for all activities carried out in the delivery framework.

In order for such a position to add value to offshoring management, certain conditions need to be in place. They include:

- A clear vision and mission for offshoring at both a strategic and operational level.
- Complete CEO support for the purpose and responsibilities of the COO.
- Buy-in of the COO's scope of responsibility from operational areas that are candidates for offshoring initiatives.
- Total organizational understanding of the COO's gatekeeper and consultative role.
- Dedicated staff, depending upon company size and the scale of offshoring activity.
- Technology support is critical. What interactive and collaborative offshoring management software environment exists to manage the entire initiative and offshoring portfolio (the collection of existing offshoring initiatives) lifecycle? A hodgepodge of desktop productivity tools is too cumbersome to manage the entire range of strategic, tactical, and operational issues. An offshoring platform that looks at offshoring holistically and in an integrated fashion is required given its potential complexity.
- A clear governance structure. Who gets to overrule whom? Does the offshoring idea stop at the CFO's desk if he or she doesn't seek the

value in the proposal? Or, does a COO and CFO weigh in and offer recommendations to proposals that, if created, require submission to an executive committee?

- Procurement alignment. Are current enterprise procurement practices in conflict with provisioning offshoring services?
- Budgeting alignment. How is offshoring support going to be paid for? Who will pay for the valuable services of the COO and his or her crew? Will the organization adopt a chargeback system for COO services? Is a shared services model for the COO and organization an effective arrangement to implement budget and finance policies?

As blue sky as this vision is, organizations are likely to adopt a more centralized and structured offshoring decision-making and management system as offshoring matures as a management discipline and as the level of offshoring activity increases. If nothing else, the COO model clarifies the resources and elements required for successful offshoring, even if the organization does not buy into the COO concept.

GOOD TO GREAT, THEN OFFSHORE VERSUS OFFSHORE, THEN GOOD TO GREAT

Another way to view company/service provider relationships is through the prism of business process change and improvement by virtue of offshoring. Does the organization look to optimize and reengineer business processes first, then offshore the results or does the organization seek to offshore steady state processes and then look to improve processes in collaboration with the service provider? This issue was raised in the context of establishing a shared services organization but many organizations might not have a shared services model in place so the question is raised again around the subject of the relationship with the service provider.

While the international business process offshoring marketplace is relatively new, youth has not deterred the market from slowly evolving into offering two distinct types of partnership arrangements when a company contracts with a service provider for offshoring services. According to Gartner, one model is "Support-and-Transform" and the other flavor of service provider value proposition is "Transform-and-Support."[1] While Gartner's expertise is confined to management issues in information technology and this identified pattern revolves explicitly around IT offshoring, companies exploring any kind of business process offshoring should determine if this vendor pattern holds true in their domains, be it finance, HR, or R&D. Thinking about service providers in terms of this duality might crystallize for the organization both how to proceed with offshoring—reengineer first and offshore or vice versa—and what to look for in a service provider; what pattern holds with other customers? Does the vendor predominantly support and transform customer processes, vice versa, or neither?

In the former case, basically, a company looks to an offshore service provider to support business processes it seeks to move outside the organization. The company actually forklifts out the assets that make the business processes functional. Those assets can include people, processes, and technology. Once those assets have been firmly embedded within the infrastructure of the service provider, the vendor can improve and transform the business processes it is now responsible for. The service provider can introduce new technology and leverage the knowledge it captures by virtue of managing the same processes across a number of client organizations.[2] The idea is to cross-pollinate good ideas across the entire customer base. An example of this might involve a multinational that offshores stable finance processes to the service provider on the Oracle platform. Over time the service provider figures out some hooks and tweaks to these processes, either through technical innovation or hard-won wisdom it earned from servicing many other customers on the same IT platform, wisdom it can offer the organization. Most offshoring relationships, in fact, evolve this way. Companies offshore existing processes as they are, then seek improvements and innovations at some point after the service provider has reached business process administration and management steady state.

The second value proposition has just the opposite effect. Companies who seek to exploit a new business capability will contract with a service provider and implement new technology that supports the new business processes. After a transition phase in which workers are brought up to speed on the processes and the technology driving them, the service provider's value is to support the combination of people, processes, and technology that the client hopes to leverage improved performance from. Take the smallish manufacturer (notice we're not talking about manufacturing processes and the workers who are engaged with them but rather back office *services*) that decides to forge a relationship with a service provider who can deliver more sophisticated supply chain functionality than the company has been able to muster on its own. It moves internal staff to the service provider organization and reengineers old processes into new ones that map well to the service provider's technology. Now the manufacturer can manage capacity far more efficiently because, amongst other things, it has visibility into the demand for its products. Supply chain automation does not necessarily provide the company with a competitive advantage since this is not a new class of packaged application. However, the manufacturer experiences a measurable improvement in an array of operational areas. There is less waste, fewer raw materials sitting around, and better alignment between payables and receivables because supply hasn't been created for demand that doesn't exist.

In Gartner's estimation, the first scenario is best suited for larger, slower-moving organizations that cannot quickly ramp up new technology in the service of business process innovation but who might capture these benefits over time as the service provider acts as a kind of collaborative enabler of new capabilities. Conversely, the "Transform-and-Support" organization believes in the big business process payoff from new technology and aligns itself with a service provider who is schooled in it.

RELATIONSHIP DEFINED BY PRICING

Organization/service provider relationships are also defined by several fundamental pricing and payment arrangements. Different offshoring initiatives are best suited for one of these models. They might be recognizable to some managers because this classification has a long history in defining IT service relationships.

Cost Plus

In this arrangement the vendor is paid for the actual cost of doing the work plus a fixed fee for its profit and, in some cases, an additional incentive fee for delivering extra value. In the case of offshoring, such extra value might be completing a project ahead of schedule. Another Cost Plus approach is to structure vendor prices around the offshoring company's historical cost of conducting the work the vendor will assume responsibility for. Use of this approach assumes that the organization has a very good grasp of its historical costs in delivering internally the offshore candidate business processes.

Fee for Service

Pricing and payment is based on transaction volume, which works best when transactions are discrete as in payroll processing, medical transcription, or credit card bad debt collections.

Time and Materials

The vendor is paid based on a negotiated hourly rate plus reimbursement at cost for additional materials used in delivering service. This approach has appeal when project specifications are not entirely clear at the outset of the relationship. But anytime an organization opens its checkbook to time-based billing it exposes itself to rising costs if it does not have a very granular understanding all the way down to the individual vendor employee level of the work the service provider is performing on a regular basis.

Fixed Price

Negotiated payment at regular intervals. The value of this approach is its consistency and predictability as well as its ability to shield the customer from assuming any service provider cost overruns. The drawback is the possibility the customer will overpay for offshored services or that the service provider, perhaps motivated to cut internal costs as aggressively as possible, will attempt to cut corners, with the knowledge that its revenue stream is fixed. Service level agreements can help mitigate overly aggressive vendor cost cutting because specific quality levels for the fixed price are contractually guaranteed.

Gain Sharing

The customer and vendor share in the gains achieved over time after the relationship begins. Gains might take the form of cost cutting or some strategic impact—revenue, marketshare, and so on. This model assumes the real possibility of future value captured by virtue of the relationship, which may or may not be the case in more cost-cutting-oriented offshoring arrangements. In fact, many companies who bother with and pay attention to a formal business case providing transparency into the real upfront costs of offshoring, will look for immediate savings from the relationship instead of potential future savings, given that breakeven is reached further out on the time horizon than the organization originally believed.

Shared Risk/Reward

The material difference between gain sharing and shared risk/reward is that in the latter vendor and customer both invest in the cost of the project and share the revenue that is generated proportionally to each party's investment. In offshoring, one scenario suitable for this model involves a vendor who invests in the resources to manage the customer's business processes and receives compensation based on cost savings that materialize over time. If future value is not cost savings but revenue, you might find this model applied in the unique but not unheard of scenario where a corporation that has developed best-of-breed delivery of some domain of business processes internally ends up partnering with an offshoring expert to package and sell offshoring business process management services to the market as a new profit center. This model is ideally suited for this arrangement.

Business-Benefit-Based

In this model the vendor is paid in proportion to the business value generated by the project in the form of cost savings or revenue. This model is a term of art not materially different in outcome from gain sharing or shared risk/reward.

Every example above shows that how the final offshoring deal is structured will have a profound impact on how the company/vendor relationship will look. More future-value-oriented pricing models, by their very nature, require a more collaborative relationship between the two organizations because a lot is at stake around successful mutual execution. More collaboration might mean more frequent communication, travel, or physical presence at each other's headquarters. As was already shown, future-value relationships put the focus on different metrics than those used in approaches that emphasize cost cutting.

A fixed price model, however, is predictable and unconcerned, at least explicitly, with future value. Of course both the vendor and organization might be keenly interested in exploring how business process delivery innovations and improvements invite the possibility of future value, but that agenda item is not the subject of present management focus. In fact, any pricing models that naturally define the customer/vendor relationship should be flexible enough to accommodate the natural evolution of that relationship as the goals might shift. An example of this is the emergence a couple of years ago of Offshoring Development Centers (ODCs). Mentioned earlier in the book in the context of knowledge retention, Otis Elevator established an ODC with Wipro just a few years ago. An ODC describes a relationship in which the vendor dedicates resources to one IT client in exchange for a volume of work that justifies those dedicated resources. Otis was giving Wipro so much IT work that both parties believed that a deeper relationship, which included a dedicated Wipro work team devoted to Otis projects, could benefit both sides. Among the benefits of such an arrangement beyond knowledge retention and speedier ramp-up times is the better negotiating leverage the customer enjoys, given the scale of the work provided the vendor. Piecemeal fixed-price or time-and-materials jobs morph into an ODC proposition in which a cost-plus arrangement subjects the vendor to delivering services in line with the customer's historical delivery costs and equal to the customer's internal level of quality.

EXIT STRATEGY

As a profit making industry, the biggest thing going for information technology is the lock–in created out of the customer's investment decisions. Should the customer want to switch platforms, the cost is steep and so is the disruption in business continuity. Anyone making any kind of IT investment decision is faced with lock-in. Would that this were not the case in offshoring but, alas, 'tisn't so. Companies face potentially big lock-in issues once the service provider relationship has begun, and they are not all technology-driven. Should the contract expire and the organization decides either to forklift its business processes to another service provider or as the Beatles say, "get back to where you started from"—in-house—the organization faces the time-consuming and perhaps costly task of extricating itself from the current relationship like Houdini breaking out of a steamer trunk wrapped in chains 20 feet underwater.

Leaving aside the relationship's ending because of breach of contract, the company has the choice of continuing its relationship or the other two options mentioned above. The decision to leave a service provider comes with no decision framework or magic set of templates that tells the organization when to exit. Different companies have different thresholds of pain. Good Natured and Resource Strapped Inc., whose service provider missed service levels 20% of the time decides to give it another chance with a second-year option. The missed service levels rarely caused any major disruption or financial losses. The labor market is tight, and there is little appetite for taking on another big initiative with other important projects going on. The vendor for Uptight Global missed service levels 6% of the time and the marriage is off. It's moving its business to the competitor across the street.

Whether to leave an offshoring relationship is a highly customized decision—once again, context is king—but there are plenty of reasons, of which missed service levels are a symptom, why this unfortunate eventuality could occur: angry customers and suppliers, vendor overpromises, lack of offshoring organization's understanding of business process complexity, changing market conditions, and many more. Organizations must look at the following issues carefully before making that ultimate exit decision. Exhibit 11.1 summarizes exit strategy issues.

As counterintuitive and as pessimistic as it seems to prepare for this eventuality, particularly in the midst of the excitement of embarking on a new service provider relationship, it must be done in the name of risk mitigation and contingency planning. An argument for an exit strategy does not suggest that a high likelihood exists that an organization will need to execute one. It does suggest, by inference, the importance of a thorough vendor selection process to find the vendor who is a best fit. This minimizes the need for an exit strategy in the first place.

Issue	Action Item
COST	Work up some kind of budget summarizing exit costs: Contract – if exiting before expiration how much does the vendor get? Transition – knowledge, technology. Internal change – organizational reengineering to accommodate business process reentry, new people. Legal – calling all lawyers. Technology – any additional software needed in new relationship? Also, impact of moving licenses again. Training – if processes are coming back, how much new training is required to reach comparable service level quality?
CAPABILITY	If work is coming back in house, does the intellectual capital exist anymore to do the job?
SPEED	How long will it take to reach a new steady state, either internally or through a new service provider?
EFFECT ON STAKEHOLDERS	What are the potential impacts and disruptions of another business process offshoring (BPO) move on suppliers, customers, partners?
OLD SERVICE PROVIDER ROLE	What role can the jilted service provider expect to play when the organization begins the process of moving the business away from it? Contract language should spell out the terms of vendor cooperation before, during, and after exit, as needed.
RISK	Noncompliance in reporting during exit. Data corruption or loss during transition. Incomplete or lost data during transition. Service provider data theft sabotage.

EXHIBIT 11.1 CRITICAL ISSUES WHEN EXPLORING EXITING AN OFFSHORE SERVICE PROVIDER RELATIONSHIP

CHAPTER TAKEAWAY

Here are some key concepts to leave this chapter with:

- If offshoring is expected to be a regular activity viewed with potential strategic importance, a chief outsourcing or offshoring officer might make sense, particularly as the dollar total and volume of individual offshoring initiatives escalates. This COO will oversee all offshoring activities and liaison directly with the highest levels of management. Organizations must determine if it is a board-level position.

- Is the organization going to rely upon the service provider to deliver reengineering value by virtue of offshoring or is the organization intent on reengineering business processes internally and then offshoring them? An answer to this will turn on a host of issues. How deep is the vendor's expertise and the company's confidence level in its offshoring ally? Is the company equipped to reengineer first before offshoring? Some companies will offshore to fob off onto a service provider a problem area. Instead of getting rid of a problem, this simply adds another—the problem of managing a third-party who has inherited internal dysfunction.

- What kind of economic model will the organization strike with the service provider? What has been the organization's experience using these various approaches in other vendor situations? What goals the company seeks from the relationship will heavily influence the economic model chosen.

- Organizations who seek to paint their backsides white and run with the antelope away from an offshoring vendor relationship face some potentially vexing challenges. Understand completely all the implications— legal, operational, and business continuity—of departing a relationship before it starts. Being aware of exit challenges, some organizations might take a deep breath and attempt to fix their existing situation instead of leaving. Better the devil you know than the one you do not.

NOTES

1. Robert Brown, "Evaluating and Selecting a BPO Provider: Be Careful What You Wish For," Gartner presentation, Outsourcing Summit 2004, May 17–19 2004, Las Vegas.
2. Ibid.

Phase 4

ONGOING MANAGEMENT: EXECUTE & MANAGE

The good ship offshoring is about to be christened now, and the organization and service provider are just about to embark on a beautiful adventure, right? The work is not finished, of course. In Phase 4 of the Offshoring Value Delivery Framework some critical execution issues still loom, chiefly, how is the organization going to transition technology and/or knowledge to the service provider? While technology transfer is straightforward enough, knowledge and expertise transfer is more complicated and its successful execution is a cornerstone of good offshoring management practices. When a company offshores its business processes a significant amount of experiential and operational knowledge must go along for the ride in order to equip the new workforce to administer and manage the business processes successfully. The transition period from inception of business process transfer to service provider steady state must be managed with the discipline and eye for detail the organization would invest in any other large-scale project. Quality of execution in the transition period can have a large impact on the Payback Period of the offshoring initiative. It also sets the tone of the relationship between customer and service provider and a relationship that launches on the basis of mutual distrust and dissatisfaction arising out of flawed business process transitioning is a lousy way to start.

12

Start of a Beautiful Friendship

TRANSITION

If there is one place that represents the most vulnerable point of failure in an offshoring relationship, it might be during the transition phase, defined as that period of time when the client organization engages in all of the necessary steps to turn over daily business process management responsibility to the service provider. The organization has journeyed far from developing strategy to selecting a vendor to negotiating the contract. All that good work is undermined, however, if the transition is not handled with the proper focus.

Story of ON Semiconductor

ON Semiconductor was discussed in Chapter 5. The Phoenix-based chip manufacturer with operations around the globe took the offshoring plunge several years ago when it transitioned mainframe application maintenance and support for approximately 50 legacy business applications from a domestic outsourcer situated near its headquarters to an operation in India comprised of a partnership between ON Semiconductor's domestic outsourcer for these services, ACS, and an established Mumbai, India-based company Larsen and Toubro InfoTech Limited (L&T). At one time these application were strategic but ON Semiconductor's three-to-five year plan was to mothball some 50 programs in pricing, distribution, receivables, order management, and a host of other critical business process programs and replace them with modern, client-server applications around Oracle, i2 supply chain, Matrix One product lifecycle management, and others.

The story of ON Semiconductor describes the often overlooked effort required to transition business processes out of the organization and into a service provider. For ON Semiconductor, the central issue was capturing the dramatic cost savings of 50% from the existing contract the domestic outsourcing service provider insisted it could deliver at the same level of quality the company received. On one level, quality assurance was at less risk to the extent that ON Semiconductor would be working with the same service provider. They had forged a good working relationship and ACS understood its customer's needs. However, other risks manifested themselves in the fact that the total service package would be delivered in partnership with a new service provider who enjoyed an established presence and track record in India. An entirely new team of technical professionals would be picking up the work from the domestic crew scheduled to be relieved from this customer engagement. And, ACS was new to offshoring, its plunge into this new mode of service delivery coming at the behest of ON Semiconductor, who was prepared to end the domestic outsourcing relationship if it could not win significant cost savings. A chip market recession in the 2000 to 2002 time frame mandated that CIO David Wagner completely reengineer his IT organization's cost structure. In this way ACS, who had considered building an offshore capability, was thrust into the arms of L&T.

A global manufacturing footprint gave ON Semiconductor a sophisticated attitude about offshoring. It had no problem with the idea of a service provider managing these critical business processes many times zones away. Rather, in the mix of contextual issues involved in moving legacy application maintenance overseas, the one rising above all others was this: "One of the fundamental assumptions in the whole cost-cutting imperative was that cost needed to be cut but quality needed to be maintained," says Wagner.[1] This assumption is a fundamental principle in any offshoring effort and is important enough to state explicitly, as obvious as it may seem. The cost reductions any company like ON Semiconductor seeks is predicated on a quality of services at least equal to that the company already enjoys no matter what business processes are subject to offshoring: HR, finance, fulfillment, and so on. The company sought drastic cost reduction in the management of certain business applications but not at the expense of the skills of the workers managing these applications or the skills of managers overseeing the work and maintaining the service relationship. This point becomes vivid when readers see the effort ON Semiconductor put into vetting worker quality as it transitioned these business processes to Mumbai. Labor quality assurance emerged as a central feature of ON Semiconductor's transition plan.

ON Semiconductor's transition consisted of five steps. It started with a detailed plan about how knowledge of these custom applications would be transferred to the new ACS/L &T staff. Steps 2 and 3 consisted of work processes involved in certifying that the new crew gained mastery of the acquired knowledge. Step 4 could be characterized as a kind of subtransition stage in which the new team began assuming responsibility for these business processes with ON Semiconductor oversight. The last step ON called steady state. Here the company confirmed that the new relationship was completely operational and that the full terms of the relationship have been forged. The entire transition had a completion deadline of approximately five months, and ON Semiconductor assigned a program manager to oversee the entire transition. Exhibit 12.1 is a modified but representative depiction of a high-level view of ON Semiconductor's transition plan for offshoring legacy application maintenance and support business processes.

Business Process Transition Execution

Phase 1: Knowledge Transfer. The knowledge transfer phase consisted of a breakdown of all functionality areas within each software application. Responsibility for comprehension and mastery of groups of software functionality was assigned to individual members of the new offshoring team. In addition, members of the old ACS outsourcing team in Phoenix with subject matter expertise were assigned to new team members as mentors responsible for oversight of complete knowledge transfer. Take an application called Demand Management. Specific processes include order processing, quote for purchase, and quote sales order. These areas of functionality might be assigned to one ACS/L & T offshore professional, while his ACS mentor would oversee the offshore professional's drive toward competency in the subject area. Knowledge itself took the form of manuals, flowcharts, and other written documentation as well as VHS tapes featuring instructor-led teaching.

The cause-and-effect interdependencies of each step in the transition (can't conduct certification unless knowledge transfer is completed) demanded that ON Semiconductor establish target and actual dates for the start and completion of all tasks in each phase. In the knowledge transfer phase, for

APPLICATION: DEMAND MANAGEMENT	L&T/ACS KNOWLEDGE TARGETS		KNOWLEDGE TRANSFER	LEVEL 1 CERTIFICATION	LEVEL 2 CERTIFICATION	PREP FOR OFFSHORE SUPPORT	STEADY STATE ENTERED
Specific functionality							
Order processing	Jim	—	Target begin: Target end: Actual begin:	Target begin: Target end: Actual begin:	Target begin: Target end: Actual begin:	Target begin: Target end:	Target begin: Target end:
			Actual end:	Actual end:	Actual end:	Actual begin: Actual end:	Actual begin: Actual end:
Quote for purchase	Jane	Bill					
Quote sales order	Joe	Bart					
Audit	Jill	Betty					
Price list	Jack	Bob					
Ship and credit	Jenna	Bev					

EXHIBIT 12.1 ON Semiconductor's Offshoring Transition Plan

SOURCE: David Wagner (CIO of ON Semiconductor) provided an Excel spreadsheet of the transition plan. This figure is a stylization of that report.

206

instance, ON Semiconductor allotted five to six weeks for new workers to study the materials in their competency areas around specific application functions and processes and confer with their ACS outsourcing team mentors. The actual start dates were later than initial target starts in most cases; therefore, the actual end dates were bumped by an equal number of days. However, the estimation of the total number of days that knowledge transfer would require for any functional category proved mostly on target. Some knowledge transfer completion dates took longer than budgeted, some less time. The purpose of documenting target and actual start and finish dates was to give ON Semiconductor visibility into overall knowledge transfer activities against plan. This was important because the offshore contract specified a hard start date just several months away, and successful knowledge transfer was critical for completion of successive stages of the transition effort. If this fell far off schedule, so would the entire transition effort.

ON Semiconductor had experience on its side in terms of both some of the execution in knowledge transfer and well as its choice of training content. The company executed the same knowledge transfer approach it used when originally contracting with ACS for outsource management of these applications upon the company's spinoff from Motorala. It had high confidence that these knowledge transfer techniques—both from a planning and content perspective—within a larger transition plan would serve the company well as it moved application maintenance from Phoenix to India. The training materials had been used for years in Motorola and had proven effective tools for technical training.

Phases 2 and 3: Certification.   ON established two levels of competency for the process of certifying that offshore technical workers could do the work of its domestic outsourcing personnel. This represented the next two phases of the transition. The Level One certification, Phase 2 in the overall transition, which followed on the heels of the knowledge transfer exercise, was designed to validate that the new offshore technical workers understood how the legacy applications worked. Level Two certification, Phase 3 in the transition, sought to confirm that the workers could apply that understanding in a real-world production environment.

Leveraging testing techniques Motorola had built and used for its own training, a combination of written exams and simulated problem scenarios requiring a systems fix, ON Semiconductor tested the offshore candidates on a variety of application-specific subjects, which included familiarity with their functionality and business logic, in addition to their problem solving skills in troubleshooting real-world scenarios. The company established a work timetable as a subset to the overall transition plan that prescribed the details of the testing work. Each application functionality area subject to testing was assigned to an ON subject matter expert. Each ON Semiconductor subject matter expert (SME) conducted the tests, then certified that the new offshore workers had reached competency in their assigned knowledge domains. Just as ON Semiconductor assigned required timetables for knowledge transfer, so too did it assign the two phases of certification target and actual start and completion dates. Level One certification was budgeted a short amount of time, less than two weeks in many instances, given the relative simplicity of the testing. Level Two certification was budgeted for much longer, approaching two months in some instances of application functionality. In some function areas, the time to competency, a key performance metric in the training world, was reached well ahead of schedule. A good sign as ON Semiconductor closely watched the testing results come in.

Despite some vocal criticism about the legitimacy of certification testing, particularly in the Microsoft world, where companies found certified workers were good at test taking but paralyzed in a real-world production environment, ON Semiconductor was highly confident that their customized testing regime would accurately gauge offshore labor preparedness to manage these custom programs, even if the risk existed that the work candidates were not up to learning these new skills.

As testing results emerged, ON Semiconductor prepared itself to build a contingency plan in the event that test takers failed at a higher rate than was acceptable to stay on beam with the transition. A formal contingency plan did not exist during the transition but the company was prepared to construct one rapidly if questions arose about the abilities of the new Indian technical workers to handle the demands of these applications, which would emerge in the certification results. The likeliest contingency scenario would involve folding these business processes in-house in the company's Malaysia operation, where workers had long proven their technical proficiency. In Wagner's estimation, certification measurement and worker quality validation represented the single most vulnerable point in the whole offshoring process, as his company never worked with L&T before, and the vendor would be responsible for hiring the offshore team that would service this account. ON Semiconductor accepted the real risk that the service provider staff might not pass certification to its expectations. Happily the results were strong. An 80%-plus first-attempt pass rate. Wagner found the

Indian technical worker skills were excellent. They demonstrated a mastery of coolgen, an older development environment for mainframe applications and possessed good design and systems analysis skills as well. It helped that they also spoke fluent English.

While the two phases of certification were under way, the company began to transition help desk activities to the India operation. This activity does not appear as a discrete phase in the transition plan but was viewed as a mentoring activity and folded into the overall skills development and certification process. Trouble tickets generated from help requests initiated by a user of these legacy applications somewhere around the globe would route to India where they were fielded by members of the new technical team, while the old team back in Phoenix listened in to ensure service quality.

Phase 4: Preparation for Offshore Support. This is also referred to as a transition readiness test. At this point in this transition, ON wants to know what dates will "the switches flip" on the actual business processes in the offshore organization? This phase is not unlike the final preflight check before an aircraft takes off. The pilot and copilot review a list of conditions each of which must be in a certain state before the plane can take off and fly safely. Runway lights: on; flaps: in position; fuel flow: within normal parameters; and so forth. In the same way, ON Semiconductor conducts its preflight, asking if all the necessary elements are in place for this new offshoring relationship to take off on an adventurous trip to the subcontinent. Again, the company organized this phase around application functionality. For each functional area within each legacy application taking the trip to India, it wants to confirm the new work team is ready for their responsibilities, that the company is in possession of the correct contact information for each L&T team member. By virtue of the new relationship, ON Semiconductor changed the reporting path for escalating trouble tickets. Is the process documentation completely updated to reflect new processes as well as the fact that new personnel are responsible for stable processes not changing in the new relationship? The timetable for this phase is short within the overall transition plan, representing one day to a week. The actual end date for this phase was no later than the day before the official offshoring contract went live. Although somewhat of a pro forma exercise, this is nevertheless an important phase in the transition plan. It represents the last chance to validate that all the conditions for successful offshoring are in place; when the company flips the switch, the last thing it wants is a blown fuse that brings down the lights.

Phase 5: Steady State Entered.   In the transition timetable, ON Semiconductor entered a steady state condition the day after the actual end date to complete Phase 4 activities within each application functionality area. The transition is completed. The offshoring relationship is airborne. The ongoing relationship is just beginning.

Other Transition Principles at ON Semiconductor

Although not reflected in the transition plan, ON Semiconductor prioritized plan rollout based on application complexity. The steeper the learning curve to reach competency in an application, the earlier the company began the transition processes—knowledge transfer, certification, and so on. If any application proved particularly difficult for the new team to master, requiring more time than budgeted, the bigger the cushion ON could lean on in an attempt to catch up. Successfully managing the cause and effect linkages in each successive phase of the transition would ultimately determine the effectiveness of the entire transition. Fortunately, the new team proved well up to the challenge of mastering all of the offshored applications.

ON Semiconductor also prioritized knowledge transfer rollout based on sequential processes within each application. For example, in the Demand Management application, one of the first candidates for knowledge transfer because of its complexity, the company transferred knowledge of order management processes only after an L&T/ACS team member grasped pricing functions, since a customer would need to know the price of chips before placing an order for them. Order functions preceded ship and credit application processes because a customer order must be generated before shipping activities are engaged in, and so on. ON Semiconductor also prioritized sequentially by entire application, after complexity was accounted for. Some financial reporting applications were introduced far later in the transition process, since these are influenced by transaction-oriented programs like Demand Management. The company was driving holistic comprehension of applications and their functionality. This was best achieved using a sequential approach whereby the new team would see both how each program fit into total system workflow, while also gaining understanding how a collection of sequential functional processes composed one entire application.

Offshore Transitioning Is a Relay Race

A useful way to think about transition planning is to view the collection of activities that compose the entire transition as a two-person relay race. The baton handoff in a relay race is a finely synchronized activity that requires perfect execution from both participants. World-class runners spend a lot of time on the mechanics of baton handoff because it represents such a huge vulnerability to the goal of winning the race. A familiar sight to most readers is watching a relay race on TV where the handoff is fumbled. When this occurs, the race is essentially over.

Runner one, the offshoring organization, is coming around the track, his attention drawn toward his partner, the offshoring service provider. When both runners synchronize their movements—the first runner reaching out to the second and the second beginning his run before the first runner reaches him—they both occupy a passing zone not unlike the timeframe bounded by a transition plan. In ON Semiconductor's case, the specific tasks of knowledge transfer and certification represented this runner synchronization as both prepared for handoff. By the time the company had reached the Prep for Offshore Support stage, it was in the act of handing off the baton to L&T. When the baton has passed fully from customer to service provider and the service provider accelerates his run, the relationship has reached steady state. The significant feature of this metaphor is the concept of synchronization; the two runners are required to coordinate their efforts as they enter the passing zone to ensure a successful handoff. In the same way ON Semiconductor and L&T coordinated their efforts to ensure a successful handoff of domain knowledge from customer to service provider; ON Semiconductor determined the extent of knowledge transfer and certification and the timetables involved. L&T took its cue and prepared its team accordingly for the work ahead.

The other salient feature of this metaphor is a handoff at a speed greater than zero. The whole point of a relay race is to hand off the baton with a minimal amount of disruption to the speed at which the team is moving. Runner one could stop completely, then hand off the baton to his teammate. The results are predictable. The everyday operational necessity to the organization to engage in the very business processes undergoing offshoring dictate the same kind of handoff from customer to service provider, even if it is done at a velocity lower than top speed. Luckily for ON Semiconductor, it did not need to concern itself with labor force decommissioning issues facing many companies because the domestic team handling these business processes already belonged to a service provider. It was the job of ACS to determine the right balance between the draw down of the domestic application maintenance work team and the ramp-up of the offshore workforce. The company could have decided to construct a transition in which all activities from knowledge transfer to readiness for full offshore support received one deadline date for total handoff of responsibilities and the next day represented full green light offshore operation but this approach would have been impractical and impossible given the totality of the preparatory work involved to equip the service provider to do the job it expected. This is why the relay race baton handoff conceptualization is highly applicable to offshoring transition planning.

Driving Transition Planning: Knowledge Transfer

Answering the questions in the following two grids teases out the rough outline for a transition plan.

Driving Transition Planning: Knowledge Transfer	
Issue Category: Knowledge Transfer	**Action Item**
How extensive is the required knowledge transfer to the offshore service provider for it to gain mastery of the work to be performed?	Knowledge transfer intensity is influenced by: • Uniqueness of the business processes offshored—ON Semiconductor offshored custom applications requiring a high level of knowledge transfer. • Service provider familiarity with these processes—are they managing them now? • Service provider workforce quality—best measured by track record of successful management for other customers • IT sits under *all* business process offshoring, is workforce competent in company's choice of platform?
How is knowledge transfer targeted?	• Train the trainer: gatekeeper approach in which service provider leads replicate know how to staff. • Direct to team: higher mastery levels but low scalability.
What forms will knowledge transfer take? Binders, CDs, books, tapes, RealAudio feeds, in-class instruction	• Forms influenced by: • Process complexity—more mentoring, less self-directed training as complexity increases. • Process maturity—less mature, usually less complete documentation • Availability—is process documentation complete, up to date? How about IT documentation? If IT is headed overseas with processes how complete is the platform knowledge base? • Quality—depth and breadth of material in clear English prose. • Timetables: mentoring, low teacher-to-student ratios is high impact but time-consuming and less scalable.

Driving Transition Planning: Validating Knowledge Transfer	
Issue Category: Validation of Knowledge Transfer and Competency	**Action Item**
How will the organization certify service provider mastery of business processes?	• Pilot project—effective way to certify but will organization get the same service provider workers when full offshoring begins? • Third-party training and testing—does it teach to a test only or provide problem-solving skills testing? • In-house testing. If testing is the process by which quality and readiness are determined, is the organization confident of its predictive value? HR training track record over five years is a good barometer. ON Semiconductor was very confident of internal testing regime's predictive value.
How will organization gauge time to competency needed as transition plan is constructed?	• Companies with deep in-house training expertise won't have a problem answering this. Smaller companies might. • Consider prioritizing—more complex processes taught first, builds cushion if timetable deviates.
How is competency defined?	• Establish score that defines a passing grade. • Establish total percentage of workers company wants to see pass on first attempt—ON Semiconductor achieved 80% pass rate. • Remedial plan—everyone gets a second chance. • Don't obsess subjective scoring—seasoned in-house SMEs are good judges of whether offshore workers have mastered the problem-solving skills not easily quantified in a test score.
How are knowledge transfer and competency validation timetables arrived at?	While knowledge transfer and validation are discrete activities, managers can begin to measure the time involvement by starting with an end game date (by what date does the organization want transfer and certification completed by?), then work backward. Arriving at timetables can be achieved by: • Company history—what does internal training experience say? • Benchmark data—hire training firms to answer one question: How long on average does it take to train and test workers on these business processes? • Vendor—What has it observed? Ask to confer with other customers. Knowledge transfer is too important for the contract start date to dictate its deadline. Knowledge transfer drives contract start—not the other way around.

TRANSITION COSTS DESTROY VALUE PROPOSITIONS

When transition costs are introduced into a financial model the organization will discover, in certain contexts, that offshoring is simply not worth it. Mercer Human Resources Consulting walked a European consumer goods company through a cost benefit analysis in 2004, where this very determination was made.[2]

Bottom-line focused entering the offshoring debate, the company explored the idea of consolidating a number of offices across the globe into one operational center across HR, finance as well as marketing and sales functions—marketing campaigns, channel and brand management—in order to capture some savings by eliminating operational redundancies. A number of captive locations in North America including Canada, Mexico, and even the United States were considered; the company operated in very high-cost U.S. locations and the idea here was perhaps a relocation into a lower-cost U.S. location would prove attractive. Approximately 500 positions were targeted for offshoring, 80% of which consisted of pure labor arbitrage and worker replacement, while 100 positions consisted of employees the company would make offers to relocate. The captive offshoring move presented an approximate 16% cost savings and many millions of dollars—before transition costs.

After the company factored in transition costs, break even pushed out to several years beyond operational steady state. Suddenly the offshoring move looked far less attractive, particularly when in fast-moving business environments it is difficult to predict what kind of economic climate the company would find itself in at that breakeven point. Even a couple of years can represent an eternity in dynamic markets. In helping the company model some of the cost implications from the initiative, Mercer showed the company that a high likelihood existed that most of the percentage of the workforce that it planned to offer relocation—20% out of the 500 would leave the company. Several elements were at play. One, the economy. Mercer found that this subpopulation of the total targeted offshoring workforce would not have difficultly finding new positions near their existing place of employment. Given its expertise in workforce issues, Mercer also demonstrated that other drivers would likely influence the low mobility rate of this worker population, including their age (the older, the less mobile), whether they had school-age children, and whether the employee had civic ties to the community (active in church, rotary, Kiwanis, and the like).

Not only did this possibility represent a real human capital loss of experiential knowledge, as difficult as it is to quantify in hard dollar terms, but the company would also face the cost and time required for new recruitment while keeping the executives targeted for replacement on the payroll during the transition to ensure continuity and a minimal disruption to retailer relationships. During the transition, there could exist no vacancy gap in the jobs of the population of executives who turned down a relocation offer and who were scheduled to leave the company, given their importance to operations and customer relationships. Once the company reached steady state, the costs ramp up again in the form of severance for the departing executives, a total amount exacerbated by the relatively high position and salary that many of this workforce population fetched. Then Mercer introduced into the discussion the possibility, however small, of retailer relationships disruptions during the transition. Whose idea was this anyway? All in all, costs ballooned and the early savings numbers looked meager upon reflection. The offshoring idea was scrapped.

A company can recover from most transitions executed badly—as long as money is no object. The transition phase is not a make-or-break proposition operationally, since most organizations can, with enough effort, right a ship that is listing, but much more a make-or-break proposition financially. If cost reductions are central to the offshoring value proposition, an organization must have visibility before the transition phase into all the business levers at work that can affect those early rosy estimates when the transition is actually executed. Offshoring easily breaks up on the rocks of incomplete and ill-considered transition planning.

PERFORMANCE TRACKING AND VALUE AUDITING

Tracking vendor service level performance was covered in detail during the discussion of service level agreements (SLAs) in Chapter 10, but it is in this phase of the Offshoring Value Delivery Framework^{TM} where this work is actually conducted. Performance tracking is joined by a sister management principle in this phase: value auditing. Auditing for value simply means that the organization will investigate whether the cost reductions and/or revenue enhancements suggested in an offshoring business case have actually been captured. This kind of audit requires little if any operational assistance from the service provider. The value audit is a project conducted in-house, and most of the relevant information that comes from the service provider has been reported out through the SLA process and through invoices.

Argument for a Value Audit

The roots of value audits come from information technology management. The poor financial showing of so much IT over the years caught the attention of senior management and particularly the CFO, all of whom sought to inject more discipline in both IT capital investment making and the exploitation of that technology. A minority of companies realized that an important activity in the search for value creation was the idea of validating whether the rosy scenarios that decorated the evangelization of proposed technology initiatives were even remotely accurate. One of the most pronounced assumptions in IT management practices today is that the cost savings or revenue-enhancing returns forecasted in a return on investment (ROI) exercise will materialize on schedule or at some point. How else to reconcile the fact that most organizations do not bother to validate the forecast at some point after deployment to determine whether impacts meet plan? However, much effort is invested in constructing an economic model as a decision-making tool that becomes so much clutter taking up hard drive space.

Of course, the other reason value audits are conducted by a minority of IT organizations is the fear, uncertainty, and doubt about the ramifications should the real-world impacts fall below forecast. No one enjoys evaluations, especially when the outcomes are less than expected, and those who are in a position of accountability—the project champions, those who control the budget—fear reprisal from a project gone bad.

But if organizations are going to invest the resources and effort in offshoring, they should be encouraged to operationalize a consistent, repeatable post-offshoring investment value audit capability. A value audit is useful because it answers such questions as: what costs emerged that were unanticipated? Why were the expenditures required? Did any additional unforeseen benefits emerge? A value audit also has larger, more strategic benefits. If you accept the lofty principle that one of the most powerful drivers of enterprise performance is capacity of employees to learn and turn the learning process into improvements in their work, audits are an effective component of offshoring management for this reason. The benefits do not accrete from simply confirming that the offshoring returns match or exceed forecast but from management improvements undertaken by virtue of an understanding of what mistakes were made and how the organization can learn from them. All this toward better offshoring management. Even the simplest of offshoring initiatives like a single application development project deserves a value audit, which might be as basic as summarizing financial performance and impacts in a Word document. It is the act of asking what the organization captured by virtue of offshoring in a formal, documented, systematized way that is important here. Building a culture of self-awareness and improvement is an important component if the organization regards offshoring as potentially strategic.

The good news is that unlike IT value audits, offshoring value audits are probably easier to conduct. Some of the benefits of enterprise software are diffuse, causally indirect and hard to measure. An offshoring value audit provides a clearer measurement path because much of the cost/benefit impact in rolled up in what the service provider delivers. Understanding the points of value in software might require identifying numerous systems from which data can be pulled for metrics calculation purposes. The service provider assumes the responsibility for resource allocation decisions that bear on whether some metric was achieved or not. In this way, the benefits from an offshoring initiative are more contained—either the service provider cut our costs or brought in revenue or it did not. For this reason some organizations might argue there is little need for a value audit because the value is clear to the organization.

But again, this misses the point of the value audit function. While in IT the purpose of a value audit might be the discovery and validation of value, the purpose of an offshoring audit are these, in addition to providing a deeper understanding of the management decisions that bear on value creation. How effective is the organization's service level management? If the offshoring is captive, how effective is recruitment and retention at our in-country location?

For organizations who see the value in the concept of a value audit a basic work breakdown structure is provided in Exhibit 12.2, as guidance to building a project-oriented audit capability.

Some high-level considerations in operationalizing an offshoring value audit function are:

- Design the audit around a handful of important metrics rather than get bogged down in hair pulling over impacts that are less significant. In many offshoring initiatives, the bulk of the value is found in a few select benefits. By virtue of conducting an audit, it is possible that other economic drivers will be unearthed. When this occurs a decision can be made whether to pursue further investigation of that newly discovered performance indicator.

- Build consistent criteria threshold: decide on a dollar figure above which an audit kicks in as well as the extent of the business impacts

1 - Plan The Audit		2 - Conduct the Audit		3 - Analyze, Report Audit Results	
		Work Breakdown Structure for Each Milestone			
Tasks	Finish √	Tasks	Finish √	Tasks	Finish √
Put together audit team		Pull relevant data into offshoring mgmt platform (if available)		Conduct status meeting after data collection is completed	
Assign specific KPIS to team members		Calculate results against economic value forecast		Review each team member's data collection for completeness and accuracy	
Identify data sources for each key performance indicator		Monitor team progress at specific scheduled points throughout audit		Review own data collection for completeness and accuracy	
Confirm existence of reporting capability to generate data		Sign off on team data collection before closing audit		Investigate why results exceed, fall short of forecast	
Establish data collection deadlines for each team member				Populate results interpretations into offshoring MGMT platform	
Establish timetable to verify audit progress				Prepare final audit findings report	
Launch kick off meeting with audit team – review audit plan				Present audit findings to senior management	
Get buy in from it/is to assign an audit liaison for technical support around data collection				Prepare remedial action plan based on sr MGT input – get signoff	
				Reaudit at future date	

EXHIBIT 12.2 OFFSHORING VALUE AUDIT WORK PLAN OVERVIEW

218

that would necessitate such an exercise. A simple application development project might dictate the documentation of value in a simple summary. A complex, multicountry migration of finance or HR would warrant a far more rigorous investigation of value.

- When the results are in, what will be done with the information? Know what you are going to do with the results before embarking on a value audit. Is the audit a continuous learning and process improvement vehicle, a means by which offshoring management owners earn bonus compensation? Both? Will the results become an element in someone's personnel file, whether good or bad? The purpose of an audit is to validate offshoring economic forecast against real-world results but the existence of measurable results can create a cauldron of political intrigue unless management knows exactly how they are going to act upon the results before the audit is conducted.

- Who owns and is responsible for the audit? The unit whose processes are being offshored? The finance department? A value audit is an interdepartmental and interdisciplinary exercise, but someone is ultimately responsible for the audit function and its funding.

GOVERNANCE

In Phase 1 you saw how offshoring decision-making governance might look. How would ongoing service provider governance work? Exhibit 12.3 offers one perspective.

A number of challenges emerge in making an offshoring relationship work, not the least of which is adjusting to the large time zone difference in which the service provider is off-duty when the customer is going through its work day, and vice versa. Cultural differences manifest themselves too. In India, when someone says "yes" this does not mean he or she either agrees with you or will follow through on a request but rather that what you are saying is understood. This is certainly an improvement over Japan where yes can mean no. U.S. managers must also adjust to foreign accents, which can be quite exotic and difficult to understand.

Governance Plan

It's a good idea for the organization to build a governance plan before the ongoing relationship is launched full time. The plan could describe and visualize the organizational governance model the company is adopting,

Strategic	Tactical	Just-in-Time
Executive Committee	Offshoring Management Office	Offshoring Management Office + operational people
Responsibilities	Responsibilities	Responsibilities
Sets vision and strategic direction	Oversees all facets of the Offshoring Value Delivery Framework:	Just-in-Time governance describes those day-to-day activities that make the offshoring relationship function. This includes such things as conference call coordination, tracking down ongoing information needs and generally ensuring the smooth operation of the offshoring relationship. Coordinating meetings can be painful drudgery, but the work is essential: scheduling times, who is on the call, confirming agendas, who kicks-off the meeting and who needs to attend
Articulates mission and charter	**Phase 1**	
	Works with project sponsor— business case development	
Authorizes & architects budgeting—who pays for what	**Phase 2**	
	Supports, consults in selection process	
Outlines operational responsibilities across the enterprise—HR, finance, legal, IT, etc.	Constructs, collects analyzes RFPs	
	Coordinates all due diligence	
	Drives management to selection decision	
	Phase 3	
	Coordinates pilot where applicable	
	Supports contracting	
	Validates vendor security	
	Phase 4	
	Oversees transition	
	Supports/conducts performance tracking and value audit	

EXHIBIT 12.3 OFFSHORE GOVERNANCE AND MANAGEMENT ARCHITECTURE

such as the one above. The plan would identify budgets and the key personnel responsible for the various governance activities the model comprises as well as describe the activities and their schedules. A description of activities needs to include those that are contractual obligations, such as weekly conference calls at a specified time between customer and service provider management. All governance activities that are contractually binding need to be flagged in the plan so that all involved understand the relationship's mutual obligations. This awareness also makes it easier to document those occasions when obligations were missed. Those become discussion "mights" with senior management at review time. In documenting any governance problems, the governance plan is the vehicle for suggestions on how the relationship can be improved.

Continuity Plan

In the context of overall relationship governance, an organization should have in place a business continuity plan specific to offshoring initiatives before one is launched. A business continuity plan is a risk mitigation and preparedness tool that attempts to minimize disruption to daily business operations should a disaster strike. Disasters could include tsunamis, earthquakes, a political coup, or the most likely scenario, an extended power outage. We saw in Phase 2 of the Offshoring Value Delivery Framework that some companies have the option to include these risks in an offshoring location assessment because none of these scenarios, however remote, are impossible in many service provider countries. Discontinuity risks, moreover, are not just confined to natural disasters. One unthinkable risk is that your service provider suddenly goes out of business.

The continuity plan should include a probability risk assessment of the likelihood of occurrence for each identified disruption event, the scope and type of business discontinuity that such a disruption could cause, the impact risks—lost revenue, regulatory noncompliance, dissatisfied customers, supplier disruptions—and a description of business process workarounds that would keep business operations going during the disruption. The continuity plan must also include a description of tactical responses should a disaster materialize. Include the names of key service provider personnel who would be contacted (it is likely their names appear in either/or an SLA or the contract) as well as organization personnel and their responsibilities and roles during the disaster. Finally, the organization might also want to include a statement acknowledging the adequacy and completeness of insurance coverage that would protect it from losses continuity planning confronts.

FINAL THOUGHTS ON THE OFFSHORING VALUE DELIVERY FRAMEWORK

A structured approach to offshoring cannot guarantee success, but if its tenets are followed it can minimize the risk of failure. The Offshoring Value Delivery Framework provides a methodical and methodological roadmap for executing any offshoring initiative from the simplest application development project to the most sophisticated strategic, intellectual-property-producing joint venture relationship. One of the most powerful attributes of any systematic framework is its repeatability. As organizations ramp up an ever-increasing number of offshoring projects across all business functions, loyalty to a framework that has proven effective cultivates organically a collective organizational competency for offshoring, while building a library of tactics that can be mined and reused in support of executing off-shoring strategy. Loyalty to certain work methods also acknowledges implicitly that employees have trust in the framework, a belief that it will help them in their everyday work. Employee buy-in is essential if management is to work at all.

CHAPTER TAKEAWAY

Some key concepts to leave this chapter with:

- Beware of transition hell, a place into which the organization is consigned when little planning is devoted to that time when the business processes are moved into the vendor organization. This destination is characterized by blown deadlines, cost overruns, finger pointing between the company and vendor—and the relationship hasn't even started yet.

- An audit that validates and confirms that value from the relationship has been created is as important as the organization wants to make it. They take time, effort, and planning. Organizations that decide audits are worth it are in a position to elevate organizational performance and their offshoring IQ from the collective learning experience the act of auditing provides. Documenting this learning through audits provides the basis for organizational improvements.

- Think about ongoing governance in terms of strategic, tactical, and day-to-day responsibilities for managing the offshoring relationship. Delineating responsibilities this way clarifies who should have what decision authority and what job at any given time. It is also the basis for how governance can be designed if organizations are just getting started with offshoring and its management challenges.

- Continuity planning is an important component of overall offshoring management. Although a conscious decision was made to place this activity in the context of relationship management, it is really a risk mitigation and contingency tool. No matter its context, an organization should think deeply about those events that would create serious business disruption with a service provider and have some contingency plan in place were such a disruption to occur.

NOTES

1. ON Semiconductor offshoring story was told by CIO David Wagner in a number of interviews in March 2005. Individual footnotes are too numerous to document. Wagner vetted all references to ON Semiconductor in the name of ensuring the accuracy of the information provided in this text.
2. Interview with Jay Doherty of Mercer Human Resources Consulting, April 5, 2005.

13

CALLING ALL LOW-COST REPS

The Offshoring Value Delivery Framework is just as relevant in choosing the right contact center service provider as any other service provider to manage a set of business processes. Vendor and site selection, contracting, service level agreements, security, and ongoing governance are all critical issues in managing a vendor relationship that will deliver measurable value over and above existing domestic contact center operations at a comparable quality level.

As it happens, the existing literature in contact center strategy is wide and deep. Hundreds of texts exist that attempt to point the way to success in all facets of contact center operation in both in-house and outsourcing contexts. The key to contact center offshoring success is to join the principles of the Offshoring Value Delivery Framework with the collective knowledge and expertise around contact center management reflecting the accumulated result of years of trial and error in operating them. Taken together, the organization possesses a solid foundation for offshore contact center initiatives. Therefore, a repeat of the available literature in the hows and whys of outsourcing this function would be both redundant and beyond the scope of this text. Rather, the purpose of this chapter is to highlight any important differences that distinguish outsourcing contact center functions from offshoring these functions. What are the important strategic and operational differences facing organizations in moving contact center operations from an existing U.S. or other North American location to a low-cost offshoring country such as India, differences that could serve as a baseline for understanding the implications in moving this activity from a domestic location to one overseas? Because contact center business processes represent one of the most popular and visible offshoring activities, this subject deserves its own chapter.

Several subjects specific to contact centers that can enlighten managers in decision making covered in this chapter are: India's operational advantages over the United States, comparing and contrasting key performance indicator (KPI) results from offshore locations with a company's internal numbers, and differences in capital intensity between offshoring and domestic contact center operations. Comparing and contrasting domestic contact center experience within these subject areas should help organizations answer key questions about the value creation of offshoring contact center operations. But before we dive into these issues, it is worth discussing the conflicting attitudes of organizations toward contact centers as a necessary business operation, attitudes which reveal why these business processes are such a popular offshoring target.

MIXED ATTITUDES ABOUT CONTACT CENTERS

The subject of contact centers brings out the schizophrenia in corporations. This single activity is arguably one of the most important functions a company conducts because it is often the only point of direct contact which a customer will ever have. The collective contact center experiences a customer commits to memory can affect, over time, the customer's attitudes about the organization and her willingness to sustain the relationship with repeat business. This is particularly true in our new commercial universe of online buying where contact center communication is not only perceived as critical but the only viable choice the customer has to speak to the company she patronizes (notwithstanding email, but more on this in a minute). Yet many organizations, through failure or a failure to try, have not turned the contact center into a "profit center" of any kind, either in the cold verdict of a profit and loss statement or in the judgments of C-level executives who might otherwise believe in the ultimate value of a well-run in-house contact center operation and would argue for a sustained financial commitment to it, even though a real profit might never materialize.

Some companies deserve at least some credit for trying. A profit-centric contact center generally involves outbound calls where the company believes that it can prevent a loss in revenue or generate additional revenue. It decides to set up an outbound contact center operation for the express purpose of preventing churn where predictive models tell them a customer defection is likely by calling on this vulnerable customer segment. Another scenario has contact center reps reaching out to a customer segment by pitching additional products or services after a relationship has been established. If you bought our widgets, you are going to love our gadgets! Despite high hopes and the commitment of management, the return on investment needed to justify the additional expenditures in labor and training to generate incremental revenue never materializes for many organizations. This situation is not helped by the fact that many Americans have declared that the telephone is an irrelevant and ill-suited sales channel. A ridiculous number of Americans signed up for inclusion on the federal do-not-call list *on the first day.* And so midnight strikes and the contact center turns into a pumpkin again.

It is fair to say that companies who could make money on contact centers beyond the fully loaded investment to operate them would be less inclined to consider offshoring because this business activity would drive profitability not simply incur costs. But profit has proven a hard nut to crack. In one study, actually, it was found that about 35% of companies surveyed would never outsource customer service calls.[1] But this decision is not necessarily because the contact center is a source of revenue. There are some managers who actually believe that contact centers are mission critical, a core competency and worth spending the time and money on to perfect procedures and workflows that make them world class—whether the contact center explicitly makes money or not. Yet this leaves 65% of companies who would at least consider offshoring and, in many if not most cases, offshoring is an option precisely because companies wish to get the costs to operate them under control. Depending on whom you talk to, the fully burdened hourly labor rate per seat in the contact center runs $40 to $70 an hour. For example, say a company operates 100 seats total. A company operating a 12-hour-a-day, 5-day-a-week contact center faces an annual cost upward of $22 million. To be fair there are several other reasons why the contact center function is a good candidate for offshoring, which will be explored shortly. But cost considerations are what makes the mare run, particularly in this business process domain.

Technology has attempted to lighten the financial load but with mixed results. Website self-service, email, and live web chat were eagerly anticipated by organizations as tools to serve as a customer service proxy for the contact center; get people to adopt these alternative channels of interaction and watch contact center resource needs, and therefore costs, decline. Certainly the rise of e-commerce self-service has been a hit with customers. Instead of waiting 20 minutes on the phone to place an order, customers dive into website pages to buy what they want when they want it and get out fast. Some retailers have become very adept at keeping customers apprised of their orders through customized page updates or e-mail. The more effective the Internet environment, the fewer the calls to a contact center. Although my personal experience can hardly be considered representative of the entire online buying population, I have bought a considerable dollar volume of books and gear at Amazon and have, in the past five years, been compelled to pick up the phone and call its contact center exactly one time.

These new technologies have hardly proven a panacea to total contact center cost reductions, however. Websites can be unwieldy. Ever try wading through pages on pages of information only to not find what you are looking for? For example, try resolving any technical issue using the "knowledge base" at Microsoft's elephantine website Email can be just as ineffectual because it often lacks the immediacy that customers expect in resolving some problem; it only took four days to get an email response to a billing question this time as opposed to last time when your email got lost in the blackhole of some Exchange mail server never to meet the eyes of a customer service rep at all. And web chat, with its dependence on typing, is often too rigid a communication medium. Rep and customer talk past each other as both busily clack away on keyboards attempting to resolve a complicated customer issue that is better left to a live telephone exchange.

For many organizations these tools have been consigned to goals around customer satisfaction; they aren't expected to move customers off contact center interactions but are, rather, simply an expansion of choice as to what means and which channel they would like to use in talking to the organization. That these alternative channels haven't delivered structural contact center cost reductions for many organizations just heightens management's desire to look for cost reductions in other ways and offshoring may be the answer. This is certainly the perception. Only time and extensive empirical data will tell managers if these cost reductions are substantial, permanent, and pose no risk to quality. For many organizations the verdict is in. They simply cannot forklift the contact center fast enough out of the organization, and contact center offshoring specialists are ready to oblige. They have made a nice business out of taking the burden off the hands of the client, who writes a monthly check to these service providers and is done with it. No one should be surprised that the interest in contact center offshoring is red hot and will continue to be so. The picture painted here might be slightly bleaker than reality for some companies but not much. A contact center is a cost center for many organizations, and off-shoring this function offers eye popping savings, since 50 to 80% of a contact center's budget consists of labor,[2] and contact center labor can be had much more cheaply overseas.

It's Not Just About Money: Other Reasons to Offshore

There are other reasons beyond just cost why companies are offshoring contact center operations today. Many revolve around capacity issues. Retailers and catalogue houses see a big call spike at Christmas and need additional inbound contact center capacity to handle order taking and fulfillment. So do electronics retailers, who see a substantial inbound call increase after people receive obscenely complicated DVD players and reach out for help. Instead of assuming the fixed costs of adding this capacity year-round, companies wisely choose to handle additional capacity as the variable cost it is—a cost tied to sales. Technology firms might add additional tech support capacity after a new product release or software upgrade.[3] In every case, companies increasingly procure these contact center/tech support services from third parties in realization of Ronald Coase's vision. Search and information costs are relatively low, negotiation and bargaining costs are low, and the entire short-term relationship can be managed at arm's length just as Coase argued, across town or across a continent.

A longer-term commitment to increased contact center capacity can revolve around growth in the size of the organization through acquisition—when a company buys another company, it is buying the acquired organization's customers too. Some companies with a global footprint are also attracted to contact center offshoring because it offers a "follow-the-sun" capability to support functions; when one target population is sleeping another is awakening. The ability to offer 24 by 7 contact center availability through the placement of operations across multiple time zones has a lot of appeal, since companies can align contact center availability with the normal business hours of any geographic location. Still other companies will add offshore inbound or outbound contact center capacity to address new markets defined by geography, ethnic background, or language. In Chapter 1 you saw how one service provider, anticipating growing demand for offshore contact center services from companies attempting to communicate with the huge population of Spanish-speaking Americans, invested in an offshore contact center in Tijuana. A combination of capacity coordination, geographic availability, market and demographic need, relative ease of deployment, and cost make offshoring contact center functions a compelling proposition for any company not attitudinally fixed to a belief that contact center operation is so strategic that it could not possibly be left to the management of strangers. Since the population of companies who would at least consider offshoring, if not doing so already, is considerably larger than the population of those that would not, this is another justification for contact centers receiving their own chapter.

Focus on India

As seen in previous chapters, India represents the perfect economic storm that attracts offshoring activity. Labor cost are very low, contact center workforce quality is high because it is educated and English-speaking, the country offers a reasonably stable business environment and rapidly declining telecom costs, and the government is committed to creating a social and economic environment that will continue to attract future offshoring investment.

Into this confluence of country-specific conditions are a couple of additional supply-and-demand economic realities that should keep India at the top of the list of go-to contact center locations. In the estimation of Cincom iOutsource Systems, a diversified business process offshoring, application management, and contact center services company with a presence across the globe, there exists a capacity gap between the number of domestic workers participating in the U.S. contact center industry and what the industry needs. Approximately 7 million people work in the domestic contact center industry when the need is for an additional 700,000 workers, creating a capacity gap of 10%.[4] The gap, of course, could be filled quite quickly. All domestic companies need do is announce positions on an Internet job board promising wages of $20 plus an hour. They would find themselves inundated with well-spoken, quick thinking, and more highly educated people than those who commonly work in the call centers today. This is unlikely to occur, since companies pay contact center workers roughly about half that in the name of cost containment; U.S. companies have proven very resistant to investment commitments that would significantly raise the wages of its workers because of the operational cost implications. If they did, the capacity gap might vanish. Consequently, India is the place that many domestic companies will turn to in meeting domestic contact center labor supply needs at a fraction of the cost; India is expected to help fill the capacity gap.

Cincom iOutsource also contends that Indian contact center workers enjoy a 30% capability premium versus their U.S. counterparts. In almost every performance metric category that quantifies this 30% performance

gap—and the contact center industry has a wide range of performance metrics, as any manager involved in its operation will tell you—Indian workers
come out ahead of their domestic counterparts because the majority of
folks working in the industry have college-level educations. One example
that manifests this capability differential: Cincom iOutsource says it requires
agents to achieve 98% scoring in speaking and listening comprehension, a
measure of how well they communicate to callers as well as how well they
understand customer problems and needs.[5] Testing is conducted by third
parties. This same score hovers around 85% for domestic contact center
workers. U.S. companies can secure contact center workers from India that
are more capable yet fetch a far smaller wage than their U.S. counterparts.
Comparable or better quality at lower prices.

Costs are so low for some organizations in India that by virtue of offshoring there they can reshuffle operating expenditures and not only cut
contact center costs but actually increase profitability around their business and perhaps gain a competitive advantage. In some instances a few
companies have transformed cost-centric contact centers into money-making
centers—a goal not achieved in the United States—by virtue of the cost
savings from offshoring. Ashish Paul, CEO of Cincom iOutsource's global outsourcing services, cites one debt collection customer who deployed
a team of approximately 100 U.S. lawyers to handle legal filings against
debtors, while a contact center of about 50 reps conducted skip-tracing
activities to track down the debtors' whereabouts. The company offshored
both the legal help and skip-tracing operations to India. Instead of 100
lawyers, the collection company now employs four U.S. attorneys who
work directly in the U.S. legal system. The remaining legal staff is based
in India. These attorneys prepare legal documents and much of the intellectual contents that compose the cases against debtors. Offshoring the
legal help resulted in immense savings, some of which the company
plowed into a hefty contact center ramp-up from the original 50 reps to
500. A factor of 10 increase in contact center labor conducting skip trac-
ings has resulted in a measurably greater debt collection success rate,
because as a result of drastically increased manpower the company can
track down a far greater population of debtors.[6] Multiple offshoring
opportunities allowed one organization to reallocate operational resources
in such a way as to increase the intensity of contact center activity and
improve its profitability directly by doing so.

Paul also asserts that India offers another differentiating point of value
that can't be matched by most other offshoring locations. Indian college

graduates view a job in a contact center as an introduction to a career. They seek to advance from agent, to supervisor, to manager. For most reps in the United States, a low-paying contact center job is a stop gap to other aspirations. Domestic contact center workers are college students earning extra money, housewives motivated by the same goal, laid-off professionals in transition to a new gig, the self-employed sweating out a revenue drop until new projects arrive; all of these are versions of the actor-waiting-tables cliché. Because Indian reps look at their first contact center job as a career opportunity, the intellectual capital specific to the industry and the industries of the customers they serve is nurtured and contained. Accumulating experiential knowledge about handling customer calls effectively grows with experience while remaining contained within the country's borders, because a dedicated population of employees remains and advances within the industry. Contact center reps might leave one service provider for another, but at a macro level, a large reservoir of contact center expertise is being built in India. Paul believes this ever-increasing experiential knowledge in multiple business process domains will prove a differentiator from other offshoring candidate countries as well as an attraction to organizations in search of not only contact center operational competence, but industry-specific expertise inbound and outbound activities. India's compelling offshoring value proposition and popularity as a contact center destination is the reason why the chapter's focus is directed here.

Understanding the Offshoring Performance Differentials

Because cost animates the contact center offshoring discussion like no other consideration, it stands to reason that organizations would want to compare their domestic cost experience with that in India. Investigating the cost differentials in specific operational areas provides managers a clean slate to understanding in fairly granular detail what those operational costs will actually look like were they to offshore domestic operations.

Managers might also like to understand the potential greater productivity of foreign contact center workers versus their domestic counterparts. Exhibit 13.1 breaks down key performance indicators important to the contact center industry across a number of important operational categories, mostly with a cost orientation. Benchmark Portal provided the metrics and Cincom iOutsource provided its specific results for contact center operations in India. One note: the information in the exhibit assumes at least a working knowledge of contact center performance metrics and their calculations. Although highly

Contact Center KPIs for India:	One Vendor's Experience			Remarks
AGENT PRODUCTIVITY				
Replacement Costs (% of Total Personnel Cost)	Total Personnel Cost, Agent Personnel Cost			(Total Personnel Cost – Agent Personnel Cost) × 100/total Costs)
	$2,443,233	$1,363,636		**17.79%**
Cost per Agent Hour	Total Costs, Agent Hours			Total Costs/Agent Hours
	6068271.111	720000		**$8.43**
Agent Productivity	Net Agent Hours, Average Percent Occupancy, Total Agent Paid Hours[a]			(Net Agent Hours × Average Percent Occupancy)/Total Agent Paid Hours
	630000	87.50%[b]	720000	**77%**
Excess Staffing	Excess Call Handling Capacity, Net Individual Agent Capacity, Total Agents[c]			(Excess Call Handling Capacity × 85%)/(Net Individual Agent Capacity × 90%/Total Agents
	2880	40320[d]	250	**16.87%**
ASSET MANAGEMENT				
% Availability	Total Reserved Stations, Total Station Capacity			(Total Stations – Total Reserved Stations)/Total Stations
	250	300		**16.67%**
Workstation Area	Cubicle Size (Length & Width)			Cubicle Length × Cubicle Width
	6ft	4ft		**24 Sq Ft**
Workstation Area Including Office Space	Total workstation Capacity, Total Call Center Area			Total Call Center Area/Total Station Capacity
	300	30000		**100 sq ft**
Workstation Density per 1000 Sq Feet	Workstation Space including Common space			1000 Sq Feet/Workstation Area (including common space)
	100 sq ft			**10**

EXHIBIT 13.1 CONTACT CENTER KPIs FOR INDIA: ONE VENDOR'S EXPERIENCE

Contact Center KPIs for India:	One Vendor's	Experience			Remarks	
Ratio of Workstations to Total Space	Workstation Area, Total Call Center Area[e]	7200	30000		Workstation Area/Total Call Center Area	**0.24**
RETENTION						
Turnover Rate (Annualize)	Annual Turnover (less promotion and transfers) from human resources[f]	120			Annual Turnover	129
New Hire Costs	Annual Turnover, Cost of New Hire Training per Hour, Length of Training in Hours[g]	129	$2.49[h]	154	Annual Turnover × Cost of New Hire Training per Hour × Length of Training in Hours	**$49,422.93**
COST RATIOS						
Cost per Production Station	Net Cost, # Production Stations	6068271.111	250		Net Cost/Production Stations	**24273.08[i]**
Cost per Talk Minute	Net Cost, Talk Hours[j]	6068271.111	535500		Net Cost/(Talk Hours/60)	**$0.189**
Cost per 60 Minute Paid Hour	Total Cost, Call-Handling Capacity[k]	6068271.111	10080000		Total Cost/Call Handling Capacity	**$0.602**
Cost per Paid Agent Hour	Total Cost, Total FTEs, Net Individual Agent Capacity[l]	6068271.111	341	40320	Total Cost/(Total Agents × Net Individual Agent Capacity)	**$0.441**
Cost per Call	Net Costs, Call Handling Capacity, Calls Handled per Hour per Agent[m]	6068271.111	10080000	16[n]	(Total Cost/Call Handling Capacity)/Calls Handled per Hour per Agent	**$0.038**

EXHIBIT 13.1 CONTACT CENTER KPIS FOR INDIA: ONE VENDOR'S EXPERIENCE *(CONTINUED)*

Contact Center KPIs for India:	One Vendor's Experience			Remarks	
Direct Labor	Direct Labor Expense, Total Costs			Direct Labours Expense/Total Costs	
	2443233	6068271.111			**0.403**
DIRECT TELECOM Telecom Rate per Minute	Telecom Rate, Minutes of Call Time Recorded by ACD Annually[o]			Telecom Rate/ Minutes of Call Time Recorded by ACD Annually	
	1080000	494424000			**0.002[P]**
Total Telecom Cost per Minute	Total Direct Telecom Cost, Total Annual Minutes from ACD[q]			Total Direct Telecom Cost/# Annual Minutes from ACD	
	1346666.666	494424000			**$0.003**
Total Telecom Cost per hour	Net Cost/Hours per Year[r]			Total Direct Telecom Cost/(# of Annual Minutes from ACD × 60)	
	1346666.666	8240400			**$0.163**
Service Level	Calls handled, Calls Offered, Busy Calls[s]			Calls Handled/(Calls Offered – Busy Calls)	
	10080000	10281600	100800		**99.01%**
Average Length of Calls (min.)	Talk Time, After-Call Work Time[t]			Talk Time + After Call Work Time	
	3	0.225[u]			**3.225**
Calls Handled per Calls Offered	Calls Handled, Calls Offered			Calls Handled/Calls Offered	
	10080000	10281600			**98.04%**
Total Call-Handling Capacity	Net Individual Agent Capacity, Total FTE			Net Individual Agent Capacity × Total FTE	
	0	341			**0**

Exhibit 13.1 Contact Center KPIs for India: One Vendor's Experience *(continued)*

Contact Center KPIs for India:	One Vendor's Experience			Remarks
Extra Call-Handling capacity Required	Total Call-Handling Capacity, Required Call-Handling Capacity			Total Call-Handling Capacity – Required Call-Handling Capacity
	0	0		**0**
OTHER RATIOS				
Net Individual Agent Capacity	Net Agent Hours, Calls Handled per Hour, No. of Days per Annum			Net Agent Hours × Calls Handled per Hour × No. of Days per Annum
	7	16	360	**40320**
Manned Hours per Paid Hours	Manned Hours, Paid Production Hours (Excluding Paid Leave)			Manned Hours/ Paid Production Hours (Excluding Paid Leave)
	8	7		**1.14**
Talk Hours per Paid Hours	Talk Time, Paid Production hours (excluding leave)			Talk Time/Paid Production Hours (excluding leave)
	5.6	7		**0.80**
Agent Occupancy	Work Time, Manned hours			Work Time in Hours/Manned Hours
	7	8		**0.88**
Expected Occupancy	Call-Handling Capacity Required, Total Call-Handling Capacity			Call-Handling Capacity Required/Total Call-Handling Capacity
	0	0		**#DIV/01**
Error Rates	Entry Errors, Total Calls Handled[v]			Entry Errors/Total Calls Handled
	4000	10080000		**0.04%**

EXHIBIT 13.1 CONTACT CENTER KPIs FOR INDIA: ONE VENDOR'S EXPERIENCE *(CONTINUED)*

[a]Net Agent hours = 7 Hrs/Agent × 22 Days * 12 Months X 341 Agents

[b]Avg Occupancy % = (7 hr of Actual Calling / 8 Hrs total*100)

[c]Net Individual Agent Capacity (7 Hrs × 16 Calls/Hr X 360 Days

[d]Excess Call Handling Capacity (.5hrs*16 Calls/Hr*22 Days*12 Months)

[e]300 Workstations × 24 Sq ft

[f]For 341 agents (Turnover is 33%). Around 113 people will leave annually. If 2.5% agents move to the next level (9 agents). For 34 supervisors (turnover is 25%). Around 9 people will leave annually.

[g]Length of Training = 7 Hrs × 22 Days

[h]Cost of New Hire Training per Hour = Annual Total Cost/360 Days/8 Hrs/341 Agents

[i]Cost per Prodn Station/Hr ($8.43)

[j]Talk Hours = Net Agent Hours X 85% Will Be Talk Time (Avg of I/B-98% & O/B-72%)

[k]Call-Handling Capacity = Net Individual Agent Capacity (See Note j) × 250 Agents

[l]Net Individual Agent Capacity (see note k)

[m]Total Calls Handled = Call-Handling Capacity (See Note k)

[n]Calls Handled per Hour per Agent = (I/B Calls/per Hour/Agent X O/B Calls per Hr per Agent)/2

[o]Minutes of Call Time Recorded by ACD = (I/B Talk Time Hrs + O/B Talk Time Hrs) * 60 Minutes

[p]Telecom Rate as per Infrastructure Sheet

[q]Total Direct Telecom Cost = Telecom Rate + IPLc Cost/Yr

[r]Total Hours per Year

[s]Calls Offered Including 2% Abandons

[t]Talk Time = 80% X (60 minutes/16 Calls Hr/Agent)

[u]ACW Time = 30% of (Net Agent Hours – Talk Hours), Rest 70% Is Wait Time

[v]Errors Assumed for 400 People Making 10 Errors P.A.

familiar to contact managers, this data might prove less understandable or relevant to other readers. They are invited to skip this section.

For managers conversant in this data, the purpose of providing KPI data is for managers to compare one vendor's experience against internal results in their domestic operations. While one vendor's experience cannot be considered a true benchmark, these results can be leveraged as a starting point in building a baseline, particularly in light of the fact that no comprehensive contact center benchmark data in popular offshoring locations exists yet. And while Cincom iOutsource is not as large in the contact center offshoring universe as some other vendors, it does cover the waterfront with customers in financial services, manufacturing, travel and leisure, health care (insurance and hospital), billing, debt collection, and IT help desk. Another potential takeaway is the fact that BenchmarkPortal's KPI list is fairly comprehensive. If some organizations have not bothered to measure certain performance drivers in domestic contact center operations, they are now equipped to when migrating these business processes overseas.

A comprehensive KPI snapshot assumes that organizations comprehensively measure and track the rich set of contact center metrics available, and use these data points as the basis for both strategic and tactical decision making. However, in one study conducted by Purdue University and BenchmarkPortal, they discovered that many managers routinely understated the true cost of running a contact center upward of 30%,[7] an indication that managers did not have a grasp of costs for workflow functions that inform measurement calculations or hadn't bothered to use readily available and detailed metrics at all. And while some might argue that having detailed cost metrics is less important in an offshoring relationship, where these costs are borne by the service provider, the exact opposite may be true. Because an offshoring service provider's cost structure is mostly hidden from customers for competitive reasons, the organization who makes the effort to collect detailed metrics data domestically will be able to compare at a very granular level its cost structure line by line against some quasi-benchmark to reach a fuller understanding of exactly where the cost reductions are going to come from. Are these reductions predominantly from the labor arbitrage and telecom? How about differences in asset structures and deployment? How much does the productivity disparity between a company's in-house agents and the service provider's account for total cost savings? A KPI-by-KPI comparison between some aggregated vendor data from India and the company's experience domestically might surprise managers.

Capital Intensity

Remember in Chapter 4 when the radical idea of deautomation was introduced? Labor in some countries is so cheap that companies may be better off lessening the amount of capital invested in business processes and investing more in people. In contact centers, this concept can manifest itself in actual elimination of interactive voice response (IVR) technology, that dreaded system that confronts callers with a sometimes endless and confusing set of options they must vault before reaching a hold queue that can last 5 to 10 minutes or longer. The use of IVR technology speaks to the basic challenges of running a contact center today: One, matching the general nature of a caller's issue whether it involves billing, problems using the organization's website, or a technical issue around product use, with the rep possessing the domain expertise to resolve the issue quickly. More fundamentally, the need for IVR technology reflects the capacity gap between the number of available reps an organization is willing to finance and the number of callers who need assistance. While the capacity gap can fluctuate hour by hour, the gap is likely to exist in perpetuity in the United States for the simple fact that there will always be more need for contact center help than companies are willing to fund.

Cincom iOutsource has a number of clients where this problem has been eliminated. The drastically lower labor cost in India has allowed some organizations to deautomate by replacing technology capital with people. In the case of IVR technology, so many Cincom iOutsource reps can be assigned to a company account that the technology is not needed. When customers call, they are engaged immediately with no hold times. The KPI impact is that hold times, now effectively zero, mean eliminating call abandonment rates, an important metric that many companies watch. Alternatively, Cincom iOutsource estimates that abandon rates in U.S. contact center operations might be as high as 10 to 20% because of the capacity gap.[8] Another impact is that some metrics are rendered meaningless. A metric that measures the percentage of calls answered in less than X minutes, for example, is no longer valid in this scenario.

Deautomation can deliver other less obvious but important business-contextual impacts. Before hiring Cincom iOutsource, another debt collection company found that debtors calling into an IVR in response to requests to contact the company in order to arrange payment for past debt would only wait in the hold queue a very short time, believing that they had fulfilled their end of the bargain to attempt contact.[9] Some debtors would use these arguments in court proceedings" "But your Honor, I called the debt collection company several times but could never reach anyone." Or, often debtors would just leave voice mails for collection agents to return. Either way, the debt collection rates were lower before the company had the opportunity to eliminate the IVR by offshoring to India. Replacing this capacity-balancing technology with labor has increased collection rates because debtors—often to their surprise—are reaching live agents after just a few rings of the phone.

The deautomation proposition might not be valid in very large contact center situations, but the concept is worth considering in every contact center scenario: Can expensive capital that an organization might otherwise deploy in either a captive or service provider offshoring initiative be removed from the entire contact center service delivery platform by virtue of the attractiveness of substituting labor for capital? Capital that would otherwise cause a drag on the total cost-savings value proposition? As you have seen, deautomation can actually impact revenue or income that the contact center generates.

CHAPTER TAKEAWAY

- Offshoring contact center operations should not introduce any exotic issues or surprises in most aspects of the negotiation phase—predominantly SLAs and contracting. Company experience, business process domain knowledge, and the Offshoring Value Delivery Framework together serve as a foundation for managing offshore contact center relationships.

- India is poised to fill a large capacity gap for the number of agents needed today. In the estimation of Cincom iOutsource, the country also offers a compelling agent capability premium over domestic contact center workers. Overall Indian agents are highly educated, which can be reflected in productivity metrics. The company also asserts that for cultural reasons India will develop a domain expertise competitive advantage over other contact center locations, an advantage that if it materializes will result in faster ramp-up times for offshoring companies, fewer knowledge transfer and transition challenges, and fewer operational disruptions from agent attrition.

- When investigating offshoring's potential, organizations should be eager to see if the sometimes drastic labor cost differential will allow them to invest in more contact center labor resources—and still enjoy total savings over domestic operations—which in turn generates measurable increases in income or revenue, where applicable and within the business context. (For example, with a tech-support-type contact center, this issue is irrelevant, but not in a debt collection or sales-order-taking context.)

- Because industry-wide benchmarking data does not exist today, companies would do well to ask vendors in the request for proposal or information phase for aggregated performance data across all customers and along every metric that they consider important, as a limited proxy for true benchmark data—as Cincom iOutsource does in this chapter. Companies can then match this data against their own for two purposes: one, the organization can gain a deeper understanding as to what specific elements of operations might an offshore service provider reduce costs. Two, vendor KPI data for its customer base provides a very helpful baseline in service level agreement construction.

- If the labor cost differential is drastic, another idea that the organization should at least explore early in the process is the opportunity to deautomate the total contact center technology platform by shifting total resource commitment to more labor and less capital.

NOTES

1. Dr. Jon Anton, "Offshore Outsourcing Opportunities," Anton Press, 2002, p. 2.
2. Ibid, p. 20.
3. Ibid, p. 6.
4. Interview with Ashish Paul, Cincom iOutsource, February 9, 2005.
5. Interview with Ashish Paul, Cincom iOutsource, February 23, 2005.
6. Ibid.
7. Anton, "Offshore Outsourcing Opportunities,: page 30.
8. Interview with Ashish Paul, February 23, 2005.
9. Interview with Ashish Paul, Cincom iOutsource, May 19, 2005.

14

TOWARD BEST PRACTICES

The Capability Maturity Model (CMM) is a widely adopted framework for best process practices in software development.[1] Created by Carnegie Mellon University, the model consists of five levels of maturity and process excellence designed to attack common problems plaguing the software development discipline: blown deadlines, cost overruns, and low quality of the final deliverable. The purpose of this final chapter is not to explore the CMM as it pertains to software but rather to ask a simple question: Can the logic behind the CMM be transposed to the business of offshoring business processes?

Of course (but you knew this or why even raise the question). While no formal CMM exists for offshoring, it offers a powerful conceptualization for how organizations can evolve offshoring management from a poorly considered, ad hoc set of business decisions to a world-class, value-driving corporate strategy that delivers long-term value. Exhibit 14.1 visualizes how it is possible to co-opt the principles of CMM to the business of offshoring management.

In Exhibit 14.1, Level 1 represents the least optimal offshoring management conditions in the organization, while Level 5 represents offshoring best practices. You can see through successive levels of the model the increasing amount of sophistication, formalization, effort, and discipline introduced into offshoring management until Level 5 is reached. It is here that all the best of the previous levels are merged into a total value framework encompassing active senior management involvement, a company-wide understanding of offshoring's fit within the context of strategic goals of the organization, a formal decision-making and participation governance

Level 1	Level 2	Level 3	Level 4	Level 5
Ad hoc decision making Myopic contract negotiation focus Poor SLA design and management Little vendor selection rigor Little communication with vendor High risk of cost overruns, overestimation of savings Little or no Offshoring Value Delivery Framework adoption	Just-in-time decision making: costs are high, let's offshore Little senior management involvement Cost-driven focus only, no attention to other value Cursory cost/benefit analysis Some planning Little Offshoring Value Delivery Framework adoption	Some senior management involvement Forward-thinking planning: What future offshore do we prepare for now? Acknowledgement of offshoring's potential strategic value Formal business case, comprehensive value analysis Solid SLA/relationship building & management Some Offshoring Value Delivery Framework adoption	Embraces planning throughout the offshoring lifecycle business case, selection process, contracting, transitioning, relationship management Commitment to benchmarking Extensive Offshoring Value Delivery Framework adoption	Offshoring corporate vision Transparent understanding of goals across the organization Formal and flexible governance structure Rigorous planning Collaborative intranet work environment for data input, analysis, and decision making Win-win relationship model with vendor Comprehensive Offshoring Value Delivery Framework adoption

EXHIBIT 14.1 CAPABILITY MATURITY MODEL FOR OFFSHORING MANAGEMENT

process for every step of an offshoring initiative, and the existence of collaborative data collection and analysis tools to guide managers through all facets of the work involved. In other words, the organization has embraced and operationalized the Offshoring Value Delivery Framework or some internally created version of it.

Admittedly the hard boundaries between each of the five levels is somewhat arbitrary. For example, if poor communication with an offshoring service provider is a characteristic of a Level 1 organization, how much measurably improved is communication for a Level 2 organization? Communication should be at least somewhat improved. Or, it can be argued that formal business case development practices are just as much a characteristic of some Level 2 organizations and do not necessarily begin at Level 3 organizations. It's just that these organizations don't do what the analysis in a detailed business case tell it, which contributes to why the company's total offshoring condition is Level 2 and not Level 3.

But then the purpose of the CMM for Offshoring is not to suggest that the absence or inclusion of any specific characteristic along the way from Level 1 to 5 will automatically place the organization at any specific maturity level. Rather, a collection of characteristics will generally and broadly define an organization's offshoring management practices in one of five levels. Also, the CMM for Offshoring is not a standard. The Financial Services Technology Consortium began an effort in early 2004 to establish industry best practice and service baseline standards for offshoring.[2] The formalizing of process and management techniques into widely accepted practices that companies can leverage to maximize offshoring value is a need yet to be fulfilled across all industries but one with great appeal. Therefore, in the absence of standards, no widely adopted baselines exist that might clearly define the characteristics that compose each level. The CMM for Offshoring is meant as a conceptualization to get managers to think about the management processes, techniques, and resources needed to take their organizations to Level 5 from whatever starting point they find themselves in. As a conceptualization, its power is in helping managers to comprehend the evolutionary path to offshoring excellence that they can travel should they choose.

Perhaps this conceptualization will provoke managers into asking and answering the following questions: Where is the organization's offshoring management today, and given the future competitive landscape, in what direction should it head? Hopefully, this book has shown you the way to answering them.

NOTES

1. Technically the new model is called the Capability Maturity Model Integration. The original Capability Maturity Model is no longer supported by the school's Software Engineering Institute. See www.sei.cmu.edu/cmm.
2. "Banks Plan Offshore Sharing," *ComputerWorld*, Patrick Thibodeau, February 23, 2004.

INDEX